TELLING
TRUE STORIES

TELLING
TRUE STORIES

A NONFICTION WRITERS' GUIDE

FROM THE NIEMAN FOUNDATION AT

HARVARD UNIVERSITY

Edited by

Mark Kramer and Wendy Call

A PLUME BOOK

PLUME
Published by Penguin Group
Penguin Group (USA) Inc., 375 Hudson Street, New York, New York 10014, U.S.A. •
Penguin Group (Canada), 90 Eglinton Avenue East, Suite 700, Toronto, Ontario,
Canada M4P 2Y3 (a division of Pearson Penguin Canada Inc.) • Penguin Books
Ltd., 80 Strand, London WC2R 0RL, England • Penguin Ireland, 25 St. Stephen's
Green, Dublin 2, Ireland (a division of Penguin Books Ltd.) • Penguin Group
(Australia), 250 Camberwell Road, Camberwell, Victoria 3124, Australia (a
division of Pearson Australia Group Pty. Ltd.) • Penguin Books India Pvt. Ltd.,
11 Community Centre, Panchsheel Park, New Delhi – 110 017, India • Penguin
Books (NZ), 67 Apollo Drive, Mairangi Bay, Auckland 1311, New Zealand
(a division of Pearson New Zealand Ltd.) • Penguin Books (South Africa) (Pty.)
Ltd., 24 Sturdee Avenue, Rosebank, Johannesburg 2196, South Africa

Penguin Books Ltd., Registered Offices: 80 Strand, London WC2R 0RL, England

First published by Plume, a member of Penguin Group (USA) Inc.

First Printing, February 2007
30 29 28 27 26 25 24 23

These writings are adapted from the authors' presentations at the Nieman Conference on Narrative Journalism.

Each selection is the copyrighted property of its respective author and appears in this volume by arrangement with the individual writer.

℗ REGISTERED TRADEMARK—MARCA REGISTRADA

LIBRARY OF CONGRESS CATALOGING-IN-PUBLICATION DATA

Telling True Stories : A nonfiction writers' guide from the Nieman Foundation at
Harvard University / edited by Mark Kramer and Wendy Call.
      p.   cm.
    ISBN 978-0-452-28755-6
    1.   Reporters and reporting.   2   Journalism–Authorship.   I.   Kramer, Mark.
II.   Call, Wendy (Wendy Louise). 1968-   III.   Harvard University. Nieman Found-
ation for Journalism.
    PN4781. T45 2007
    070.4'3—dc22   2006026809

Printed in the United States of America
Set in New Baskerville
Designed by Eve L. Kirch

Mark Kramer and Wendy Call dedicate this book to their families, Susan, Will, and Eli, and to Aram, Marilyn, Douglas, Alan, and Kate, respectively.

ACKNOWLEDGMENTS

Mark Kramer and Wendy Call give their deepest thanks to the many people who made this book possible and to the organizations that supported it. All fifty-one contributors generously donated their precious words and then their help and patience through many rounds of edits. Jina Moore read the entire manuscript, asked sharp questions, kept track of countless pieces of paper, and made this a much better book. Buck Ewing and Mary-Helena McInerney recorded and transcribed more than half a million words. Geri Thoma always had cool and calm advice. The entire Nieman Narrative team—Lisa Birk, Jenny Davis, Liliana Ibara, Dasha Kusa, Nell Lake, Jessica Pierce, Pauliina Pope, Martha Synnott, and Prat Thakkar—offered all sorts of support over more than three years. Chuck Collins, Jim Collins, Laurie Hertzel, John Temple, Patricia Weaver Francisco, and Dick Weiss each read portions of the manuscript and made excellent suggestions. Jacqui Banaszynski and Adam Hochschild added insight and enthusiasm at regular intervals. Trena Keating, Emily Haynes, and Lavina Lee deftly turned our manuscript into this book. Bob Giles, curator of the Nieman Foundation and the Knight Foundation, provided essential support. Thanks to the Poynter Institute, which lent its name and savvy to our narrative journalism conference early on, and to the *Boston Globe,* the *Oregonian,* and the Harvard Book Store, also generous conference cosponsors.

Mark also thanks Susan Eaton, Sid and Esther Kramer, Will and Eli Kramer, Wendy Call, Sean Ploen, Joe Lavalle, Lesh Avens, Bob and Joan Weiss, Roy Peter Clark, Ranald Macdonald, Samuel McCracken, Sheryl Jackson, David Anabel, Nick Mills, Noel Perrin, Sam

Splace, Bruce DeSilva, Walt Harrington, and many years of Nieman Fellows.

Wendy also thanks Douglas and Marilyn Call, Aram Falsafi, Sandra Ruiz Harris, Pam Kasey, Mark Kramer, David Palmer, Carol Rose, and Sasha Su-Ling Welland.

CONTENTS

Acknowledgments   vii

Preface   xv

Part I: An Invitation to Narrative

Stories Matter BY JACQUI BANASZYNSKI   3

Delving into Private Lives BY GAY TALESE   6

The Narrative Idea BY DAVID HALBERSTAM   10

Difficult Journalism That's Slap-Up Fun BY KATHERINE BOO   14

Part II: Finding, Researching, and Reporting Topics

Introduction BY MARK KRAMER AND WENDY CALL   19

Finding Good Topics: A Writer's Questions
BY LANE DEGREGORY   20

Finding Good Topics: An Editor's Questions BY JAN WINBURN   22

Reporting for Narrative: Ten Overlapping Rules
BY MARK KRAMER   24

To Tape or Not to Tape? BY ADAM HOCHSCHILD,
JACQUI BANASZYNSKI, JON FRANKLIN, AND GAY TALESE   28

Interviewing: Accelerated Intimacy BY ISABEL WILKERSON   30

The Psychological Interview BY JON FRANKLIN   34

Participatory Reporting: Sending Myself to Prison
BY TED CONOVER   35

Being There BY ANNE HULL   39

Not *Always* Being There BY LOUISE KIERNAN   45

Reporting Across Cultures BY VICTOR MERINA   46

Reporting on Your Own BY S. MITRA KALITA   48

Field Notes to Full Draft BY TRACY KIDDER   51

Doing Enough Reporting? BY WALT HARRINGTON   54

From Story Idea to Published Story BY CYNTHIA GORNEY   55

(Narrative) J School for People Who Never Went
    BY ADRIAN NICOLE LEBLANC   59

Part III: Name Your Subgenre

Introduction BY MARK KRAMER AND WENDY CALL   65

Profiles BY JACQUI BANASZYNSKI   66

The Ladder of Abstraction BY ROY PETER CLARK   70

Every Profile Is an Epic Story BY TOMAS ALEX TIZON   71

The Limits of Profiles BY MALCOLM GLADWELL   73

Travel Writing: Inner and Outer Journeys
    BY ADAM HOCHSCHILD   74

The Personal Essay and the First-Person Character
    BY PHILLIP LOPATE   78

First Personal Singular: Sometimes, It Is About You
    BY DENEEN L. BROWN   81

Columns: Intimate Public Conversations BY DONNA BRITT   83

Writing About History BY JILL LEPORE   86

Adventures in History BY MELISSA FAY GREENE   88

Narrative Investigative Writing BY KATHERINE BOO   89

Public Radio: Community Storytelling BY JAY ALLISON   92

Part IV: Constructing a Structure

Introduction BY MARK KRAMER AND WENDY CALL   97

What Narrative Writers Can Learn from Screenwriters
    BY NORA EPHRON   98

To Begin the Beginning BY DeNEEN L. BROWN   100

Narrative Distance BY JACK HART   103

Hearing Our Subjects' Voices: Quotes and Dialogue
  BY KELLEY BENHAM   104

Hearing Our Subjects' Voices: Keeping It Real and True
  BY DEBRA DICKERSON   107

A Story Structure BY JON FRANKLIN   109

Summary Versus Dramatic Narrative BY JACK HART   111

Weaving Story and Idea BY NICHOLAS LEMANN   112

Endings BY BRUCE DeSILVA   116

Part V: Building Quality into the Work

Introduction BY MARK KRAMER AND WENDY CALL   125

Character BY JON FRANKLIN   126

Details Matter BY WALT HARRINGTON   128

Developing Character BY STANLEY NELSON   129

Reconstructing Scenes BY ADAM HOCHSCHILD   132

A Reconstructed Scene BY ADAM HOCHSCHILD   135

Setting the Scene BY MARK KRAMER   136

Handling Time BY BRUCE DeSILVA   139

Sequencing: Text as Line BY TOM FRENCH   140

Writing Complicated Stories BY LOUISE KIERNAN   145

How I Get to the Point BY WALT HARRINGTON   148

The Emotional Core of the Story BY TOM WOLFE   149

Telling the Story, Telling the Truth by ALMA GUILLERMOPRIETO   154

On Voice BY SUSAN ORLEAN   158

Part VI: Ethics

Introduction BY MARK KRAMER AND WENDY CALL   163

The Line Between Fact and Fiction BY ROY PETER CLARK   164

Toward an Ethical Code for Narrative Journalists
  BY WALT HARRINGTON   170

Playing Fair with Subjects BY ISABEL WILKERSON   172

Securing Consent BY TRACY KIDDER   176

Truth and Consequences BY KATHERINE BOO   177

Dealing with Danger: Protecting Your Subject and
    Your Story BY SONIA NAZARIO   178

A Dilemma of Immersion Journalism BY ANNE HULL   182

Ethics in Personal Writing BY DEBRA DICKERSON   184

Taking Liberties: The Ethics of the Truth BY LOUNG UNG   187

The Ethics of Attribution BY ROY PETER CLARK   189

What About Endnotes? BY SONIA NAZARIO AND
    NICHOLAS LEMANN   192

Part VII: Editing

Introduction BY MARK KRAMER AND WENDY CALL   197

On Style BY EMILY HIESTAND   198

A Writer and Editor Talk Shop BY JAN WINBURN AND
    LISA POLLAK   202

Revising—Over and Over Again BY ANNE HULL   205

Transforming One Hundred Notebooks into
    Thirty-five Thousand Words BY SONIA NAZARIO   208

How to Come Up Short BY TOM HALLMAN   212

Narrative in Four Boxes BY JACQUI BANASZYNSKI   216

Serial Narratives BY TOM FRENCH   218

Care and Feeding of Editors and Writers
    BY JACQUI BANASZYNKSI   221

Part VIII: Narrative in the News Organization

Introduction BY MARK KRAMER AND WENDY CALL   227

Beginning in Narrative BY WALT HARRINGTON   228

A Brief History of Narrative in Newspaper BY JACK HART   230

Nurturing Narrative in the Newsroom BY JACK HART   233

A Storyteller's Lexicon BY JACK HART   235

Narrative as a Daily Habit BY LANE DeGREGORY   239

Building a Narrative Team BY MARIA CARRILLO   243

Two Visions, One Series: A Writer and an Editor Talk About What
    They Do BY JACQUI BANASZYNSKI AND TOMAS ALEX TIZON   246

Team Storytelling BY LOUISE KIERNAN   251

Photographer as Narrative Storyteller BY MOLLY BINGHAM   254

Subversive Storytellers: Starting a Narrative Group
    BY BOB BATZ JR.   256

Part IX: Building a Career in Magazines and Books

Introduction BY MARK KRAMER AND WENDY CALL   263

Making It as a Freelancer BY JIM COLLINS   264

Not Stopping: Time Management for Writers
    BY STEWART O'NAN   268

Lessons from the Jury Box BY JACK HART   271

Working with an Agent BY MELISSA FAY GREENE   272

What Makes a Good Book? BY HELENE ATWAN   274

From Book Idea to Book Contract BY JIM COLLINS   276

Your Book and the Marketplace BY GERI THOMA   278

Crossing Over: From Advocacy to Narrative
    BY SAMANTHA POWER   281

A Passion for Writing BY SUSAN ORLEAN   284

Suggested Reading   289

Web Sites and Internet Resources   297

About the Editors   299

About the Contributors   301

Index   309

PREFACE

Writing well is difficult, even excruciating, and demands courage, patience, humility, erudition, savvy, stubbornness, wisdom, and aesthetic sense—all summoned at your lonely desk. *Telling True Stories* offers a step-by-step guide that can help you at every stage, from idea to publication. This anthology includes advice from fifty-one respected writers who are among the most experienced practitioners of narrative nonfiction in the country.

The genre of telling true stories goes by many names: narrative journalism, new journalism, literary journalism, creative nonfiction, feature writing, the nonfiction novel, documentary narrative. It appears in a range of media including the daily newspaper, monthly lifestyle magazines, weekly alternative papers, and annual lists of "best nonfiction books." It captivates public radio listeners, film and video documentary fans, and television viewers. On university campuses some form of narrative nonfiction is taught in departments of anthropology, communications, creative writing, history, journalism, literature, and sociology. Often, faculty members of the various departments don't know about others' common methods and interests. The writers included here represent varied narrative traditions, from investigative reporting and magazine editing to filmmaking and poetry. As a result, *Telling True Stories* is quirkier than most textbooks and yet more practical than many books of advice about the writing craft.

This genre, which we'll call narrative nonfiction (or just "narrative"), challenges audiences as well as practitioners. It mixes human content with academic theory and observed fact, allows specialized understanding of everyday events, and unscrambles and sorts the

messages of a complex world. It begins with practitioners going out
into the real world to learn something new. *New Yorker* writer Katherine Boo notes:

> This is difficult journalism. It's lonely journalism. I was once on a
> Greyhound bus trip across the South, reporting. I was using the
> Memphis bus station as my Hyatt Regency. My back ached and
> my butt hurt. I hadn't had a proper night's sleep in four days. But
> intellectually and emotionally, I was as far as I could possibly be
> from bored. It's stressful work, but when you read . . . the writers
> who have done this work so well for so long, you can't help but
> know that this work is also mind-stretching, life-enhancing, slap-
> up fun.

Like Katherine Boo's call to action, nearly all the material in
Telling True Stories derives from presentations the contributors made
at the Nieman Conference on Narrative Journalism. Every autumn
the Nieman Foundation at Harvard University hosts one thousand
mid-career writers and editors, from every U.S. state and from countries on nearly every continent, for three days of lectures, workshops,
and discussions on the art and craft of narrative nonfiction. (See
www.nieman.harvard.edu/narrative for much more information including recordings of the conference sessions.)

This book offers the counsel and experience of the conference
speakers, distilled and updated, to a much wider community of storytellers: practitioners, students, and teachers of narrative nonfiction.
In editing the ninety-one pieces included in this volume, we've tightened, extracted, and rearranged, and then worked with the writers
fine-tuning and augmenting their original words. Along the way we
have condensed 600,000 transcribed words to one-fifth that length—a
bouillon of experience and explanation. This broth had many cooks—
not only the fifty-one writers whose names appear in the credits, but
also their teachers, colleagues, and students, and the audiences at the
Nieman Conferences because some of the material in this book orig-
inated in workshop question-and-answer sessions, with the speakers'
ideas focused and refined by thoughtful group discussion.

Telling True Stories offers nonfiction storytellers a sourcebook that
helps name and describe many aspects of this difficult but rewarding
work. We start with an overview of the field and then explore topic
selection and data collection (reporting and research). We consider
cousin genres (memoir, travel writing, the essay, and commentary),

narrative structure, literary quality, ethics, the editing process, newsroom storytelling, and career-building.

Some of you will read this book from this page forward, start to finish. More of you will use this book as a reference, an on-call tutor. We have designed the book to reward both of these approaches.

It's so hard to do this work well, and then it's hard again next time. We aspire to keep you good company as you strive to tell better stories. We wish you the gumption and the inspiration to do this important work as well as you possibly can.

Mark Kramer and Wendy Call
Cambridge, Massachusetts
April 2006

PART I

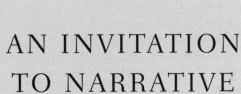

AN INVITATION
TO NARRATIVE

Stories Matter

JACQUI BANASZYNSKI

I want you to travel with me to a famine camp in Sudan on the Ethiopian border. You have seen the dreadful television footage of the starving babies, their bellies bloated. Flies crawl in and out of their eyes and mouths, jealous for the last drops of moisture that cling there as long as these babies cling to life. Now you are among them, as a reporter for a midsized daily newspaper in the upper Midwest, charged with writing about a place you have never been before, about an event you can't possibly understand, for readers who will never go there and don't know what it has to do with them—beyond writing a check to charity.

You've been at the camp for several days. You walk its ground each day, stepping around and over 100,000 people who have come because they heard there was water. By the time they arrived—some of them walking three weeks from their Ethiopian villages—the water was no more than a well of mud in a dry riverbed.

You watch the little girls walk to the river and dig in the mud, soaking their rags with moisture that they wring, drop by drop, into their plastic jugs. You sit in the clinic where the waiting line is hundreds long. Desperate fathers thrust their babies at you, thinking that because you are a *khawaja*, a foreigner, you must be a doctor. You must be able to help. But all you have to offer is a poised notebook and some questions—suddenly too little to accommodate this reality.

You wander to the edge of the camp, to the vast defecation zone where those healthy enough to walk go to heed nature's call. It is oblivious to the need for a little human dignity. Women squat inside their skirts, their heads covered in veils, trying to create some sense of cloister.

You stumble to the rocky hillside where clusters of men claw at the hard earth, creating holes just deep enough to cradle the shrouded bodies they gently place there. The holes don't need to be deep, for the bodies are very thin. They bury seventy-five each day, sometimes more. Most are babies.

At night you retreat to the other side of the straw wall that encloses this awful world. You collapse—ashamed of your small and temporary hunger, of your selfish fears—on a cot in a small straw hut. You're grateful that it's dark, that you will not have to look at things for a few hours, but you can still hear. You hear coughing and vomiting and whimpering and keening. You hear shouts, angry bursts of life, and rasps that rattle to silence as seventy-five more people die.

Then you hear something else: *singing.* You hear sweet chants and deep rhythms. Each night, over and over, at about the same time. You think you are hallucinating. You wonder if you have gone quite mad from your fear. How could people sing in the face of this horror? And why? You lie in the dark and you wonder until the mercy of sleep claims you. Daylight comes again, and you open your eyes.

I went to Africa in 1985 to report on the Ethiopian famine for the *St. Paul Pioneer Press.* I had never been outside of North America.

The singing intrigued me. It took me several days to find out what it was. I had to go through several translators before someone finally told me that it was *storytelling.* When the villages in Ethiopia and what is now Eritrea finally got too parched or too bombed for people to survive there, they got up, en masse, and walked to the famine camps. Then they settled, in whatever little huts they could find, as a village. They continued whatever rituals they could. One of their rituals was their nightly storytelling. The elders gathered the children around, and they sang their songs.

It was their version of school. It was how they carried their history and culture and law with them. It may have been my first conscious awareness of the power, history, and universality of storytelling. We all grew up with stories, but do we ever stop to think about how much they connect us and how powerful they are?

Even, or especially, in the face of death these stories live on, passed from elder to younger, from generation to generation, carried with as much care as those precious jugs of water. Events pass, people live and die, life changes. But stories endure.

Several years after I went to Sudan, I stumbled across what has become one of my favorite books, Tim O'Brien's *The Things They Carried.* He writes, "Stories are for joining the past to the future. Stories are for those late hours in the night when you can't remember how you got from where you were to where you are. Stories are for eternity, when memory is erased, when there is nothing to remember except the story."

I asked Tomas Alex Tizon, who used to work with me at the *Seattle Times*, why human beings need stories, and he replied:

Thank God for stories—for those who have them, for those who tell them, for those who devour them as the soul sustenance that they are. Stories give shape to experience and allow us to go through life unblind. Without them, everything that happens would float around, undifferentiated. None of it would mean anything. Once you have a version of what happened, all the other good stuff about being human comes into play. You can laugh, feel awe, commit a passionate act, get pissed, want to change things.

My friend and fellow writer Katherine Lanpher, who wrote for the *Pioneer Press* and is now with Air America, told me this about stories:

Stories are the connective tissue of the human race, whether you are dissecting a school levy or South Korean politics. At the heart of every issue is a human element that leads to the three most beautiful words in the English language: *What happened next?* If you answer that question, you are a storyteller.

They say language makes us human. That notion is being challenged as we discover that apes have language. Whales have language. I welcome them into our fold. I'm not threatened by them, quite frankly, because I think that stories make us human. Only by telling them do we stay so.

Stories are our prayers. Write and edit them with due reverence, even when the stories themselves are irreverent.

Stories are parables. Write and edit and tell yours with meaning, so each tale stands in for a larger message, each story a guidepost on our collective journey.

Stories are history. Write and edit and tell yours with accuracy and understanding and context and with unwavering devotion to the truth.

Stories are music. Write and edit and tell yours with pace and rhythm and flow. Throw in the dips and twirls that make them exciting, but stay true to the core beat. Readers hear stories with their inner ear.

Stories are our soul. Write and edit and tell yours with your whole selves. Tell them as if they are all that matters. It matters that you do it as if that's all there is.

Delving into Private Lives
GAY TALESE

The fiction writer, playwright, and novelist deal with private life. They deal with ordinary people and elevate these people into our consciousness. The nonfiction writer has traditionally dealt with people in public life, names that are known to us. The private lives that I wanted to delve into as a young writer at the *New York Times* would not often be considered worthy of news coverage. I thought those people had a sense of what was going on. I believed if we could bring them into the larger consciousness, they could help us understand the trends happening around us.

My father was a tailor. He had come from a small village in southern Italy, but he was very fine with a needle and thread. He brought a sense of his own style to his work. He had a great sense of caring about a perfect buttonhole, of measuring perfectly, of making a suit that would fit on the body and would elevate the man's presence. He was an artist of a needle and thread who didn't care whether he made a lot of money.

We were people of the underclass, people who went out and observed but were not ourselves observed. My father was an eavesdropping tailor. He knew a lot about the people who came into his shop. I grew up hearing about the lives of ordinary people, and I thought they were interesting.

My father learned the English language by reading the *New York Times*. During World War II my father's relatives back in Italy were all on the wrong side of the war. His brothers were fighting with Mussolini's army against the invading Allies in 1943. My father read the *New York Times* with a certain sense of concern. I saw in that little house of mine how major events affected us. Each day the *Times* had maps and arrows showing the armies getting closer and closer to my father's village. I saw a great sense of drama.

This is nonfiction; this is my life.

I never had a happier time than when I was a reporter in the *New York Times* newsroom. I left with a tear in my eye when I was thirty-two years old, after working there for a decade. I left not because of any disenchantment with the newspaper, but rather because of the limitations of daily journalism: space and time. The limited time one could devote to the indulgence of one's curiosity made it somewhat frustrating to stay on a daily newspaper. I wanted to spend more time with people who were not necessarily newsworthy. I believed then— and I believe now even more—that the role of the nonfiction writer should be with private people whose lives represent a larger significance.

When I left the *New York Times* in 1965 to work at *Esquire,* the first thing I did was go back and write about some of the journalists there, those wonderful characters in the city room, who weren't news. The first person I wrote about was an obituary writer, Alden Whitman. He would wander around the city room with a little green cap, smoking a pipe, thinking about death, thinking of people who were about to die. He would interview them and tell them that he was going to update their files—a sort of advance obituary. He made his living in this very distinguished way. What was it like to be a man who interviewed people whose time on earth was worthy of space in the *New York Times* when they died?

Now in my seventies, I still have as much of that curiosity as I had at age twenty-two. Curiosity is the beginning. That's not something we are going to get from the Columbia School of Journalism or the University of Missouri. As a nonfiction writer I indulge my curiosity in private lives. I write nonfiction as a creative form. Creative, not falsified: not making up names, not composite characters, not taking liberties with factual information, but getting to know real-life characters through research, trust, and building relationships. You come to know them so well that they are like part of your private life. I respect these people even though I have written about gangsters and pornographers. I saw the world as they see it.

I find a way to write with respect, a way to write truth that is not insulting. I don't make allowances for their dalliances or deviations, but I slide those facts in without being harsh. Precise writing allows that; sloppy writing does not. I get this care for language from reading the great fiction writers: F. Scott Fitzgerald, John O'Hara, Irwin Shaw.

By 1999 I had spent eight years working on a book but was unable to finish it. I wanted to write about failure. It interests me because it is a learning experience. When I was a sportswriter, the locker room of a loser was always more interesting than the locker room of a winner.

I wanted to write about John Wayne Bobbitt, the guy who lost his penis. He was a loser in every sense of the word, yet he got no sympathy from anybody. His wife was treated as a virtuous woman, because he got what he deserved. That was interesting. I wanted to know John Bobbitt, and I hung around with him for six months. I drove him around, got to know his doctor, and eventually got to know his wife, Lorena. I traced the knife she had used to Ikea, where she had bought it three years earlier.

On a Saturday in July 1999, I happened to be watching a baseball game on television. On that same day was a highly advertised game between the United States national women's soccer team and the national team of China. I was channel surfing because I was interested in this soccer game, too. Mia Hamm was said to be the greatest soccer player in the United States—not only among women but among men. I started flipping between baseball and soccer, trying to avoid work, so I could get my mind off the miserable life that I was living.

I had never watched soccer in my life. Like most people my age, I don't understand soccer. My father might have understood it, but for all the wonderful things that were imported from the old country, they did not import soccer. Ninety thousand people in the Rose Bowl were watching it. I don't know what they were making all the noise about, but they were clearly excited.

I was interested because of the adversarial relationship between the United States and China. It wound up being a nothing-nothing game. They had a shoot-out of penalty kicks. One Chinese woman ended up missing the penalty kick, and the game was over. If I were a sportswriter, I would have been in that locker room, and I wouldn't have been talking to Mia Hamm but to the woman who missed that kick.

She had to get on an airplane in Los Angeles, spend twenty-some hours in the air, and return home to a China eager to knock off Americans, angry at our meddlesome foreign policy. It struck me that this was the way to write about China. This woman was twenty-five years old and she lost. What was it like for a twenty-five-year-old woman to screw up in this Communist regime emerging as a world power?

I thought, "Oh, the *New York Times* will have that tomorrow." But there was nothing in the paper about the woman who missed the kick. That week both *Newsweek* and *Time* had cover stories about the

Women's World Cup, but nothing about what I wanted to know. It was all about the American victory and how the Chinese team missed the kick, but nothing about that woman—number 13.

I know Norman Pearlstine of Time-Warner, so I called him. "Norman," I said. "In the article today there was nothing about the Chinese woman." So I sent him a fax and told him what I thought would be a good story. I said, "If you write about this woman, she will tell you something about how the Chinese react, what the neighborhood said about her, what her mother had to deal with. The Women's World Cup was televised around the world, and she missed. How do they deal with defeat? These women were part of the great achievement of China's being a world power. She might have had a great-great-grandmother with bound feet. She is using soccer to represent the new China, but she misses the damn ball and now represents disappointment."

I thought she could be a real key to representing the story of China. I would be glad to do that story. They thanked me for my idea, but nothing happened. The summer passed. I was in Frankfurt, celebrating my fortieth anniversary with my wife. And I decided I was not going back to New York at the end of the week. I changed my ticket and went to Hong Kong. I had to find Yu Ling. I went to Beijing—speaking not a word of Chinese, knowing no one. I checked into a good hotel because surely someone would speak English there. I asked the concierge.

This was not like calling the public relations department of the New York Yankees for an interview with Derek Jeter. I wanted to talk to someone who had missed a kick. I stayed in China for five months looking for her. Finally, I got to meet her. I saw her again and again, working through interpreters. I saw her on the field, met her teammates. Soon I had put a year into it.

In 2000, the Chinese mainland team went to Taiwan, and I went with them. This is the type of nonfiction that I indulge in, hanging around people. You don't necessarily interview them, but you become part of the atmosphere.

The girl who missed the kick is featured in the book. Not only has that story come together, but all that other stuff—John Wayne Bobbitt, the storefront that can't ever host a successful restaurant, a redneck sheriff in the post–Selma South, all that—is now the story of my trying to deal with reality, with all its misadventures, its wrong turns, with an ever-energized quest to know something about people who tend to be ignored.

The Narrative Idea

DAVID HALBERSTAM

As narrative writers we care deeply about sustaining quality journalism in an age that is rather inhospitable to it, for both technological and economic reasons. Television came along in the 1960s and 1970s and replaced print journalism as the quickest, most powerful instrument for news. On the occasion of cataclysmic events—the crashing of a NASA shuttle, John Kennedy's assassination, the September 11 attacks—people turn to television. It is the prime carrier of news. So we, the print journalists, have had to go where television cameras could not. We must answer the questions that the television's images pose. We're lucky, though: Television news raises more questions than it answers.

Print journalists have to be better than they used to be. With network television, cable television, the Internet, and even video games it's tougher to compete for people's time. There are more and more sources of information out there, and they demand less and less intellectual energy. People work harder; they have less time. When I started as a journalist, fifty-two years ago, I operated in an age with a single-income middle class. Now it's a two-income middle class. The writer must get better and better, become a better storyteller.

To write good narrative you must be able to answer the question: *What is the story about?* The *idea*, the concept, is critical to narrative journalism. Moving the idea from genesis to fruition is what it's all about.

Let's start with the book idea that became *The Teammates*. In February 2002, I had dinner in Palm Beach with Emily and Dominic DiMaggio. Dominic had been a center fielder for the Boston Red Sox back in the 1940s. In 2002, he was eighty-four. In 1989, I'd written about him in the book *Summer of '49*. We had kept up a friendship. That night Dominic told me about driving from Boston to Florida with John Pesky, his former teammate. They'd gone to see Ted Williams, another teammate, who was dying. They all knew it would be the last time they would be together. Dominic described how he walked into the room, how desperately frail Ted was, and how he started singing to his old teammate.

I listened to Dominic's story that night, and then went home and thought, "That's never going to happen again. Four men, essentially one team, staying friends for sixty years, paying attention to one another, phoning one another, and caring about one another late in their lives." I thought, "That could be a really nice, small book." I called Will Schwalbe, my editor, and outlined the book and my idea. He immediately got it. "Perfect!" He said. "*Tuesdays with Morrie* meets *Summer of '49*." Bingo!

Writing *The Teammates* was pure pleasure. I liked all the men; I'd worked with them before. There was a richness to them and their lives. They understood themselves and what had worked for them, and yet they had a certain modesty. They'd reached the age of eighty, so they knew the book would be a summing up—not just for Ted Williams but of their own lives. Later, my friend and colleague Frank DeFord, a wonderful writer for *Sports Illustrated*, got hold of the book and said, "Damn! Why didn't *I* have the idea?"

That's precisely the point: The book *is* the idea. Once you have the idea, it just flows out. This is perhaps the best advice I can offer. Taking an idea, a central point, and pursuing it, turning it into a story that tells something about the way we live today, is the essence of narrative journalism.

I'll give another example. In the fall of 2001, Graydon Carter of *Vanity Fair* called and asked me to go to our neighborhood fire station, about three blocks from my home on Manhattan's West Side. On September 11, 2001, thirteen men had gone out on two rigs. Twelve had died. Like so many New Yorkers, I wanted to do something in that terrible moment after the tragedy. I was delighted to do it; I jumped at the assignment. I went to the firehouse and talked to the other firemen, all of whom were in considerable emotional pain. They were extraordinarily open and generous toward me. I did about eight or nine days of reporting, and I thought, "This could be a wonderful, small book."

This is the key to the book: In a city that had been hit by an apocalyptic event, in the midst of it all, was one small institution, a place where relationships were intensely humane, very old-fashioned. Men ate together and slept together and risked their lives for one another. Yet that one institution had paid disproportionately with its suffering. I thought that I could measure some of the pain inflicted on the city by looking at that firehouse. The tone of that book, *Firehouse*, is very understated. It had to be. The book's language had to suit the occasion. You don't "hype up" in the wake of tragedy. You underwrite, letting the events speak for themselves. You treat everyone with respect.

The result is a very simple story of a terrible day in a city and who pays the price for it. The book, in fact, is the only one of my books that is not dedicated. The dedication was so self-evidently to the men who died there.

I got the idea for my first—and still best-known—book, *The Best and the Brightest*, in 1969 after I returned from my second tour as a reporter in Vietnam. I knew that U.S. policy in Vietnam wasn't going to work out. I thought, "When the Kennedy administration swept into office, they were called brilliant, the best, most able group to serve in a generation. And yet, clearly, Vietnam was turning out to be a tragic miscalculation, as painful as anything this country had experienced since the Civil War. How could it have happened? How could men so allegedly brilliant be the architects of so great a tragedy?" I envisioned a mystery novel, a detective novel, with a great cast of characters.

I figured it was a four-year book. I got a rather small advance that came out to about $10,000 a year. I thought the book would take two and a half years of legwork if I went out and did two long interviews a day. That's almost exactly the way the equation came out. To my surprise, the book became a huge best seller. It spent thirty-six weeks on the *New York Times* bestseller list. Doing the book changed my life. I didn't get rich, but because of its success, I received generous book advances, giving me the time to do future books the way I wanted to do them. *Time* is the crucial ingredient for a nonfiction writer. The more time, the more interviews you can do, and the greater the density of your work.

I'd like to give one critical bit of advice to those who are drawn to this work and want to succeed: *The idea is vital.* Telling a good story demands a great conception, a great idea for why the story works— for what it is and how it connects to the human condition. It is about ideas, about narration, about telling a story. You must be able to point to something larger.

The legwork of reporting is critical and most of the fun. It turns an idea into an entertaining and substantive story. The more reporting—the more anecdotes, perceptions, and windows on a subject— the better. Writing is secondary. Sometimes when I lecture to journalism classes at colleges, I tell them I'm about to divulge the best question a reporter can ask a source. For the first time (in some cases) their interest perks up and out come the notebooks. And I say, "At the end of the interview always ask, 'Who else should I see?'"

It's very simple: The more views of any subject that you get, the better. The more reporting you do, the more authority your voice has. I can always tell when a journalist is cheating. I can tell when it's a two-phone-call story. If you were an executive producer of a football game on television, would you have a better product if you had twenty cameras on the field or just two? The more people you talk with, the more perspectives you gather, and the more interviews you do, the better. Your writing will flow from the material you've gathered. Chances are, you've come into this work because you genuinely like talking to people. If not, you should probably find other work. The legwork must be fun. Think of it as part of a continuing education; we're paid to learn. It isn't just getting a byline that drives you; it isn't just where the story lands in the paper. Fifty-two years later, I still like what I do.

Here's my last bit of advice, garnered from those fifty-two years: *Read.* Read good nonfiction books. Read very good newspapers: the *New York Times, Wall Street Journal, St. Petersburg Times, Los Angeles Times, Washington Post.* When you find a reporter whose work you admire, break his or her code. Examine the story and figure out what the reporter did, where he or she went, how that reporter constructed the story, and why it worked.

Read good detective fiction. I don't think anybody does narrative structure better than good detective writers. Read the work of Gay Talese, one of the journalists who broke through the barriers to narrative writing in the 1960s. You'll find density in all of his work. He took the time to observe, to be a fly on the wall. His work is great cinematic journalism. When you read his work, you can almost hear a little camera whirring away. I belong to a generation of people like Talese and others who struggled against more limited forms of journalism. Our editors just wanted the who, what, where, when, and why. Often, the work we thought was our best got cut away.

Things are changing. Narrative nonfiction is on the rise, and I feel lucky to have spent more than fifty years doing it. I've been paid to learn, to ask questions, to think. What could be more enjoyable and more rewarding than that?

Difficult Journalism That's Slap-Up Fun

KATHERINE BOO

The greatest potential—still largely unrealized, I believe—of narrative reporting is communicating the very hardest news. Narrative can convey vividly and potently the greater failings of government and industry, inequities of class, and fractures in the infrastructure of opportunities in this country. It can engage the public, almost against its will, in crucial questions of meritocracy and social justice.

Over the years my editors and I have wrestled a lot with the tension between narrative and news. After I turned in a story draft for a series about neglect in Washington, D.C., group homes for disabled adults, one of my editors, a very smart, experienced, and tough woman, said, "You have uncovered serious crimes here. You are burying them under a bunch of distracting writing." A literary approach to the story, she argued, sabotaged the prospect that those crimes would be taken seriously, that justice would be done.

In the face of these risks, why do we choose narrative?

For some subjects, *not* choosing narrative means not being read at all. When your subjects are grim and your characters destitute, disabled, or extremely unintelligent, and the wrongs against them are complicated, how many people are going to relish tucking into your story with their bagels and cream cheese on Sunday morning? I choose narrative, sometimes with ambivalence, to further the goal of our profession: readers finishing the story and maybe giving half a damn.

Go to a place in your community that you don't know very well, ride a few buses, get off them, explore, and ask yourself questions about what you see. I guarantee you will find something that the public doesn't know about because too few journalists bother to make these trips anymore. It's considered inefficient. When editors ask what you have been doing, they don't want to hear, "I've been riding buses and thinking all day."

Doing this work might involve some subversion of your editors, of the process, and of the marketplace. Serious subjects don't sell newspapers anyway. Narrative about serious subjects might not be a popular craft, but it's essential. Without the telling, well-reported detail, the narrative form is an empty seduction. It's us listening to ourselves talk, falling in love with the sound of our own voices.

How do you find those telling details, the earned facts, and then convey them? It involves two opposite sets of skills. While reporting, you must lose control so you can accumulate the facts. While writing, you must exert maniacal control over those facts. You begin by being laid-back and hanging out. Take the great inhale so that when you exhale, you will have among your notebooks that detail that conveys so much, so economically. Weave that detail into the warp and weft of your hard facts.

A friend once told me that I find my stories because I never learned to drive. It's true. I take the bus. I walk around. By being out there—not the driver of my story but the literal and figurative rider—I have the opportunity to see things that I would never otherwise see.

I found the group home story because I missed a bus in a housing project. Someone gave me a ride home. He had to stop at a group home because he was having some disagreement with the staff there. I entered the group home at eight in the evening. What I saw there led to my story.

When I do interviews, I never take my subjects to a restaurant for lunch. It's one of the worst things a journalist can do. Stay on their turf. Interview them in *their* world. If they say, "Now I've got to go and pick up my kids from day care and go to the grocery store," you say, "Great. I can write while we're on the bus." I'm not just hearing their stories, I'm watching them live. I find my truth in the dialectic between what they say and how they live.

You prepare for that kind of reporting by *not* preparing, by *not* scheduling three interviews a day. Carol Guzy, a photographer at the *Washington Post,* likes to say, "When you go for coffee, bring a tent." I carry a big purse because if I need to get on a bus and go to Georgia, I can. It's very difficult to do this work halfway. It's very difficult to say, "At five o'clock every day I'm going to be home." For a lot of us that creates practical problems, problems with our families.

Reporting gets easier over time. A friend of mine at the *Chicago Tribune* says, "Curiosity is a muscle. The more you use it, the more it can do." The more you force yourself out into the world, taking chances, and the more times you call the public official to get that document he doesn't want to give you, the easier it becomes and the more pleasure you get in doing it. That pleasure and passion will show when you get down to the business of writing.

I'm not sure that writing gets easier over time. It still seems very hard. The hardest thing is figuring out how to keep the reader from throwing it down and getting a beer instead. You must choose, and choose aggressively. One of the most painful things about writing is all you *can't* say in your stories. I think about the people who died in Washington, D.C.'s neglectful group home system, the terrible stories that I chose not to include. By watching readers' reactions to narrative stories, I've come to believe that three well-articulated, nuanced examples—backed by sharply documented evidence of a broader problem—are far better than twenty examples that raise more questions than they answer. Stories that run in one, two, or three parts, not sixteen, are more effective.

We often talk about story-making as a two-part process: reporting and writing. This leaves out the third part: thinking. I spend a great deal of time holding my themes and scenes up to the light and asking myself: *Which facets are intuitive? Which facets say something meaningful?*

As I do this thinking, this distilling, I talk a lot to my friends—not journalists but painters, poets, and stockbrokers. I listen carefully to what interests them and what irritates them. Listen to the questions people ask after you give them a two-sentence synopsis of your reporting day. In those questions and reactions you get closer to the most important ideas and arguments that you need to show in your scenes. Once you understand the heart of the matter, you will have a much better sense of how to refine and arrange the parts.

This is difficult journalism. It's lonely journalism. Not long ago I was on a Greyhound bus trip across the South, reporting. I was using the Memphis bus station as my Hyatt Regency. My back ached and my butt hurt. I hadn't had a proper night's sleep in four days. But intellectually and emotionally, I was as far as I could possibly be from bored. It's lonely and stressful work, but when you read Adam Hochschild, H. G. Bissinger, Darcy Frey, Joan Didion, Jessica Mitford, A. J. Liebling, or any of the other writers who have done this work so well for so long, you can't help but know that this work is also mind-stretching, life-enhancing, slap-up fun. Go out and find some of it.

PART II

FINDING, RESEARCHING, AND REPORTING TOPICS

Introduction

MARK KRAMER AND WENDY CALL

Before you can construct a factual narrative or develop a strong main character or identify a theme—or even know that you have a useful story—you must *report*. The process always begins with empirical data collection.

This section of the anthology might be the most important. It covers a complicated range of skills and practices: intuiting what might be an apt topic, finding the right place in the vast world to pursue it, developing working relationships with the people you find there, and interpreting the mixed-up, ongoing clutter of activity that constitutes the real world. The writer must transform observation and data into comprehension and then develop tactics for transmitting that understanding to readers.

This section doesn't recite general principles of reporting; many other books have done that work. We've gathered and culled observations, experiences, and musings of fine reporters. They tell you how they thought up topics, identified the right locations for reporting and research, settled in for the long haul, recorded what was happening, decoded it, added background research and their own intelligence, and finally began to write.

The practitioners included here have written for or edited the country's top newspapers and magazines, authored award-winning books, and taught in several fine journalism schools. Their work takes different forms, presents different worlds, and addresses diverse audiences, and yet it all rests on the same foundation: reporting.

A narrative writer with a good story idea is a solo entrepreneur doing a start-up. Until the piece is published, the risk is mostly on the writer's shoulders. Even a staff reporter at a magazine or newspaper is in large part an independent practitioner while working on a story—especially one done at the writer's own initiative. Nonfiction narrative writing may be artful, human, and even poetic, but it's also a business proposition—a very personal one. The writers here all report with their heads, their hearts, and their deep practicality.

◆

Finding Good Topics: A Writer's Questions

LANE DEGREGORY

How does a writer decide whether a news story is worthy of narrative?

First, there must be some sort of unfolding action. Something has to *happen* so the story can progress from one point to another. To follow current, unfolding action, the writer has to be there. You can almost never write narrative over the phone. You need to be at the scene—to smell it, taste it, hear the dialogue, see the body language, look the people you will write about in the eye.

Second, the writer must gain access. If you talk to people, will they open up to you? Will they let you come back to their house, look through their closets, see what's in the refrigerator? If you don't have that kind of access, you must find someone else close who can provide the insights. Otherwise, you end up utterly frustrated.

Once these two conditions seem likely—but before I propose a narrative story to my editor and write a budget line for it—I ask myself seven questions.

Can I go along for a ride or take a walk or be at a meeting, a trial, or a funeral?

Action moves the story along. Can I be a fly on the wall at an already scheduled event? I do my interviews before or after, so I don't interrupt the action. If my subject has a regular routine, I go along. I see the person doing things that I would never have thought to ask about. If there isn't anything going on, I can *make* something happen. I'll flip through photo albums with the person, taking a walk down the proverbial memory lane. Anything I can do to keep the person moving *and* comfortable provides more material for my notebook.

Is something going to happen?

If I can't be present for some unfolding action, has something significant *already* happened? If so, can I look back and witness its effects on the person or the event I'm writing about? Is there a video of the event, or did someone take pictures?

Is the place important, is the action important, or is the person important?

What am I going to focus on? Is the scene or the movement most important? Is it a "finding the answer to life" sort of piece, or is it a quiet moment about a quiet person?

Will there be interaction between my character and others?

Dialogue is fun to read. It's so much more real and alive than my questions and the subject's answers. I try to find out if the person I'm writing about will be taking their grandma out to lunch. If so, I want to go with them and hear how they talk naturally, not how they phrase their responses to me.

Do I want to tell the story around one scene or five minutes or a whole day, or perhaps follow someone over a period of time?

I wrote a story about a transgendered person after I followed her for ten months. Originally, I planned to follow her as she got electrolysis done, changed her name, picked out a new wardrobe, and changed the oil in her car with her new manicure. I kept following her around, but she was a lonely person and didn't really have friends or acquaintances who accepted her. I saw people reacting with surprise when she walked by on the street, but how could I write about that?

So I waited and waited and waited. Finally, she went to the driver's license office to get a picture with her new look, changing from Andrew to Madalynn. We spent about two hours at the office, including an hour waiting in line. People were forced to interact with her. When I sat down to write the story, it was the only scene I needed. Ten months of work following her around were condensed to two hours at the driver's license office.

Do the characters experience epiphany?

Do the subjects learn something about themselves? Do they become more confused about their place in the world? What kind of realization do they have or lack at the end of the story?

What's the big idea?

I ask myself this because my editor always does. Here's an example: I wrote a story about a man in a bar telling his buddies he had been flashed by two women. Why is that important? What does it say about our culture? Well, it shows a universal truth about the importance of storytelling: The guys at the bar goaded another guy to tell a story. They had stopped in after work for a moment to themselves, their break between driving the garbage truck and going home to feed the dog and make dinner and pay the bills.

If you can find a universal truth in a story, even if it's as silly as "people like to be entertained at a bar," that's important. Thinking about universal truth frames your subject and moves it from one guy at the bar to a symbol that everyone can appreciate.

When I find that meaning, linked with action, I know I have a narrative.

Finding Good Topics:
An Editor's Questions

JAN WINBURN

In our newsroom we often read great narrative stories from other newspapers and wonder, "How did they get that idea?" Sometimes we call the writers and ask them. Finally, we realized we could develop a methodology for finding story ideas. We devised a set of questions. As journalist James B. Stewart said, "What are the smart questions?" Here are the seven that we use.

What are the enduring issues of the day? What are the universal subjects?

For narrative writing, this question suggests a follow-up: How can those issues be seen from inside one person's life? To give an example: The death penalty is an enduring subject. It's in the headlines, as it was twenty-five years ago and will be twenty-five years from now. A fresh take on an enduring subject is always timely. When the DNA exonerations of people convicted of murder began, I thought, "These people were nearly put to death. What would they do with the second lives they had been given?"

I wanted to find one of the oldest cases of a person released based on DNA evidence. I asked a reporter to write about what the man had done with his second life. The story surprised me. I thought he would go as far as possible from where his name was known. He went right back to the eastern shore of Maryland, where his father had been a waterman and he was a waterman.

Is there someone whose life is like that of someone in the headlines? Can this headline story be better understood through the eyes or experience of an ordinary person?

While Monica Lewinsky was in the news, a reporter could have looked at the personal life of other White House interns.

What truism is being presented in the news, and does heading in the opposite direction suggest a story?

We write about all sorts of conventional wisdom. Sometimes, you can take one of those truisms and look in the opposite direction for a story. One of my favorite writers at the *New York Times*, Dirk Johnson, wrote a piece called "When Money Is Everything Except Hers." During the 1990s economic boom, he visited Ronald Reagan's hometown, Dixon, Illinois—a place that was supposedly very prosperous. He wrote about a person there who wasn't prosperous.

Where would it be worth going deeper? Where is the close-up on a story? Where does mystery remain?

When a story has been heavily covered, reposition the camera. Pull in from the wide, news-gathering angle. Look for a close-up angle on the story that hasn't been told.

Where is there ambiguity in a big story?

Look for what author Gary Smith calls "emotional truth." One night in October 1994 a Baltimore man named Nathaniel Hurt went out on his balcony and fired a gun four times into the darkness. Hurt, who was sixty-two, killed a thirteen-year-old boy. He lived in a neighborhood where open-air drug markets operated and kids vandalized cars and homes. Was Hurt a symbol of the beleaguered homeowner in a city under siege or just a vigilante?

Eight months after the incident, as Hurt's sentencing approached, the *Baltimore Sun* features writer Laura Lippman visited Hurt at his home. She saw the pristine carpet protected by plastic runners and the creamy white sofa. Hurt reenacted that night for her. Her story revealed something new: the man himself. "Listening to Hurt," she wrote, "one begins to understand what it means to be honest to a fault."

Is there an untold background tale?

In 2002, Joseph Palczynski went on a rampage in Baltimore after his girlfriend had broken off their relationship. He kidnapped her and killed four people who got in his way. He took her family hostage. The events unfolded over two weeks, ending with the police killing Palczynski. Nearly lost in the coverage of this complex story was the fact that it had started as domestic violence. Four writers at the *Baltimore Sun* saw that connection and located six of Palczynski's former girlfriends—all of whom had been abused. Using evidence that spanned thirteen years, the writers wove a chilling narrative exposing Palczynski's long pattern of battering women and threatening their families.

Is an ending really another beginning?

Endings mark the beginnings of new stories about to unfold. A farmer's wife lost her husband in a house fire. That was the end of one story but also the beginning of another: her life on the farm without him. We wrote about her first year alone on the farm.

Reporters and editors should ask themselves all these questions and then *listen*. Listen to what people in your own life say to you. Keep yourself open to all of life; take your head out of the newspaper. Sometimes I have to stop reading newspapers because I have a hard time opening up that other chamber of my mind—the one that invites ideas in from life.

Reporting for Narrative: Ten Tips

MARK KRAMER

When you write, and especially when you write narrative, you create a sequential intellectual and emotional experience for the reader. From your perspective as the writer you are doing other things: describing an event, creating a record, imparting information, explaining that information's source, or doing what my high school teachers called "showing your work"—as in "Solve this problem, show your work." But whatever else you are doing, the fact remains: Your readers will have an intellectual and emotional experience as they read your work. If that experience isn't pleasurable or exciting, they will stop reading.

To keep them reading, you must create a worthwhile experience and also a logical one. In narrative work, characters move through an experience or a set of experiences. That movement crosses the topical categories of any subject outline the author could possibly devise. In narrative writing, characters take action over time, and events unfold. In order to present an organized account of something, however, the author must cover it topic by topic. To make both these things possible, the writer must gather all the topical information *and* all the action. That requires a different reporting style. Here are ten steps to follow.

1. Before selecting a topic, think carefully about what will intrigue readers. Story conception is critical. Is the topic's emotional temperature high or low? A reader brings a lot of emotionality to "high-valence" stories. The most common high emotional valence news story is about an endangered baby: a stolen car with a kid in the back. It takes very little work to energize readers' concern in a story about an endangered baby; as a species we are hardwired to care. Once you have readers engaged and concerned, you have them in the palm of your hand. You can digress to give background information. Your readers will forgive you nearly anything. Stories with high emotional valence require no context, no characterization.

It is more difficult to write narrative about low emotional valence topics. The writer must marshal other tools, including more accomplished writing. Perhaps the slowest topic ever in narrative writing is the flow of rocks; John McPhee wrote four books about it. You can do an exercise to help you figure out McPhee's secrets for keeping the reader with him. In the margin of one of his books—*Basin and Range*, for example—keep a running tab of the questions that come to mind. You will find that the question changes with nearly every paragraph. McPhee inserts them cunningly to mesh with his sharp images, strong characterizations, and anecdotes. These operant questions aren't the big thematic questions of the book but small puzzles to keep the reader going while he deals with the flow of rocks.

2. After selecting a good topic, secure good access. Say you're considering travel to Paris or Buenos Aires or Boise. If you don't know anyone in Paris or Buenos Aires but have met some fascinating people from Boise, go there. Access is everything. The best idea will become a lousy story without deep access to people living their lives. This access takes charm, guts, and aplomb. Potential subjects will take you at the level of sophistication that you bring to the subject. If you're naive and gawky, you will receive the basic public-relations version of the subject. Do your homework beforehand; the more you know, the more collegially you'll be treated.

For any story you must have access to people at what Henry James called "the felt life level." In his preface to *Portrait of a Lady*, he addresses "the perfect dependence of the 'moral' sense of a work of art on the amount of *felt life* concerned in producing it." *Felt life* is the level of informal comprehension that you have of your subject at the end of a day spent reporting.

You sit, dog tired, at the edge of your bed, and your significant other says, "How was your day?" You reply, "That road commissioner was a real ass. He's so vulgar and vain. Yet there's something sweet about him." The next day you go to the newsroom and write, "A new road intersection at the corner of Holmes and Fourteenth was announced yesterday by the road commissioner."

Narrative demands felt-life-level access, which is extremely difficult to get. You call a surgeon and say, "I hear you're doing a new kind of neck surgery, and I'd like to find out more about it." He says, "Fine. I have time for a cup of coffee Thursday afternoon at two o'clock." You need to say, "I don't want an interview. I want to watch you living your normal day. What about Wednesday when you're too busy to see me? I won't be a bother. I'll just follow you around."

If you obtain that access because the surgeon is your uncle, don't do it. That's contaminated access. If you learn that your surgeon uncle is an obtuse egotist and that's relevant to the story, you can't include it because it will upset your mother. You need the uncle of a distant friend.

3. Find the unfolding action that will provide the narrative line. Once you secure good access, you must find good examples of unfolding action. Ask your source about her schedule for the coming week and then find something interesting you can experience with her. You won't know the true subject of your piece until you get on site and see things happen. In this case, *subject* doesn't mean topic, location, or main character; it means what the story is about, on a deeper level.

You don't have to follow chronological order, but whatever order you follow must make sense to the reader. For example, following the reporter as she gathers material does not make good narrative. It's the story of how an ignorant person—the reporter—became slightly less ignorant. Your narrative should center on your subject's life. You can't falsify the sequence of events, but you can start at the end if you tell your reader what you are doing.

4. Find hints of character in the action. I wrote a piece about a builder of ship models, an old, meticulous man of great brilliance but not the kindest man, as he would tell you himself. One of his sons, a rather famous writer, expressed resentment, off the record, of his father's self-absorption and insularity. Those personality traits became the story's core.

5. Find the right scene details through careful sensory reporting. Sight, sound, smell, touch, and taste will allow you to set strong scenes, which in turn develop a sense of place in your writing. Beginning narrative writers often set scenes too casually or with too much detail. Give the reader a feeling of volume, space, and dimension, but don't build a diorama.

To reconstruct long-ago events or any scene that you didn't observe, ask your subjects to help you. Don't write "George recalls trudging through the snow." Say to George, "I'm going to do something weird. I'm going to ask you fifty questions about a seemingly innocuous moment in the past. If you can answer them, you can help me build this scene for the reader." If you can't corroborate the person's memories, at least note in your text that they are recollections.

6. Pinpoint your subjects' emotional experience, not your own. The first time I walked into an operating room, while writing a book about surgeons, I thought, "Yuck, blood. This is brutal." None of the people I was writing about said, "Yuck, blood." I had to record my own emotions because they would duplicate the reader's emotions at that point in the story. But it was much more important for me to notice and record what the surgeon and others in the operating room said, thought, and felt. When I wrote that scene, I considered the reader's response, but I had to present the characters' responses.

7. Rigorously research your story's context. Narrative exists inside a social context, an economic context, and many other shells of context. Because of that, research is essential. You must digress from the running narrative to give necessary background information and frame your story. For example, the common story of the surviving family farm is made much more powerful by the author's explanation of the economics of family farms and why they aren't surviving.

If you don't do some research before you start reporting, you risk receiving a public relations snow job. Do just enough research to orient yourself, then do most of your reporting. Save most of the research for late in the reporting process. At that point you only have to find the right information for your story. If you research too early, you have to find out everything.

8. Late in the drafting process, crystallize the point of your story. *Destination* is what my high school English teachers called "the theme." I didn't understand what my English teachers were talking about until I had been a writer for fifteen years. I return to my initial contention: Narrative writing is creating the right sequential, intellectual, and emotional experience for readers. Early on, readers must have (1) an emotional attitude toward the characters and events, and (2) the sense that they are being told all of it for a worthy reason. All the set scenes, characterization, and background must head toward a destination. The ending must bring a payoff.

9. Very late in the writing process, refine the difference between your views and your subject's views. While writing *Three Farms,* I might have felt sad or angry about the loss of family farms, but I still had to write a fair profile of a corporate farm manager. Generally, you needn't mask your views, but make sure your readers can also understand your subjects' perspectives. This refinement will help you navigate the rules of balance for the publication where your story will appear; the rules for *The Nation* are different from those for *Time* magazine.

10. Cherish the structural ideas and metaphors that come to you while you are reporting. While sitting in your subject's barn or operating room or kitchen, you will suddenly think, "Oh, boy, I love this quote because I can use it to introduce that important topic." In the moment, it seems that those realizations will stick to you like notes on a bulletin board, but your mind is not a bulletin board. Peg those ideas in the moment. Write notes to yourself about how to write your piece.

To Tape or Not to Tape

ADAM HOCHSCHILD

I'm deeply grateful for the invention of the pocket tape recorder. Our profession was much harder before it came along. The recorder enables me to be on several channels at once. It takes care of the sound track in a far more accurate way than I can by taking notes. Meanwhile, it frees me to take notes on all the other details: what the person is wearing, what books are on his shelf, what paintings are on her wall, what can be seen out the window, as well as the expressions on the person's face while speaking, her gestures, and his movements. I find that people are hardly ever self-conscious about the recorder, especially if I turn it on without breaking eye contact with them and don't look at it.

When I wrote a book about how Russians are coming to terms with Stalin's heritage, I did all my interviewing in Russian. I'm not a fluent Russian speaker. Sometimes I understood almost everything people said; other times, much less. I came up with a technique that I thought was original, only to discover that every American correspondent in Moscow did the same thing. I tape-recorded my interviews and then found a Russian who spoke English extremely well. I had her transcribe the interviews in English. I received wonderful English transcriptions that were full of fascinating material I hadn't quite realized I was gathering.

JACQUI BANASZYNSKI

When I was a reporter, I tended not to tape. A tape recorder can be as intrusive as the reporter's notebook. Tape recorders make me intellectually lazy; my mind drifts because I know I'm getting it all on tape.

When I did use a tape recorder and had to go back to the newsroom and transcribe, it slowed me down enormously. During the course of an interview, my mind filters information, moving toward the core of my story. I found that when I listened to recordings and transcribed them, it was as though I had erased all the filtered, distilled information in my brain. I returned to the wide swath of *all* the information from the interview— not the selective material I had decided was important to my story. It was like having to start over.

If you can steel yourself against using it as a crutch and against the drudge of transcription, I say go ahead and tape. In this day it's a good defense. Still, tape recorders pose two other dangers, both delicate issues. First, when you tape-record and then compare the recording to your notes, you find out how much material in your notes isn't quite right. Second, if you take quotes directly from tape recordings, you hardly ever get a decent quote. People don't speak in perfect English. They "um" and "ah"; they drop subjects and pronouns. When I take notes, the quotes I record are closer to proper grammar, though the person probably didn't say them exactly that way.

JON FRANKLIN

I use a tape recorder all the time. I often don't listen to the tape, but I have it as a backup if I need it. I don't take that many notes unless the topic is technical, something I don't know well. I may write down some quotes, but I do more paraphrasing. I write down dialogue because I use a lot of it. Over the years I've become much better at remembering, once I really understand my story. When you're going out for the first time, you had better use a tape recorder *and* take notes *and* try mightily to remember, because you probably still won't get everything you need.

GAY TALESE

I do not use a tape recorder. I espouse patience in listening, trying to capture what the other person is thinking, trying to see the world from that person's view. I don't necessarily want word for word from their mouth. The exact words people say don't necessarily capture their view, especially when you have a tape recorder working.

The tape recorder was not popular when I was at the *New York Times* in the 1950s and 1960s. Journalism has become too much Q & A. The tape recorder has created a sort of talk radio on paper, a first draft from the minds of important people. It's all verifiable, yes it is, and the lawyers are happy about that. But when I'm getting to know people, hanging out with them and listening to them, I'm making them into verifiable characters.

Interviewing: Accelerated Intimacy

ISABEL WILKERSON

I don't do much interviewing in the Mike Wallace sense of the word. In a story about a ten-year-old, the goal isn't nailing the kid to the wall. You don't go up to a ninety-year-old and say, "Isn't it true that on November 18, 1942, you got a parking ticket on Forty-third Street?" My work involves spending a lot of time with ordinary people in extraordinary circumstances. It requires a different kind of interviewing, a different kind of relating to the subject.

I need to create what I call accelerated intimacy. We can't write the beautiful narrative stories that we all dream of unless we can get some things from the mouths of our sources. They must be comfortable enough to tell us *anything*. In journalism school, no one called the interactions between journalists and sources *relationships*, but that's what they are.

In thinking about these relationships, think also about your role relative to the subject's role. To help win the subject over, I try to make the most of my own traits and define a natural relationship between the source and me. The average age of the people I'm interviewing for my book is eighty-six. I come to them as a granddaughter.

To achieve accelerated intimacy I only do formal interviews when essential. I do everything I can to make my subjects feel comfortable enough to talk with me. I still ask questions—lots of them. I try to be a great audience. I nod; I look straight into their eyes; I laugh at their jokes, whether I think they're funny or not. I am serious when they're serious.

I think of these as *guided conversations*. The overall interaction is more important than the particular questions. I try to make the interaction as enjoyable as possible. No one wants to be grilled for hours on end. A formal interview isn't conducive to soul baring.

People often compare interviewing to peeling an onion. Though it's a cliché, the metaphor is instructive. Picture the onion. Its outer layer is dry and brittle. You tear off the outer layer and throw it away. The next layer is shiny, rubbery, limp, and sometimes has a tinge of green. You won't use it, either, unless it's the only onion you have. You want the center of the onion: It is crisp and pungent and has the sharpest, truest flavor. It's the very best part. It requires very little slicing because it's already small, compact. The size and quality are so perfect that you can just toss it right into whatever you're making.

The same goes for the interview process. The first thing out of a source's mouth is often of little use. It's the outer layer. Whenever we sit down with a person, we want to get to the center of the onion as fast as we can. That's accelerated intimacy. Every interview, every relationship built with a source, has a predictable arc. That arc progresses through seven phases. Each phase holds pitfalls. If we want people to tell us what's really on their minds, we need to make sure we don't give up before the seventh phase.

Phase One: Introduction

It all begins with the introduction. You flag a person down on the street, or you call and explain what you're doing, or you walk in the front door. You pull out your notebook. The person is busy. The person doesn't want to talk. The person wants to get rid of you.

Phase Two: Adjustment

You are feeling each other out. You ask the basic introductory questions to start the ball rolling. If you're on a deadline, you're thinking: "Am I getting what I need?" The person you are interviewing is thinking, "Do I really want to talk to this person? Do I have the time for this?" The source is getting used to the note-taking. He or she is looking at your notebook; you're looking at your watch.

Phase Three: Moment of Connection

You must make a connection with this person to accelerate getting to know her. You know you're making that connection when the person puts down the briefcase and leans back in the chair. The subject thinks, "Maybe this won't be that bad. I'll give it a little more time."

A lot of interviews are cut off at the very first stages when the interviewer isn't getting much. The subject hasn't yet set the briefcase down. You might think you already have a serviceable quote, but the first thing out of someone's mouth is rarely worthwhile. It is difficult to be interviewed, so give people a chance to get their thoughts together. Sometimes people need three or four chances to get it right. That next try can create poetry.

Phase Four: Settling In

In this settling-in phase the person finds that she is kind of enjoying the interaction. You both settle into what could be a very short-term relationship.

Phase Five: Revelation

At this point the source feels comfortable enough to reveal something very candid or deep. The source can't believe she's saying this to you. It is a very good sign, but not necessarily in the way you might expect. Often, what the person says is important to her but has no meaning for you. It has nothing to do with what you're writing about. Still, it suggests a turning point in the person's sense of trust. It's a sign that the reporter may now be able to get what she really wants.

Phase Six: Deceleration

Things begin to wind down. You may feel you already have the best you can get from the interview. You try to bring closure. You put your notebook away. And what happens? The source doesn't want the interview to end, because the two of you have a contract: You're a reporter, and you listen to the source.

Phase Seven: Reinvigoration

The source feels free to say almost anything and now makes the very best revelation of the interview. Suddenly, with the notebook closed, the source has grown to trust you, without even realizing it. In this final phase you have that person in the mood to actively cooperate. You have reached the center of the onion. Make the most of that moment—it's fleeting. If you get back to the newsroom and realize you should have asked something else, it won't be the same if you call back. The relationship will have changed.

This entire exchange, this seven-phase arc, can take five minutes or five hours or five months. It is the same whether you are working on a daily article or a book.

How does the reporter handle this fast-developing candor? Don't ever lead your sources—that really gets you in trouble. If you are leading and think you know what the story is, and you write it and it's not right, it will come back to haunt you.

In the ideal interview, the source feels comfortable enough to share with me all the details of an experience. I just listen. That is the ideal, but it's rarely that simple. Just as you have motives for doing the interview, your subject does, too. No one ever talks to the press without some ulterior motive: a celebrity promoting a movie, a candidate running for office, or someone seeking catharsis.

We must have tremendous humility as we interview, and also understand the enormity of what our sources are doing when they talk to us. Sometimes they don't even realize it themselves. For my book I plucked people from relative anonymity. I feel a tremendous responsibility and obligation to tell their stories accurately—and not just accurately but in a fair and balanced way. Your own sense of integrity, honesty, and empathy matters more than anything. Empathy is the balance to power. Power without empathy leaves you with manipulation—a horrible thing.

There is a tremendous power differential between the reporter and the ordinary individuals we write about. I can't even imagine what it must be like to have your life story displayed across the front page of the *New York Times*, above the fold, on a Sunday, with over a million people having access to your most intimate thoughts. Most of us wouldn't submit to such a thing. I have tremendous gratitude for the people who do that. It is important to honor the people who allow themselves to be representatives of something larger in our society. Their return is very small compared to what they give us.

The Psychological Interview

JON FRANKLIN

The psychological interview is a journalistic adaptation of the history-taking process that a psychiatrist completes with each new patient. Though they might not use the term "psychological interview," writers have been using these interview techniques for at least a century. For narrative writers this type of interview answers the question: *What made this character into the person she or he is?* Subjects have much more patience for this type of in-depth interview than you might think. I begin by asking about the person's earliest memories and then progress step-by-step through adolescence. The whole process takes two to four hours.

At no point should you ask the person to pay attention to you. This is key. Do not talk except to encourage your subject. You can begin by asking, *What is your first memory?* A first memory is a story; it has a time, place, subject, character, and mood. First memories are not random. When someone tells you a first memory, it's likely an essential story. It may not have happened exactly as told, but what the person remembers is *truly* what they think happened.

Even if someone's first memory isn't germane to your story, it opens a door. Once a person has told you his or her earliest memory, you can ask all sorts of other things: *What was your family like? Were you the first, last, or middle child? Was your family well-off or poor? Did you know? What happened at family holidays? Did your parents raise you together? Did you have a pet?* I'm interested in knowing all these things and also whether the family experienced any crises.

At this stage in the interview, you are poking around, discovering both *what* a person remembers and *how* it's remembered. Ask about the person's experiences and thoughts—not about their feelings or opinions. Through a person's stories you can begin to discern personality. Follow the person's story through to adulthood. *What do you remember about first or second grade? Tell me about middle school. Did you do well in school? What subjects did you like? Did your family move around a lot? Were you popular? Did you have a lot of girlfriends or boyfriends?*

Why do people answer questions such as this, posed by someone they barely know? Because people are most interested in themselves. Other than a therapist, who can a person really talk to with complete honesty? Your mother? You have to be kidding; she's made a career of manipulating you. Your spouse? *Really?* The truth is, nobody. It's a big advantage that you, the interviewer, have no stake in the character's life. Yes, it is in some sense an invasive process, but it is done with respect and with the subject's full permission.

This sort of interview gives you the understanding needed to empathize with the character and to tell a deep story. Once you have all this information, filtered through the person's subjective memory, you can compare it to public history and to information from other family members or friends. In the end, you will use very little of the information directly in what you write. The small amount you *do* use will be powerful, and the entire process helps you tell the story from your subject's point of view or from the perspective of the subject's world.

Every deep story involves a subjective person slamming into an objective world. Understanding both the subjective and the objective are crucial to knowing what happened.

Taken in sum, the responses you get in a psychological interview will give you a good idea of who the person is. Few people change their fundamental natures as adults. Traumatic events in adulthood can change a person, but in essence, most of us are junior high school kids who aged.

Participatory Reporting: Sending Myself to Prison

TED CONOVER

Anyone who leaves the comfortable role of the traditional journalist—the company of computer and telephone, newsroom and colleagues—risks embarrassment, awkwardness, even injury. At the same time, taking chances in research opens the door to insights not otherwise possible. If the reporter can walk in another person's shoes, why not do it?

I think some of my best work has resulted from immersion in someone else's world. As a college anthropology major, I learned about participant observation, in which a researcher visits a group of people and learns by living with them: eating their food, speaking their language, sharing their space and rhythms of life. At the same time every day she takes notes, becoming both participant and observer.

By wearing these two hats I build bridges to both my subjects and my readers. First-person narration lets me act as a stand-in for the reader, expressing surprise at what's new, discomfort at what's strange, and delight at what's cool. Early on, I have to establish the kind of person I am and my relationship to the story. Here many new writers make a mistake, thinking they have to come off as capable and competent in a foreign world. They forget that their subjects should be their teachers; sometimes they turn themselves into their stories' heroes. But a smart journalist always remembers that even though it's first person, the subject isn't *me*. It's *them*. The reader roots for a humble narrator.

Honesty is very important in the first person. Readers see right through a narrator who is putting on airs. As I traveled on freight trains with hobos for my first book, I wasn't trying to convince the reader that I was a hobo. That would have been ridiculous. (Thank God I wasn't a hobo, that I don't understand homelessness that intimately.) I was a beginner in a scary and little-known world—right there is all the drama you need.

A successful narrative involves change, a narrative arc. One of the things that usually changes in my books is my first-person narrator. I go from naive to smarter, for one thing, but sometimes I get beaten down.

Narrative journalism is one of the most difficult kinds of journalism. Getting the story requires becoming close to people—people who start to think of the journalist as a friend. But a moment of reckoning comes when the piece is published. When I'm reporting, I want people to remember that I'm the journalist so they won't be surprised later—except in the case of *Newjack*, my fourth book. I did something very different while reporting *Newjack*: No one knew I was writing about my experiences.

The book grew out of a desire to write about prison. I had recently moved to New York, and from reading the newspapers and talking to people, I knew that huge numbers of people were going to prison in New York—mainly because of the drug laws. I asked myself: *Is there a new way to write about prison? What hasn't been reported?* The answer was corrections officers, the prison guards. COs knew prison intimately, yet most people knew nothing about them. *The New Yorker* liked the idea and assigned me a piece about the families of COs in upstate New York. I planned to write about their lives at work and at home.

The New York Department of Correctional Services had other

ideas. They weren't impressed by *The New Yorker* and said I could visit a prison only once. There was no way to write the kind of in-depth piece I had in mind if couldn't see my subjects at work. They also turned down my request to shadow a new recruit through the seven-week corrections training academy. So I applied for the job of corrections officer myself. I didn't tell them I planned to write about it. I felt justified in this because of our country's incarceration crisis, with its huge expense and racial character, as well as the little-known circumstances of corrections officers.

I disclosed what I was doing to only a handful of people. Most of my friends had no idea. I'd never done that before, and I hope I don't have to do it again. *Newjack* helped me understand why so many undercover narcotics agents get divorced, go to jail, and seem to have their lives fall apart: Secrecy is destructive. Only a critically important story can justify it. (Of course, reporters rarely disclose everything. If reporters always said exactly why they were calling, they would rarely get the information they need.)

As soon as I finished *Newjack*, I called the half-dozen coworkers who were my best friends, as well as the superintendent, and told them about the book. The top brass at the New York Department of Correctional Services hates my book in part because I breached their security system.

When I had applied for the job, I thought that I wouldn't get it because I had filled out the application truthfully. I said I was a free-lance writer. I listed the menial jobs I'd held to support my writing: managing an apartment building, tutoring kids in Spanish, coaching for the SAT, teaching aerobics. I also included that I had worked as a reporter at the *Aspen Times*. I thought, "*There's* a red flag."

Miraculously, I still got hired. It turns out the real red flags for the Department of Correctional Services are bad credit and a short temper. People in debt are thought to be more susceptible to bribes from inmates, and people prone to losing their tempers will definitely do so working in prisons.

Once hired, I started at the corrections academy. On the last day I was assigned to Sing Sing, New York State's second-oldest prison and, luckily, the one nearest my home. I decided to stick with it, thinking I'd stay on the job for maybe four months. But after four months I didn't know enough to write a book; not enough had happened to me. I stayed for ten months.

During those months of immersion, I thought of myself primarily as a corrections officer. I really did. In my ninth month there, they announced the exam that was offered every five years for promotion to sergeant. I actually caught myself thinking, "Oh, I better sign up for that. If I miss it, I'll have to wait five more years."

It is a very intense and demanding job, especially for a rookie. In fact, the work made it difficult for me to see my other friends. I didn't have room in my mind for other things. I was *in* the prison. Day to day I was so busy with the job—walking inmates to and from their cells, negotiating with them—that I had little time to think about the book's progress. I didn't begin writing the manuscript until after I left the job. I couldn't write while having the experience because I didn't know the shape of it or how it would end. I needed to be able to reflect on the whole.

I occasionally had time at work to take notes, and I took as many as possible. The department recommends that each CO keep a small notebook in his or her shirt pocket to write down things the inmates need, such as "toilet overflowing, send plumber, C23 cell." That was perfect for me. I would write that down and then write, "Inmate has three gold teeth with the letters R-E-D engraved on them." I wrote down as much dialogue as I could.

At home after each workday, I unloaded all my impressions onto my computer before sending the babysitter home. I methodically emptied every drawer of my brain and tried to get prison out of my system. My notes for *Newjack*, with typos and bad grammar, are much longer than the book itself. When I began to write, those notes were the clay from which I shaped the narrative.

Two things in the book are not literally true. I point them out at the beginning: certain people's names and some of the dialogue. When I write for the *New York Times Magazine*, I cannot change names. In my books I take a bit of license because it's a more personal literary form. At Sing Sing I worked with people who didn't know what I was doing. I decided that if I portrayed them in any way they might find embarrassing, I should change their names. I changed about one-third of the names in the book.

In the culture of COs, when someone acts dishonorably, he or she "meets you in the parking lot." That's the shorthand for an after-work beating. Almost every day I feared I would be found out and met in the parking lot. I didn't have a book contract while I worked in the prison, nor did I want one. If I ended up in the parking lot, I didn't want to be responsible for a book that I couldn't produce.

When I began working on *Newjack*, I didn't have an agenda, but I did have a set of concerns. I was interested in the portrayal of corrections officers, the stereotype of brutality, the racial divide between officers and inmates. I have political ideas, but I try to wear them lightly. I didn't want to preach to a choir of prison-reform advocates, nor was I trying to please an audience of corrections officers. I wanted to describe an experience and a way of looking at the world to a general audience of intelligent readers. It seemed to me that if I could watch what the job did to me and to the people around me, if I could catalog moments of friction and accord between inmates and officers, if I could get to know some inmates and officers deeply, I would have most of what I needed.

Did my book result in any reforms in the corrections system? I like to think so, but I'm sure of only one. In *Newjack* I describe B-Block, the immense building where I worked. Housing six hundred inmates, it is one of the largest freestanding cellblocks in the world. Horrific and very dim inside, it seemed as if the windows hadn't been washed in fifty years. I included that detail in the book. The wife of a B-Block inmate sent me an e-mail after visiting her husband and wrote, "My husband just wanted you to know that a month after your book came out, they washed the windows."

So there's the power of the press for you.

Being There

ANNE HULL

Writing is always hard, and it's often made harder by circumstances. You might have to do it outside a Kosovo refugee camp with a penlight in your mouth and a laptop balanced on your knees. Some journalism happens under the most extreme conditions. Our lives depend on it—at least my life does. If I didn't write, I can't imagine what I would do. It is all I've ever done. Often, we are out of balance because we write. We don't pay enough attention to our personal lives. We are difficult to live with because we're distracted; we want to be with our story.

Writing is a tough gamble from the start. If we aren't clear in our writing, all our reporting means nothing. If we haven't done our reporting, vagueness shows through. If we're show-offs, we obscure truth. If we're overly sentimental, we wreck the piece. Good reporting is the key to success. Even now I bumble through every story. Still, I've learned some ways to try to do it right. They aren't rules, just accidents I've polished along the way.

Observe carefully.

Observation, the art of watching, is one of the most underrated elements of reporting, especially in newspaper journalism. The natural impulse is to ask questions. Sometimes that is wrong. It makes the reporter the focus of attention. Be humble. It honors the person you're trying to observe.

Think like a photographer. Watch. Change location. At a family dinner, change your place around the dining table. Keep moving, keep shifting your point of view, and keep quiet. Try not to interrupt the flow of events.

Live as they do.

A few years ago I wrote about a group of women from a village in central Mexico called Palomas. They traveled to North Carolina to work as crab pickers. They would stand at a steel table with small knifes and pick the meat from blue crabs ten hours a day. It is some of the most tedious work imaginable. It's painful, too; the crab shells are sharp.

Yet the women desperately wanted those jobs. They were part of a legal guest-worker program in the United States. They traveled from central Mexico to the North Carolina coast by bus. I took the trip with them. A reporter's dream, right? I sat with them for four days as they threaded their way across America. They knew nothing about this country; they had only dreamed about it, about what it might bring them. That four-day trip, a beautiful experience, became about ten paragraphs in the twenty-thousand-word final series.

We arrived at our destination in North Carolina at midnight. The women, the photographer, and I had not slept or changed clothes in four days. The owner of the crab house dropped us off at the trailer where the women were to live. She said, "I'll be back at five for the first day of work." *Five hours later.* I didn't see how any of us could do it. Sure enough, at five in the morning: *honk, honk.* We walked out to the van.

One woman's hands trembled because she was so exhausted. It's one thing for someone to tell you that her hands were shaking. It's another to *watch* someone's hands shaking. The best thing is to feel your *own* hands shake while watching *her* hands do the same. *They* were the ones with crabs slicing their palms, cutting themselves with the knives. I couldn't have done it for ten minutes, and they did it for ten hours. If you can feel some part of what your subject feels for even a moment, it infuses your writing with authority. It opens your heart. When in Rome, live as a Roman. Always. Suffering by proxy is no good. Be aware of what your subjects are doing. Don't drink a cold drink in front of someone who is not allowed to have one.

Try to minimize your presence.

It is hard to be somewhere with a notebook; you're already an obvious outsider. Try not to draw any more attention to yourself.

Remember, you are not one of them.

Warn your subjects of your separateness. Keep reminding them. At the very beginning of your reporting say, "I'm just going to watch. Don't feel disrespected if, when you bow your head at supper to pray, I don't do it." Or "Please, if I'm asked to dance at the party, I can't do it. If you all are drinking beer, I would love a beer, but I'm working. As much as possible I'd like to stay in the background." It doesn't always work, but at least it sets up a boundary. It's a very strict code but an important one.

Check people out.

Poor people often don't have paper trails like politicians do, but you still need to treat all your subjects with the same rigor. Do whatever record-checking you can early on. If you're working with someone over several months and find out about something halfway through, that could rearrange everything. If you find something in your research, talk to your editor first. It might not matter. There are things in all our histories that don't matter in our larger stories. Other things do.

Build a world around their world.

Working on a longer story is like being in love. To sustain myself I try to build a world around my subjects' world. I fortify my imagination with elements from their lives. I spent nine months working on the story about the Mexican women picking crab in North Carolina. I went to Mexico four times for that story. I bought CDs of the music they listened to at home in Palomas. I read *One Hundred Years of Solitude* by Gabriel García Márquez, *The Mambo Kings* by Guy Roberto Gill, and *Cutting for Sign* by William Langewiesche, which is about the United States–Mexico border.

As invested as you become in another world, as a writer you are ever the infidel. After the story about the women from Palomas was published, I went on to baseball. I created another world for myself. I switched over to reading David Remnick and David Halberstam. It's okay to have these false little helpers.

Remember, the writing process can be hell.

It is important to have someone who helps you through those lonely moments when the story doesn't go well. It is very difficult to integrate news with writing. I can only do it by rewriting. The Mexico story was a three-day series. I wrote four drafts; it took four months to reach the final twenty thousand words.

Think about each word.

A story's "why" is the entire cosmos. A story's particularity is the words. Each word matters. Each verb must work. If it feels too familiar, think about it again. You can't always do this at five in the evening with only two hours left before deadline, but if you improve even a couple of words, that elevates your story. With longer deadlines, spend time recrafting the sentences.

Pay attention to the sense of place.

A story needs to have a geographical heart. With the giant flood of information and with journalists reporting from their computers, many of our newspapers now lack a true sense of place. There is nowhere but everywhere now. Whether it's Philadelphia's City Hall or a baseball diamond, the story must be *located.* You accomplish this through basic, straightforward reporting.

While you drive around town reporting, open your eyes. Pay attention to the food that people order in restaurants. If you stay overnight, don't stay at a chain hotel. Stay where the locals might stay. Anytime you can stay in a bed-and-breakfast, chat up the owners and learn about the town. Look in phone books and write down what you find.

Push that information through a creative sieve. This is the hardest part. You want to weave a sense of place, not just give a laundry list of details.

Read the local newspaper.

Pick up a newspaper next to the cash register at the mini-mart. Here's something I found on the front page of a newspaper in Kentucky. "At Elk Lick Baptist Church this past Sunday, we were low on help. Our pastor, Charlie Wilson, is in the hospital, so he was not there to preach. But the Lord gave us David Combs to do his best, and he did a good job. We had 21 brave souls come out, and had a good time in the Lord." It's so beautiful. Imagine something that real in *your* newspaper.

Go to church.

To help capture a sense of place, I always try to attend church in the town where I'm reporting. While working on a story in Kentucky, I became half-transfixed by a traveling evangelist preacher with a guitar. I didn't have a skirt with me, so I went to a Family Dollar Store and bought one for $6.00. In a Pentecostal church, it's good to have a skirt on—if you're a lady.

I was just reporting and watching, and suddenly everyone was falling out, speaking in tongues. They gathered around me with a big bottle of olive oil and anointed me. When you set out to experience fully, expect to experience *fully*. Church is a good place to learn about community.

Use the language of the people you're trying to capture.

Language is important to a sense of place. A tape recorder comes in handy. Don't paraphrase what people say. Allow their syntax, language, and slang to blossom fully in your notebook. Put it in your story and do your damnedest to make sure it's still there when your edited copy appears in the newspaper. Include the personal words that reveal who a person is.

Be as open as you possibly can with your subjects.

You can't just sit there mutely and not share things from your own life. There has to be some give-and-take even though it can't ever be fair. As the weeks and months go by, you cannot remain a professional, distant iceberg.

Be attuned to your subjects' rhythms. If your subjects start to get annoyed or need some space, leave for a while. Even on a deadline story you can leave for a couple of hours and come back. Be attuned to their needs. They need breaks, and so do you.

When the USS *Cole* bombing happened, I wanted to write about a sailor who was presumed dead. I looked at the pictures of all the sailors, and one just begged to be written about. Her name was Lakeina Francis. She came from rural North Carolina. I called her mother at home on a Saturday afternoon. There was no sweet talking; in fact, it was bumbling. "Mrs. Francis, I'm so sorry about your loss," I said.

"I don't have a loss yet," Mrs. Francis said. "We're still waiting to hear." Lakeina had not been declared dead; she was missing. I felt terrible, of course. She told me, "No, I don't feel like talking. This isn't a good time. We've had TV people here all day. We're talked out."

I called her back later, apologizing for intruding. I said I had been thinking about Lakeina, as I truly had. I told her it would mean a lot to the readers of the *Washington Post* to learn a little bit about who she is—not *was*.

Mrs. Francis said, "Come on out. If you want to come to North Carolina, we'll be here." I didn't make it there until about 10:30 the next night. They lived in the middle of nowhere—no lights, cows leaning against the fences. I got to the Francis home and stayed for an hour and a half. I hardly said a word. I didn't need to be the reporter with all the questions and answers. There were two Navy chaplains in the room who personified death with their dress whites, white shoes, and white hats. The only question I asked that night was "May I come back in the morning?"

I returned and stayed all day, again hardly asking any questions. A procession of silver-haired women came to the house with their foil-covered plates of macaroni and cheese and fried chicken. Others came with American flags.

I wrote a story about that young woman's life vanishing from a small town, from the place she had desperately wanted to get away from. In the end, a small place called Woodleaf held her tightly. I filed the story the next day. It was simple, employing many of the techniques we use for longer-term narratives but written on deadline.

After filing, I went to Norfolk, Virginia, to cover the memorial service. The Francis family went, too. President Clinton met privately with all the sailors' families. He told the Francis family, "I feel like I know your daughter." I can't tell you how great that felt—not because he had read my story, but because he knew this woman. I hoped Lakeina's story would stay lodged in Clinton's heart and mind. Would it affect naval policy or the way we do things around the world? Of course not.

Still, the important things are the small, observed details that unfold before you while reporting. Journalists tend to be very self-centered: our questions, our answers, our timetable. Field reporting isn't about that. It's about going into someone else's home. Of course there is a time for questions. I had to know about Lakeina's background, so I asked about it. More important, though, I spent time in her bedroom, looking at the items she had collected before she went off and joined the Navy. It's the little things that really matter in our stories, part of just being there.

Not *Always* Being There

LOUISE KIERNAN

The narrative journalism beat comes with strong pressure to spend every possible second immersed in your reporting. Actually, you serve your story even better by knowing when to step out of the picture.

I wrote a two-part series about a woman who had been killed by a piece of falling glass. She had a three-year-old daughter who had seen her die, and another daughter who was a teenager. The older daughter didn't open up to me during the reporting process. I felt as if I were a flashing neon sign saying to her: *Your mother is dead, and I'm here to find out how you feel about it.*

Her family was Mexican, and she was about to have her fifteenth birthday party, a very important event. Her father invited me to the party, but I knew in my heart that she didn't want me there. I really struggled with whether or not I should attend. I decided that I would go, but if it seemed like she was uncomfortable, I would leave.

When I arrived at the party, Samora opened the door, and her face just fell. I went in and spent a few minutes chatting with her. Then I said, "I just wanted to come by and say happy birthday. Have a great party." And I left.

After I backed off, she opened up to me. The next time I visited, she pulled out her mother's jewelry and told me what the pieces meant to her. The breakthrough came from *not* being there.

Reporting Across Cultures

VICTOR MERINA

Anytime your reporting beat intersects a culture different from your own—or sometimes even your own culture—you will have to deal with a variety of issues, including language, religion, moral values, social norms, ritual, taboos, stereotypes, and history. You will also have to face that community's entire history of relations with the media.

Place is critical in many cultures. There are places where people gather, where people practice religion, where people vent, where people talk honestly. The reporter must find these places, these *listening posts*. You go to a listening post to find out what's happening in a neighborhood so you can begin to understand what's going on in a particular culture or community. At listening posts you hear the community speaking and sense the community's heartbeat.

Listening posts take us outside the normal realm of talking to the community leaders or the self-appointed experts. You don't go there to conduct interviews but to learn and to understand. Don't flip out your notebook, approach the first person, and say, "So what's going on in the community?" Talk conversationally. Be human.

Don't just plunge ahead, asking community leaders and sources unfocused questions. Think about what you're reporting. Do your homework. Read prodigiously. Talk to a variety of people. Spend time in the community. Widen your research. Seek out data. Find listening posts and *listen.*

After you have listened, you can move on to interviews. Well-developed intercultural skills are crucial to successful interviews. Be aware of how physically close you are to people when you're talking with them. In some cultures, people stand shoulder to shoulder when they are speaking to one another. As a reporter, you must resist the urge to step back. In other cultures, standing too close is considered offensive. Let them set the distance.

Many of us give a firm handshake right away, but that's not always appropriate. Let the other person take the lead. When I visited South Africa in 2002, I developed a good relationship with the person who translated for me. At the end of the trip I felt so thankful that I hugged him, and I could sense his whole body stiffen; I knew it was a big gaffe. I began to apologize. "No, no," he said. "Next time, go like this." He tapped my fist with his fist. The following year I saw him again. I tried to hit his fist, and he hugged me. We had come to some mutual understanding.

While you are speaking to people, pay attention to the expressions on your face. Be careful of what you're conveying. Understand that their facial expressions might not mean what you think. When I was an investigative reporter at the *Los Angeles Times,* one of my mentors said to me, "If you look that person in the eye and the person flinches and looks away, the person is lying or hiding something." But he was mistaken. In some cultures you simply don't look people in the eye.

This mentor also told me, "They must have a direct answer to your question, or they're being evasive." Well, I have an uncle from the Philippines who told stories to answer questions. He was indirect, but he thought he was answering the question in a much more complete way than merely saying yes or no.

Smiling has very different meanings in different cultures. Sometimes male reporters shouldn't smile at women or even address them directly. In certain Asian communities, for example, it is considered disrespectful to speak to women without permission. Think about gender differences.

Show respect. Don't automatically use someone's first name. Be aware of the reverence for elders in many cultures.

If you work with a translator, you must be very certain of the accuracy of the translation. Make sure the translator knows when you're looking for exact quotes, not paraphrases, of what people say.

Often, when we report on cultures other than the dominant one, we settle for far less than we do in other reporting. We aren't as diligent in our questioning, making sure we understand, and double checking. Don't just feel relieved that someone is talking to you. Don't go easy on yourself because your editor won't know what to ask you. Don't settle for the easy, superficial story; strive for nuance and complexity.

Perhaps most important, find a safe place to anticipate and to discuss difficult issues. Those of us who want to see better coverage of our own cultures or communities should be open to other journalists asking questions that will help them succeed in cross-cultural reporting. Better for them to ask questions that could be embarrassing or improper *inside* the newsroom, not out in the community. If you have questions about a community you will be covering, find someone with whom you can discuss traditions or language or taboos, someone who will give you honest responses.

Almost all of us can do good cross-cultural reporting if we really want to do it. Let's not abandon that hope. Sometimes we marginalize coverage of issues—particularly in communities of color—by saying, "Well, somebody from that community ought to cover it." Diversifying our newsrooms *is* a key goal, but in the meantime, we must broaden our coverage.

Our newspapers devote a lot of reporters' time to covering election campaigns, political figures, and other stories. We have to decide that cross-cultural reporting is important, too. If the stories are in communities that our reporters, readers, or viewers aren't familiar with—especially changing communities—time is crucial. If your news organization is going to consistently cover a community, it needs to devote the time needed for coverage that's as complete as possible. If your news organization isn't yet invested in doing that but you are, you might have to take a little time and do it on your own. Doing so will give you richer and more accurate stories to tell. Go in and force yourself to learn.

Reporting on Your Own

S. MITRA KALITA

In July 1998, I wrote a short piece for the Associated Press about some suburban second-run movie theaters that counter the rise of the megaplex by playing Bollywood films, drawing in a new audience. That was my first foray into writing about my own community: South Asians. I interviewed an Indian customer at one theater, asking him such basic questions as: What are Bollywood movies like? Can you summarize the plots for me? Did you grow up watching the films? After our interview, he asked where I was from. I told him I was born in Brooklyn but my parents were from India. He replied, "Then why are you asking me all this? You already know the answers."

This experience frames an issue we face covering our own communities. My colleague Mirta Ojito at the *New York Times* says it best: "The more you know, the less they tell you." That moviegoer assumed not only that I would know all about Bollywood but that I *should* know. To cover our own communities we must, of course, learn more about them, but we must also unlearn. Unlearning things I thought I knew has led me toward topics that truly lend themselves to narrative journalism.

Reporting from within my own community for a general audience, I must include the necessary background, context, and complexities. Media outlets across the country are grappling with how to tell stories from inside communities. Hiring reporters like me, from specific communities, is a start. Once there, we still need to pound the pavement on our own block to ensure that we're telling our subjects' stories, not our own.

In my book *Suburban Sahibs: Three Immigrant Families and Their Passage from India to America*, I wrote about Harish Patel. He had immigrated to the United States from India in the 1980s. In an early interview I asked his birth date, and he told me 1947. That, of course, was the crucial year of India's independence victory with the British and also of the bloody partition between India and Pakistan. My own parents had lived through the partition, and I'd read a lot about it. My immediate understanding of the significance of that birth date meant that he thought it unnecessary to explain it, but he *did* have to explain it to me so that I could portray his point of view. Narrative journalism affords us the luxury of stepping back and providing context in our stories. Journalists personally connected to that context should use extra caution to get facts and perspectives precisely right.

I have heard that a professor at the Columbia Graduate School of Journalism hands out paper bags on the first day of class and says, "Always bring your own lunch and never take a free meal. There's no such thing as a free meal." I don't think that rule and some others like it truly apply to writing about one's own community. We obviously must stay free of obligation, but we also shouldn't get in the way of our own work. I take my shoes off at the door, I drink the tea that is offered, and I cover my hair before entering a mosque.

I once saw a photograph of a young woman interviewing an imam. She wore a tank top that showed quite a bit of cleavage. I wondered if she had known about that interview when she dressed for work that day and, if so, whether she'd given any thought to the price she should pay for access. We *do* somehow pay for access—whether into another community or further into our own.

Occasionally, I've encountered institutional resistance to assigning reporters to cover their own communities. Somehow we never hear complaints about white reporters covering white institutions—

from the city council chambers in Middle America to the White House. This changed for the better after September 11, 2001, a day that forced media outlets to examine their own practices closely. I was a reporter at *Newsday* on that terrible day. The editors there looked around and asked, *Who knows the Muslim community? Who's been covering the Muslim community?* In many newsrooms the answer was no one.

As a journalist writing about my own community, I also face their expectations. When I approach South Asians as a journalist, they often tell me, "Do a good story on us." When I began covering my own community and was told that, I just chuckled and hoped the issue didn't come up again. If they asked, "What will this story be like?" I changed the subject. I've since learned that it's best to deal with such issues directly. It can be a long conversation, because people really do want to understand the institution that I represent and how it makes news decisions.

Readers in the community often tell me that my newspaper, the *Washington Post*, publishes too many stories from India about poverty, dowry deaths, floods, and earthquakes. "Could you try to write a positive story about our people for a change?" they ask. I often answer, "I'm not going to write a positive story or a negative story, but just a story." If pushed, I might add that while working, I'm a journalist first and Indian second. And if pressed even harder, I might explain that being Indian is a real asset in the newsroom. Still, the truth is, I do sometimes pitch stories whose importance a white editor might not understand and therefore might not want.

People take news coverage very personally. Questions such as "Why do you write so much about earthquakes rather than about wealthy Indians?" may seem a bit absurd. They indicate a lack of understanding about the journalist's mission. Many readers seem to assume that the media have an agenda to portray the entire Indian subcontinent with one broad brushstroke. I debunk such conspiracy theories, but I also concede that there is some truth to the complaints. While working on my book, I felt that most of the news stories about South Asians focused on people who, like my father, have done well in corporate America, moved to the suburbs, and bought McMansions— rather than people like Harish Patel who work as security guards, convenience store clerks, and gas station attendants.

Complaints are universal. When I cover the Latino community, people ask me why newspapers run more stories about day laborers than about multimillion-dollar marketing campaigns targeting the Spanish-speaking community. That is a legitimate question. We must push for complete reflections of immigrant communities. Even the so-called positive stories often oversimplify. We write the story of immigrants dancing at celebrations over and over. We publish the photograph of the immigrant serving food over and over. Meanwhile, the story about a member of an immigrant community scamming others with outrageous mortgage rates, for example, rarely appears.

Too often our stories of immigrant communities focus exclusively on the enclaves here in the United States, ignoring their home countries. To understand a community, we must understand its history and its continued relationship with the home country. In our current era of widespread communications technology and economic globalization, immigrants remain far more connected to their countries of origin than earlier immigrants could.

At the start of any story about the South Asian community, I ask myself, *Is this news to me?* If the answer is no, I won't do it. Our news coverage of immigrant communities should provide news *to* immigrant communities, not just *about* them. Ask the members of any immigrant group what they want to read about, and the answers most likely will be education, crime, and small-business law. The answers are the same for any other community. Our standards must be the same as well.

Field Notes to Full Draft

TRACY KIDDER

The act of writing is a zone I occupy, a psychological space. After a while I lose self-consciousness and all sense of time. Before I can get to that zone, though, I have to make the leap from taking field notes to writing the first draft. Imposing order on the chaos in my notebooks is hard—both to do and to describe. This is an attempt to do the latter.

When I was younger, I filled my reporting notes with my own thoughts and feelings about things. Those notes often didn't contain much information about the source of my thoughts and feelings: what I was actually *seeing*. They contained few details of clothing and place, smells, sounds, and other sensory impressions. I'm sorry about that, because I could use some of those notes now.

I've learned a few things since then. I try to write down all the visible, tactile, smellable facts as well as what I hear. With that material in front of me, I have complete access to my memories of how I felt about a certain incident or scene; I don't need to have those thoughts recorded on the notebook page.

I usually take more than ten thousand pages of steno notes for a book. Those notes include all the perishable material, the fleeting events I watched unfold in front of me. I fill another set of notebooks with library research and standard office interviews. Once I have it all, I have to organize it.

I used to make an index of all my notebooks. Creating the index forced me to review all my notes once, very carefully. I tried not to spend too much time on it; I didn't want to waste energy on something that was just a tool. The index was usually flawed, because I refused to go back and revise once I started. Now, I actually type out my notes. It doesn't seem to take much longer than making the index. Once I've done that, I review my notes several times to find the most interesting parts and to gain a sense of the whole.

While I'm writing early drafts of a book, I include everything I think might belong there. I gather from the field notes everything that seems potentially literogenic. For a particularly complicated story or one without an obvious narrative line, I make a chronological chart of events. I never write elaborate outlines, though I sometimes take a piece of paper and write a list of elements of the book. I make a plan, set deadlines for myself, and try to take the deadlines seriously.

I remember quite vividly sitting down after all my notes were in order for my book *House*. For perhaps the first time in my life I didn't feel impatient. I sat at my desk and thought about it for a while. I had a sound in my head, a sense of the way I wanted that book to feel. Knowing that sound made *House* much easier to write than any of my other books. For me, writing is mostly the sounds and cadences of sentences.

I write as fast as I can to prevent remorse for having written badly. When I first wrote articles for the *Atlantic Monthly*, I would start writing around eight in the evening, after the kids were in bed. Some mornings as the sun came up, I'd still be writing the first sentence. I had the feeling that I couldn't start until I had that first sentence right. Now, I complete an entire draft of the book trying not to look back at what I've written. I try not to worry if I've done something drastic, such as changed my point of view on page 200. I write terrible, enormously long rough drafts. The first draft takes the longest and is the most painful. Sometimes there are a few paragraphs or sentences that are actually worth keeping.

Once I start writing, I often realize how little I know about something that I *should* know about. I have to return to reporting, but I'm very directed at that point. While working on a book, I find all the ways *not* to tell a story. I can't separate out the different elements—point of view, voice, sequence, and themes—because the elements are not separate from one another while I'm writing.

When it comes to rewriting the draft, I really have to start all over again. I'm resigned to writing a book over and over again. I've written all my books many times over, sometimes as many as twelve times. In the many drafts there is an accretion. You keep five or ten sentences from the first ten million, but gradually they begin to accrete. Sometimes I have to throw away very good writing or completely mangle it because it doesn't fit with the whole.

When I am really, really sick of a book, that's usually a good sign that I've thought it through carefully enough. Still, the last 10 percent of the rewriting is terribly important. That last 10 percent is often the difference between mediocre and good. When the book is reasonably sound but still might have some structural flaws, I can pay attention to sentences and adjust timing. It becomes a quest for precision, to say exactly what I mean. That's when I go back to my notes. It takes a huge amount of time to answer questions such as: When did this guy say that? When did that actually happen?

My editor is very good to me. He makes fun of me but always seems willing to read all my drafts. I give him big chunks of a first draft. He'll wait a decent interval and then say, "It's fine. Keep going." When I finish the whole draft, we sit down for a big meeting to discuss the draft. At that point I wonder what he thought was "fine." I've learned the hard, painful way that letting go is important. I need to have one person who is much smarter than I am, who can be somewhat objective. When I have to make decisions about cutting, I trust my editor, Richard Todd, though we sometimes argue. A few times that I insisted on my way, I later regretted it. It's important to have one person for the first tender shoots of a book. If Richard Todd precedes me to the grave, I will quit writing.

While I was a student at the University of Iowa Writers' Workshop, some wonderfully talented young writers there gave up writing altogether. They quickly developed powerful critical faculties, but their writing abilities hadn't caught up yet. Every time you reenact the little drama of writing a book, self-criticism and self-motivation must stay in balance. Sometimes you have to think, "Gee, what I just wrote is really good." At other times you must be willing to say, "Wait a minute. This is nonsense. This is terrible. I'm going to throw it all away and start over."

Doing Enough Reporting?

WALT HARRINGTON

Craftsmanship plays a critical role in narrative writing. Paul Hendrickson's book *Looking for the Light,* about Depression-era photographer Marion Post Wolcott, has a wonderful chapter called "Ode to an Instrument." It's just two pages long. It describes the amazing beauty of the old Speedgraphic camera, which nearly every photographer in America for fifty years used. I read those two pages and thought, "I will never write like this."

I asked Paul how he had written those pages. He went to the Smithsonian museum. He got copies of the original catalogs and publicity literature on the Speedgraphic, going back fifty years. He bought an old Speedgraphic at an antique camera shop so he could hold it, feel it, touch the leather, run through all the complicated mechanical processes, listen to the clicks and whirs, and record it all in detail.

Paul also found an elderly photographer, Bill Snead of the *Washington Post,* who had shot with a Speedgraphic. He asked, "Bill, how does this camera work?" and Bill went into a reverie: "Ah, the old Speedgraphic." Paul said that watching Snead work that camera was like poetry.

That's how Paul wrote those two pages. That's the craft of narrative journalism. It is boundless.

From Story Idea to Published Story

CYNTHIA GORNEY

I got a story idea from doing a "plant and cut" on a soccer field: I heard my leg make a horrible popping sound, fell, and ended up in the emergency room. For the next three days my left leg folded out sideways every time I put weight on it. I'd torn my ACL, my anterior cruciate ligament.

I thought to myself, "I'm going to be in pain and rehab for a year, but at least I'm going to get a story out of it." That story ended up in the *New York Times Magazine*. Though it all ended well, the process leading up to that publication was hell for me, my editors, and everyone around me. Writing this story was a sort of tragic comedy in four acts, portraying a process that seemed simple and straightforward but went awry in crucial ways.

Think of the story process as a funnel. You start with an unformed, fuzzy idea, throw it into a funnel, and out comes a focused, purposeful story. That's the idea anyway. It takes practice. In Act 1 you toss your story elements into the funnel. In Act 4 your story emerges.

Act 1: The Glimmer

You have the germ of an idea. Let's say you get a tip at a city council meeting or meet someone whose story you find compelling or fall on a soccer field and go to the emergency room. That moment when you think, "This could be a story," is your *glimmer moment.*

My glimmer was "I'm going to do a story about knees." So I put knees into my story funnel. I already had a natural narrative vehicle for the story. It would begin with my injury. The middle would be my surgery and rehab. It would end with my return to the soccer field in my creaky brace with my compromised gait. In one respect I was lucky: At the time of my glimmer moment it was already pretty clear that I had some decent material for a magazine piece.

Act 2: First Discovery

Once you have decided to pursue an idea, you enter a stage of broad investigation into your topic. It is similar to the process that lawyers call "discovery." You have an idea—knees or illiteracy or HIV among Black women—something big and unfocused. You set out to learn everything you can about the topic. This discovery process helps you figure out whether your idea is worth pursuing and, if so, how to do that. It also helps you find out how to pitch it to an editor.

Start researching, interviewing, and observing, but don't overdo the discovery stage. You have to cut it short at some point. You're not trying to become the world's expert on your topic.

That is the first mistake I made. I learned so much about knees that with a sharpened spoon and some anesthetic, I could probably do knee surgery now. As a reporter, that is not the level of expertise you want. In the first discovery phase you're looking for your story.

I found two stories. During my visit to the emergency room and later talking to surgeons, I learned that two groups of people were tearing their ACLs: female athletes and older baby-boomer jocks. There was a measurable rise in boomer-jock knee injuries because of people like me who refuse to slow down. For reasons still not entirely understood, the ACL failure rate among female athletes in certain sports, including soccer, was two to six times higher than for male athletes.

I wrote a proposal for the *New York Times Magazine*. One of my first tasks—and a first task for anyone writing a magazine proposal—was to get a clear sense of the magazine's audience. A magazine audience is more specialized than that of a newspaper even when the magazine is part of a newspaper. Particular people read that particular magazine for particular reasons. Your job is to grab the attention of that audience.

In the proposal I had to give the editor of the magazine a sense of how my story would read, what the voice would be. The tone is a separate issue from the information you impart in a piece. I wanted the story to be very informative, not introspective, and surely not self-pitying. The piece would use my injury as a vehicle for general reporting. My initial memo to Adam Moss at the *Times Magazine* included proposals for two pieces. I let him choose.

The first piece was a standard treatment of the failure rate in knees among female athletes. The first few lines of my proposal gave the editor a sense of the piece's tone.

> Knee injuries clearly appear to be the Big Thing among coaches & orthopedists watching women's ascendance in competitive sports—everybody agrees that the number of injuries is escalating rapidly ("virtual epidemic" is the way that one New Jersey orthopedic surgeon puts it), both because of the huge increase in overall numbers of girls & women in sports (that's the Title 9—

Women's Movement—Changing Image stuff) *and* because of the way young women are now learning to play their sports: aggressive, fast & vicious, like the boys. Everybody also agrees that, for reasons not yet entirely understood, women blow the anterior cruciate ligament—the ACL—at a rate three to six times that for men. It's a devastating injury for an athlete.

The opening sentence was far too long and complicated for a published article, but it did tell why this story was news. It gave the editor good quotes from an expert. It let him know that I'd already done thorough research. One key to a magazine proposal is establishing your knowledge at the very beginning.

My second proposal was for a long, first-person, reported essay aimed at people like me: baby boomers who refuse to retreat gracefully into sedentary middle age. Those baby boomers made up a large part of the magazine's audience. This turned out to be the piece Adam wanted. He believed I would tell it better, that I would care a little more, and that my approach to it would fit well with the magazine's target demographic.

Act 3: Funnel Discovery

Once I had the assignment, I should have launched fully into what I call the *funnel discovery phase*. During this phase you refine your story focus and what you need to know to write it. My problem, my second mistake, was that I didn't stick to my marching orders. I'd been told to do a piece about baby-boomer jock knees, but I started my funnel discovery with too broad an idea: "I'm writing about knees." A "piece about knees" is not a story.

I'm a classic reporter, an autodidact. I love the research and reporting; I hate writing. I went into this story as if I were going to get a degree in orthopedics. I overdid discovery because I wanted to show what a good reporter I was, how much I had learned. And I was having a great time.

Eventually, I looked up and realized "Oh, yeah, deadline coming." By this time I had interviewed my former boss about his knee replacement—even though my story wasn't about knee replacements. I had persuaded the *Times* to fly me to Cincinnati, Ohio, where a fancy knee doctor has a miniwing of a hospital for his knee work. I went to Ohio to find scenes I could use along with all my research. That was mistake number three. I didn't ask myself, *What's the purpose of these scenes in relation to my story?*

Act 4: Writing the Draft

My stack of notes for the story grew to be two feet high. I finally sat down to write. As I always do, I started in the middle of sentences, babbled repetitively, asked myself lots of questions. I ended up with a slew of incoherent outtakes: e.g., "and in fact the whole modern sub-specialty of sports medicine owes much of its startup impetus to junk knees . . . torn ACLs, ripped menisci, and otherwise junked knees. segue into my operation now . . . what Mattson did." That's how I draft. Everyone has her own method.

Finally, I had the tone of the story. I developed a good beginning, with the voice I wanted.

> Well, I did it playing soccer at the age of 42, but before you start muttering *geez, what did she expect*, let me tell you some of the other ways over-energetic baby boomers do it: playing tennis, playing basketball, playing volleyball, playing softball, downhill skiing, diving sideways for a Frisbee at the beach, and making one rapid feint in the spur-of-the-moment touch football game that seemed like such a good idea until the part with the writhing and the screaming and the panicky-faced people running for ice and a medic. Myself, I don't remember that part so precisely.

A central task in writing a draft is to block out the different sections. I needed to identify my opening. I decided on a description of my injury: a lovely passage about traveling to the East Coast with my leg in a brace, hearing all sorts of wounded-jock-knee stories. The next section started with my trip to Cincinnati. My fourth section dealt with young women athletes at Stanford and their injuries. I ended with a leaping-onto-the-field scene in my squeaky brace.

I had written eight thousand words. I had been assigned a four-thousand-word story. I handed it in thinking, as reporters do, "They'll think this is so great that they'll just double the slot for it. They'll re-arrange the whole magazine."

Adam Moss cut a couple of thousand words and then made a hilarious charitable remark: "I think we can just nickel-and-dime the rest of it out." We could not, of course, cut an eight-thousand-word piece in half so easily. Here's what they cut: the whole section about Cincinnati (a thousand bucks in expenses—oops!), all known knowledge on knees, and about half of the information about women's knees. My personal story was cut in ways that were painful.

Later, though, I had to admit that the cuts made sense. The final story was on target: very much about jock baby-boomer knees. A brief digression into women's knees worked because my own female-knee story framed the article. At the end of the article I limp into the Stanford rehab center. Vanessa Nygaard and Christine Vokl, two injured Stanford basketball stars, limp in behind me. We compare scars. Their scars are longer than mine because their legs are a foot longer than mine. I included our conversation about knee rehab, their passion for basketball, and how they would go on playing—even though they knew it would cost them. I concur: I'll play soccer for as long as I can, on my own flawed physical frame, because it matters to me.

I had survived the knee injury and writing my knee story, too.

(Narrative) J School for People Who Never Went

ADRIAN NICOLE LEBLANC

I found literary journalism as a way to bring together my deep interests in sociology and class in America. Because I never went to journalism school, I always assumed there must be methods for approaching stories that I just didn't know. In retrospect, I see that my lack of method worked to my advantage. To do this work well, you must find your own way and make your own mistakes.

Some of my best stories grew from killed assignments. Here's one example: After reading a little clip in *Newsday* about a young heroin dealer who was being tried, I started attending the trial. I got an assignment from *Rolling Stone* to cover it and spent about three months at the courthouse. Ultimately, full access to the defendant was limited because of a pending appeal. He could be more open with me if his appeal were rejected, but that would take a year or two. *Rolling Stone* wasn't interested in waiting. They killed the story, but I stayed with it.

During my reporting I had gotten to know the mothers and girlfriends of some of the codefendants. I followed them. It was the beginning of a very long journey that culminated in my book, *Random Family*. Had the *Rolling Stone* piece run, perhaps these relationships wouldn't have continued.

I often take a straight assignment, believing that I can convince the editor to *see* the story differently if I can *report* it differently. The assignment is just a frame to get started. When I start a story, I often feel baffled. I ask myself and others such basic questions as: *What is a "gang girl"? What do people mean when they say those words? What associations do they bring to mind?*

When I begin reporting, I'm the thermometer for the story. I constantly gauge my reactions. Starting out as a reporter, I made personal journal entries while also taking field notes or making tape recordings. I wrote about how I felt about the field work, who I liked, who I didn't like, who annoyed me, who held my attention, and why. Some of that material eventually found its way into my stories, not because I found it interesting but because good editors drew it out of me. They asked me questions I could answer only by pulling from my journal entries, where I felt a liberty that I hadn't allowed myself in my professional notes.

I have learned over the years that I must draft scenes immediately. I do it right after reporting—ideally, as I'm typing my notes. I never used to do that, which may be part of the reason that *Random Family* took nearly a decade to report and write. I am now more disciplined about fleshing out my notes as soon as possible.

After the Columbine tragedy, the *New York Times Magazine* asked me to do a story about outcast kids in high schools. The editor asked me to find a school that had received a threat from some of these kids but had managed to thwart it before disaster happened. Three or four schools fit that category.

Almost everyone believes that because they were once kids, they understand adolescence. I knew that I couldn't fathom what it means to be a high school kid right now, let alone an outcast boy in a suburban neighborhood. I tried to convince the editor to do a story on what it feels like to be an outcast. I went and stood outside a high school, stopping kids and saying, "Hi, I'm a journalist. I am working on this story about outcast kids. Who are the most outcast kids that you know?" After talking to just six kids I had learned the social hierarchy of the school.

The initial reporting can be extremely difficult. I find that I hit a wall of despair because I am so much on the outside. I need to move closer to the inside, but I don't know how to get there or even where it is. I always get through that phase. The feelers I've put out in six different places finally come in. I must make a decision, because I can't continue following six groups of kids. If I have a good editor, I will call and talk about it. Or I'll call a friend. By listening to what I decide to say, I discover which story line I'm most interested in. If I keep coming back to one person, that's the one I choose. That conversation becomes an arrow pointing to where I should go.

If you do this successfully and turn in focused stories, editors will come to trust you. They will let you start with very loose assignments. How loose? That's a careful balance you have to find. If it's too loose, the story might end up getting killed—and you're the one who won't get paid.

After I had decided which group of kids to focus on, I told them, "I don't have questions yet. I really just want to shadow you for a while." They thought that was strange and funny. I did that for a couple of weeks. I became most interested in one young man. We spent time talking. I needed to let his mother know I was reporting on her son. We went to his house, and I explained what I was doing. After that, he clammed up. A few nights later he and some friends got stoned. He turned to me and said, "You are such a fraud." Why? Because I had given his mother an adult-style explanation of what I was doing. I wasn't the person I had been with him.

Usually, if I can keep my mouth shut long enough, I learn more. Moments of enlightenment take time. People need time—lots of time. Most people, regardless of age or social class, are rarely listened to without interruption, asked questions, and responded to thoughtfully.

Throughout the process of reporting I tell people, "It's *my* story." I often tell them, "Imagine I'm making a movie of your life. I have to trail you around with a camera because I'm trying to show people nothing but your life. I have to see your bedroom, meet your friends, see how you are with your mom. I'm going to watch you, and I'm going to see it differently from the way you do. I'll talk to other people about you. I'll be here for a while, and then I'm going to disappear and write my story about your life. It won't be *the* story of your life. It will be one tiny piece of what we've talked about. You will tell me one thousand things, and two of them will end up in the story." Ethically and logistically, it is important that your subjects understand the dynamic as much as they can.

I tend to think of myself as a reporter who doesn't ask a lot of questions. Still, sometimes I listen to tapes of my interviews, and I am amazed that my subject managed to get a word in edgewise. I realize that when I talk too much, it is because I am uncomfortable either with what the subject is trying to tell me or with the situation: the aggression of needing something from them. At other times I have the bigger picture in mind and am therefore resistant to my subject's deepest revelations when a topic becomes too intense.

It is important for me to understand my own responses to situations, not because they are inherently interesting but because they create a map of my unfolding understanding. It is important to know, in equal measure, what I might want to believe, what I resist, and what I'm excited to learn. The dead ends and blind spots offer terrific paths to narrative. My own confusion sometimes informs a narrative strategy. In order for the journalist to get her ego out of the story, it helps to know where the ego lives.

To help understand my own responses, I try not to fill my mind with other people's ideas. I don't necessarily do background preparation before I begin reporting. Usually, I don't read about the subject or talk to experts. Not steeping myself in secondary literature helps keep my ego in check. Otherwise, I might feel too confident that I know something and then ask questions too quickly rather than keep quiet and listen.

During my early fieldwork for *Random Family*, one young woman spoke about her boyfriend. He had lots of girlfriends, but she fancied herself his main one, which seemed to be true. She described dealing with all the commotion around his lively love life. At one point he was dating someone else, but she still visited him. While he went out with the other girl, she would go into his room and iron his T-shirts and polish his sneakers. She told me this, and I replied, "Oh, my god, that must have been so difficult for you!" I had interpreted it as a moment of subjugation.

Many years later I interviewed the other girl and asked her, "Do you ever remember so-and-so doing anything for your boyfriend around the house?" She said, "Oh, yes, I bet she told you she used to take care of him. *I* was the one who washed his clothes and took care of his food." It dawned on me that by polishing his sneakers, that first young woman had been asserting her territory. I had read the situation completely wrong. Only through fact-checking did I come to understand that the two girls were in competition.

By responding as I had in that long-ago conversation, I had shut up the first girl. How could she explain it to me, given how far off-track I was? That experience taught me to stay quiet. What book could have taught me that? I had to learn to listen, to surrender my place in the moment.

PART III

NAME YOUR
SUBGENRE

Introduction

MARK KRAMER AND WENDY CALL

The established parameters of newspaper journalism—sturdy, utilitarian, purposefully constrained in the service of the community—determine a powerful set of nonfiction practices. This set, as it has evolved over several centuries, presents news of common interest to a citizenry whose members differ in matters of faith, class, education, political perspective, cultural interests, and just about everything else. Newswriting aspires to unify and inform the public, and it accomplishes this feat (when it does) through strict rhetorical discipline. It eschews most emotional content, and channels presentation and analysis toward the obvious and away from the haunting social and philosophical questions that frame even mundane events. It doesn't stray from beliefs that all of us—rich or poor, old or young, devout or agnostic, well educated or less so—are expected to share: Community service is commendable. Crime is bad. Children merit protection. Business is good. Support the arts. Always root for the home team.

But the real world remains uglier, kinder, subtler, richer, crueler, stranger, more monotonous and chaotic, and, above all, more complex, than standard journalistic practices capture. Readers, including readers of conventional daily newspapers, know that. The people living in the messy, real world fascinate us even as they are barely knowable. Their histories, social structures, sufferings, biographies, triumphs, prejudices, conflicts, institutions, and eternal secrets have always allured writers.

Varied nonfiction genres, close or distant cousins in the literary family, have evolved as writers have embraced diverse topics over hundreds or thousands of years. Each genre offers a path for presenting true stories, with its own switchbacks, side routes, and scenic vistas. This section of the anthology takes quick looks at a few of those cousin genres, including the character profile, travel narrative, memoir, personal essay, commentary, historical writing, investigative reporting, and radio documentary.

◆

Profiles

JACQUI BANASZYNSKI

Why write profiles? Successful ones contain all the essential elements of narrative journalism. The writer must learn how to describe people *and* place: to locate characters, to describe them physically, to explain their motivations. Good profile writing demands good interviewing, a skill that transcends the form, and teaches responsible reporting. When you are writing about one other person and that person knows it, you must get it right.

Profiles provide specificity—the micro that illustrates the macro. In my "AIDS in the Heartland" series, I wrote very intimately about two gay farmers from Minnesota who were dying of AIDS. The story was not just about those two individuals but also about how people live and die with AIDS and how their community deals with it.

Profiles allow us to work at both ends of the ladder of abstraction. (See box by Roy Peter Clark on page 70.) The story's specificity—Dick Hanson and Bert Henningson, farmers and political activists—sits at the bottom of the ladder of abstraction. What these two men represented—commitment, love, death, and family struggle—is at the top of the ladder. Many newspaper stories are boring because they stay in the middle: There are no specific people and no great themes, either. These stories have nothing to ground them and nothing to raise them above the mundane.

The key to reporting for a profile is figuring out the questions. Interviews are crucial, and not just with the person being profiled. Who are the people around him or her? Who will reveal something about that person? Who knows the defining moments that shaped his or her life? You need to interview those people.

You must ask deep questions. What has defined this person? What is this person's motivation? Value system? Approach to life? Who *is* this person? To reach this deeply, you must ask questions that seem rather abstract. I once asked six men who were crossing Antarctica on foot—and almost died in the process—whether Antarctica was male or female, and why. The question helped them relate to the continent in a new and personal way. Ask people what they worry about most or who matters most to them or what makes them most afraid. Always follow these abstract questions with concrete ones to elicit specific anecdotes.

Some people love to talk about themselves. A few people love to talk about themselves but don't say much that is useful. They say such things as "The Lord made me do it" or "I've got to hand it to my teammates." Your job as an interviewer is to turn the subject into a storyteller. Ask questions so layered, so deep, and so odd that they elicit unusual responses. Take the person to places she wouldn't normally go. Ask questions that require descriptive answers. If your profile hinges on an important decision the subject had to make, ask her everything about the day of the decision. What kind of day was it? What was the first thing you did when you woke up in the morning? Do you remember what you had for breakfast? What was the weather like? What were you wearing? Who did you think about that day? Did the phone ring? Walk me through the first two hours of your day. These things might not seem relevant to the story, but they serve to put the person back in the moment. Push a bit. Make some assumptions that require the person to validate what you say or to argue with you.

I once attended a press conference with a top Olympic runner. Her résumé painted the portrait of a woman who had it all: stellar athletic career, law degree, rich and adoring husband, cover-girl looks. But she was in her thirties and still running. I asked if she was worried about what was missing from that picture: a baby. Was she racing her own biological clock? That made a far more interesting story than another analysis of her running form.

Immerse yourself in your interviews. You must focus so intently that your mind is fully with the person you are interviewing. You need to listen so hard that you can move with the person, take another step forward or pull back. Don't worry about your list of questions, your editor, or your story lede. Worry only about the person in front of you. A friend of mine calls this full-body reporting. If you do it right, you will feel exhausted when you leave the interview.

The most important thing to any writing, and especially profile writing, is the telling detail. Reporters complain that editors remove the telling details from their profiles. Sometimes editors do that because the details weren't relevant enough. If it is not showing something important, it's not essential. Keep reporting until you find the absolutely essential details. In "AIDS in the Heartland" I described the type of flowers the two men planted around their farmhouse, impatiens and sweet williams. I noted that the last food one of the men ate before he went into the hospital was a neighbor's moist zucchini bread. And I wrote about peony blossoms set in bowls of water around the house. All those details painted a portrait of the traditional rural Midwest in summer.

Reporting for profiles requires moving in close and then pulling back. When you shift from reporting to writing, you must distance yourself from the characters. When you sit down at your desk, your allegiance switches. It feels as if your characters are looking over your shoulder, but you must turn your back on them. You don't lose respect for your subjects or their story, but your allegiance must be with the reader.

After I have edited a profile, it must pass a test before I consider it finished. I ask the writer to give the piece to a reader who knows nothing about the subject. That new reader must be able to answer two questions, each in one sentence. First: *How would you characterize this person?* Second: *At the end of the piece, do you know whether or not you like the person?* If the answers aren't what the writer expected, the profile isn't finished.

There are many different kinds of profiles. I'll describe just three. In my own terminology they are cradle-to-current, niche, and paragraph profiles.

Cradle-to-Current Profile

After Gary Ridgway was arrested as the Green River Killer, responsible for murdering forty-eight women in Washington State, the *Seattle Times* wrote a profile that included everything about his life: where he grew up, when he first showed signs of pathology, when the police started chasing him. This type of profile requires knowing the full sweep of a person's life. It demands a huge investment of time. A cradle-to-current profile is needed only in rare circumstances.

Niche Profile

The niche profile is one of my favorites. It gets profiles in the newspaper quickly. You can do a niche profile under one thousand words in just a couple of days. The key to the niche profile is figuring out exactly why a person is in the news and then building on that.

While we had to do a cradle-to-current profile of Gary Ridgway, we might have included a niche profile of the defense attorney who had to represent him. The niche profile doesn't need to include where she was born or what she did in fifth grade unless that directly relates to her role as Ridgway's attorney. Her biographical information can be compressed, run as a small box or in tight form within the story. A niche profile describes how she came to the role and whether defending a serial killer presents an internal conflict for her.

To write a successful niche profile you must have a very clear idea of what you are looking for: telling detail and quotes that serve the story's purpose.

Paragraph Profile

The shortest profiles aren't really profiles at all but single paragraphs within larger stories. A paragraph profile transforms a fairly flat story into one with real characters. It helps your readers move through the story because names are no longer merely names. The paragraph profile reveals something about a person's character that is germane to the broader story.

While writing the most mundane beat stories, paragraph profiles allow you to push yourself to do the kind of reporting required for narrative writing. They force you to dig deeper and focus on what is truly relevant about the subject.

Again, if you were covering the Ridgway case, rather than just name the detective who finally cracked the case, you might include a paragraph profile of him. That profile might say that the detective had turned the hunt for the Green River Killer into a twenty-five-year obsession that had haunted his dreams while he filled dozens of boxes with dead-end leads. You might mention that the judge said a prayer or listened to a favorite song before he came into court that day.

There are many kinds of profiles, including those in which the essential character is not a person but a place or a building or a meeting. You don't profile a city council meeting by reporting on the results or who voted on what, but by profiling the personality of the meeting, its pace, even its silliness. If you profile a snowplow driver, the main character could be the truck, the road, the snow, or the driver. Regardless of the subject, regarding people carefully will allow you to elucidate it.

The Ladder of Abstraction

ROY PETER CLARK

The ladder of abstraction is one of the more useful tools for a narrative journalist, though it's not the easiest to understand. It took me about fifteen years to figure out how to apply it well.

S. I. Hayakawa, who was a linguist before he become a U.S. senator, first described this concept in his book *Language in Action*, published in 1939. Hayakawa wrote that all language exists on a ladder. The most general or abstract language and ideas are at the top of the ladder. The most concrete, specific words are at the bottom of the ladder.

In storytelling we create meaning at the top of the ladder and exemplify that meaning at the bottom of the ladder. Journalists are more comfortable toward the bottom of the ladder. Still, the problem is that we don't reach high enough, nor do we come right down to the bottom—where the goats can eat it, to use an old Alabama expression. Journalism tends to live in the middle, the danger zone—a lesson I learned from writing coach Carolyn Matalene.

The world of education offers good examples of the middle of the ladder of abstraction. Participants at school board meetings never discuss critical issues such as literacy or the development of young citizens who can participate in democratic life—ideas at the top of the ladder. Nor is there discussion about the children trying with difficulty to decode the reading in Miss Gallagher's first grade classroom—the bottom of the ladder. Instead, it's a world where teachers are referred to as "instructional units," while the conversation is about the "scope and sequencing of the language arts curriculum"—the middle of the ladder.

Writing at the top of the ladder is *telling*, presenting a summary. Writing at the bottom of the ladder is *showing*, presenting detail. The ladder of abstraction helps writers figure out how to express meaning at the top, how to specify it at the bottom, and how to avoid the muddle of the middle. When you include detail in a well-crafted narrative, it leads the reader up the ladder, in his or her own mind, to derive meaning from the story. If you show me a scene in which a fourteen-year-old girl gives away her down jacket on a chilly day to a homeless person, you don't have to tell me she's compassionate. Her act exemplifies it.

Every Profile Is an Epic Story

TOMAS ALEX TIZON

I grew up in a Filipino Catholic family. In the Philippines, Catholicism has melded with indigenous religion, creating a faith with elements of animism. I grew up with the belief that powers and principalities are at work everywhere. Neither my own best efforts nor anything I learned in school has pounded that belief out of me.

When I was about seventeen, I thought about becoming a minister. I said this to my younger sister, the smart one in the family. She said, "You'd make a great minister if you weren't such a slut." We both laughed, but she had a point. She wasn't saying I was actually a slut but that I had worldly appetites that would make it difficult. She was absolutely right. If someone had written a profile of Tomas Tizon at age seventeen, that would have been in the nutgraf—the core message.

Her incisive statement answered the basic question that any character profile must answer: *Who is this person?* For any subject that question could be answered in several ways. It is okay to be creative. For example, *Vanity Fair* in May 2004 profiled Timothy Treadwell, an activist who spent his entire life working to protect bears in Alaska and then was killed by a bear. Ingeniously, the first section of the profile, by Ned Zeman, is written from the point of view of the bear.

The way writers approach profiles grows naturally from our own personalities and interests. Still, we must stay focused on the subject. When I begin working on a profile, I remind myself of four things.

One: Your subject is as complicated as you are.

It's very easy for journalists to create one-dimensional characters in their stories, especially when they consider only the person's official role as soldier, mayor, victim, robber. To avoid that, I think about the mass of contradictions that I am and try to remember that others are, too. This helps me guard against sentimentality and simplicity.

Each person has a dark side. Glimmers of that dark side give profiles their complexity. It might not be appropriate to explore that dark side of the individual, but often I can explore the situation's

dark side. I wrote a profile of a U.S. solider who had died in Iraq.
That profile was not the place for me to explore, say, his pornography addiction, but I explored the dark side through his family. They
were against the war and hated that he was hailed as a hero, but they
loved their son. The profile's tension revolved around the family, not
the dead soldier.

Two: Your subject carries a burden as heavy as yours.

What is the one thing that gnaws at you when it's quiet and you
are alone, driving to work at 7:30 in the morning? Every time you
meet a person you might profile, remember that that person faces
something similar. It may not end up in the profile, but the writer
must look for that person's pain to understand him or her.

Three: Your subject wants something.

Every story has a protagonist who wants something, and must
work through a series of obstacles to obtain it. Every good story, and
every great profile, is a quest. The quest can be simple: to escape
boredom, to get the girl, to win the money, to redeem oneself, to
avenge something.

I recently wrote a profile of a twenty-five-year-old soldier. He had
grown up watching war movies, wanting to be a soldier and serve his
country. He was sent to Iraq, but as soon as he got there, a bomb hit
his tank. Injured, he was sent back to his little town in Montana. His
entire battlefield experience lasted seven minutes. I had planned to
write about him as an unsung hero. I sat in his living room, and he
showed me sketches he had done of the scene in Iraq: his tank blown
up at a bridge and the soldiers crawling out and awaiting rescue.
Through those drawings I could see his pain. He had prepared his
whole life to be a warrior, but he didn't fire a single shot. He felt like
a complete failure. That was his pain.

What was his quest? To come to terms with that strange turn of
events. Somewhere in the tangle of the subject's burden and the subject's desire is your story.

Four: Your subject is living an epic story.

That epic story is the larger narrative within which your subject's
life fits. I firmly believe that within two hours of talking to anyone I
could develop an idea of that person's epic story. (I'll admit that this
conviction might come from that Catholic-animist upbringing.) All
those Greek legends we learned in school *do* translate into our contemporary lives.

Sisyphus was condemned to roll a rock up a hill forever. Modern translation: *His life was constant, painful, endless exertion.*

Prometheus, the god of fire, angered Zeus and ended up chained to a rock with an eagle pecking out his liver—forever. Translation: *His was a life of constantly trying to retrieve something lost, only to have it taken away again.*

Midas got his wish: Everything he touched turned to gold. But that included *everything*, even his family. Translation: *Your deepest desire has the capacity to destroy you.*

Every person lives multiple stories, but no writer can render all those stories. We do the best we can, using everything we have—all our senses, intellect, and intuition—to choose the right story.

The Limits of Profiles

MALCOLM GLADWELL

Though I write profiles all the time, I believe some of the assumptions that guide profile-writing need to be reexamined. The idea that drives standard reportorial profiles is that we read and write them to learn about individuals in great depth. When I look back at the profiles I've written, I can safely say that none came close to describing who the individual subject really was. That was never my intent.

The standard method for reporting a profile is to find someone and follow that person around. At *The New Yorker*, famously, some writers spend much of their adult lives following their subjects around. That's how you get to the subject's core—or so the idea goes.

I have never called anyone and said, "I would like to follow you around." Often, I can get what I need in the first few hours I spend with the subject. Anything more than that is unnecessary and could even be harmful. I write ten-thousand-word profiles of people with whom I've spent only a few hours.

Why so little time? Because I'm not so interested in reporting about the individual. One reason I don't write profiles of people is that I believe we are incapable of truly describing a person's core. As writers we must acknowledge the limitations of our craft. People are more complicated than our profiles of them reflect.

We tend to focus too much on psychological explanations. Classic profiles devote a great deal of time to the subject's childhood, yet psychologists cannot find a relationship between what happens in child-hood and how a person turns out. Profiles are a form of psychological analysis and should be written with respect for the limitations of psychological work.

Psychologists talk a lot about the difference between *samples* and *signatures*. For example, you would need only about five seconds of a Beatles' song to identify it. Their music has a *signature*. With a very small slice you can know something profound about it.

Other things are only samples. If I ask you to walk outside at three in the morning and try to predict the weather for the following afternoon, you would have a difficult time doing it. Walking outside for two minutes does not provide you with a signature of the weather but only a *sample*.

Even when you spend a lot of time with people with your recorder or notebook out, you see them during only a few of the thousands and thousands of hours that make up their adult lives. We pretend that we're getting a signature, but we're not. When I write a profile of a person, I've usually also done interviews with twenty people in the subject's life. The best material comes from them, not the subject.

Though we are incapable of getting all of a person's essence, I do believe we can get at pieces of someone's personality. That's enough. In the profiles that I write, it allows me to explain the aspects of the person that bear on the topic or idea that really interests me.

I write profiles about *ideas* because I'm deeply skeptical of the legitimacy of writing only about the person. Profiles need to be more sociological and much less psychological. Many profiles that are written about individuals ought to be about subcultures. The individual is a means to examine another world—the world in which that person lives. When we limit ourselves to the individual's personality, we miss the opportunity to consider larger questions about society and subcultures.

Travel Writing: Inner and Outer Journeys

ADAM HOCHSCHILD

Travel writing is one of the oldest forms of our craft. The story of going to a strange place and then returning home is an archetype going back at least to Homer's *Odyssey*, written (or spoken) some 2,800 years ago. In this form the author tells of a geographical journey that parallels an inner journey—from illusion to understanding, from ignorance to knowledge. Two of my favorite modern books exemplify this writing at its very best: Primo Levi's *The Reawakening* and Michael Arlen's *Passage to Ararat.*

The Reawakening narrates Levi's experiences after he was freed from Auschwitz in 1945 and tried to return to his life in Italy. The book gives the reader an inside look at the chaos of Eastern Europe toward the end of World War II. Currency had no value, so everything worked by barter. Levi's book also narrates a journey from death back to life: A man begins the story as an emaciated prisoner, barely alive, and ends as a full human being in the home where he grew up.

Passage to Ararat also narrates travels of the soul. Arlen tells his story within the framework of a journey to Armenia, his father's country of origin. The narrative arc gradually rises as Arlen begins to learn about his father's roots in Armenia and the desperate exodus that occurred in the midst of the genocide. Arlen then goes to Armenia himself. The arc is completed as he travels home through Turkey, where he meets various Turks who deny that the Armenian genocide ever took place. He intersperses the book with explorations of Armenian history, his family's history, and the emotional energy his father devoted to keeping silent about his heritage.

Books like this, of course, are a far cry from what we see in most newspaper travel sections. The problem is that advertisers dictate the contents of newspapers' travel articles. Cruise lines, restaurants, travel agencies, and airlines determine what we read. I'm all for vacation traveling, but the most interesting travel has nothing to do with cruise lines and restaurants. It involves entry into worlds other than your own. You don't have to go very far to do that. For most people living in Manhattan, the world of the south Bronx is farther away—by every measure but geography—than much of Paris or London. Newspaper travel sections should have regular features about travel close to home.

As writers we can inch newspapers closer to covering travel as discovery. When you write travel pieces, seek the unconventional. Include the hotels and restaurants as a sidebar if you must, but don't make them the story's main point. If the newspaper wants articles about familiar destinations in Europe or the Caribbean, write about unfamiliar things a visitor can do there: visit an experimental school in Sweden or see a medical clinic in Canada operating with universal health coverage or see the campus of the University of West Indies that is built on two former slave plantations in Jamaica.

Writing unconventional pieces about unconventional places presents special challenges. Several years ago my wife and I lived in India as Fulbright lecturers for six months. After I returned home, I had two story ideas. I wrote magazine queries and asked my agent to circulate them for me. She told me, "Forget it. No editor is going to think they're interested in stories about India. It's too far away, and it's not in the news. You'd be better off writing the stories and letting me circulate them." That is hardly ever the right way to go about selling freelance stories, but in this case she was right. I had to convince editors, through the articles themselves, that they *were* interested in India.

I wrote two long magazine pieces about India, both somewhat unconventional topics in fairly conventional form: a profile of an environmentally minded architect who built low-cost, energy-efficient buildings, and a story about society and politics in the state of Kerala.

But I still felt that I hadn't yet captured the overwhelming *differentness* of being in India. What I mean is this: Visiting and writing about unconventional places opens up great opportunities. When I'm in a country radically different from my own, I notice much more. It is as if I've taken a mind-altering drug that allows me to see things I would normally miss. I feel much more alive.

In this kind of travel, while you're having the experience, treat it respectfully. If you have the slightest expectation that it might be something you will write about, observe it carefully. Write everything down. Keep a diary.

When I am on a journalistic assignment, I keep two notebooks. One is for the story that I am assigned or intending to write. The other is for experiences and details that move me. I may want to use the latter notebook for some future project, but I have no idea how or when. Later, that second notebook becomes very important. I can dip into it and retrieve things.

Reporting in other countries can be a liberating experience. When I interview people here in the United States, an assignment from a well-known magazine raises my prestige, while an assignment from an unknown magazine lowers it. In other countries I'm more a blank screen onto which people project their impressions. All the petty distinctions and rankings mean absolutely nothing because I'm from a different universe altogether.

Being from a different universe, it takes time for the true meaning of what we see and hear to reveal itself. Let some time pass before writing about your experiences. This is deeply important for writing about personal experience: Those that matter most are the ones we must digest, absorb, and figure out what they mean.

During the first weeks I spent in India, for instance, I mostly noticed how different it was from the United States: spiders the size of a child's fist in the cupboards, five weeks and several trips to many offices required to get a telephone installed, unreliable electricity. Early on, I filled my diary with those stories and with the exasperation I felt. In later months I found myself thinking, "Well, maybe this is a healthy experience. Have we become too dependent on things that aren't so important?" Everyday minor crises meant that we got to know our neighbors. When the water ran out, we carried buckets back and forth between our house and theirs.

After I returned from India and finished my two magazine pieces, a jumble of such experiences still filled my thoughts when I awoke in the morning. I didn't know quite how to make a coherent article, short story, or anything else out of them.

Experiences like this one came to mind again and again: One evening just after dark, I left a meeting at a remote government conference center. No taxis or rickshaws passed by. The only place I knew I could find them was a crossroads at the bottom of a mile-long hill. The electricity was out; it was completely dark. No moon, no stars. Every so often a vehicle would come roaring up the road. In the hopes that it was a taxi, I would try to flag it down, but each roared past. I didn't want to stray too far off the road because I thought there might be a ditch. I began to worry.

I heard a strange sound ahead of me: stir-frying. A food vendor was stirring something in a wok as he wheeled his cart along. I got closer and could see him, because he had stuck a candle on the front of his cart. That candle both protected him against being run over and allowed him to see a few feet ahead. I realized it could do the same for me. I fell in about twenty paces behind him and walked the rest of the way down the hill, totally relaxed. I reached the crossroads, finally, and there was a working streetlight.

I often thought about that experience but couldn't figure out how to use it in my writing. I didn't know quite what it meant to me. About a year and a half after it happened, I was looking at all the undigested bits of my India notes. I realized that each one of those chunks of experience adhered to the same theme: the clash between my expectations as a westerner and what I found in India—and some fear of that unfamiliarity. The experience of finding safety behind the food vendor's candle symbolized my letting go of fear. With that realization the disparate pieces from my notes coalesced into an essay about both my outer and inner journeys.

As writers and as readers we should look for ways that the outer journey can mirror an inner journey. That is not only what good travel writing is about; it's what life is about.

The Personal Essay and the First-Person Character

PHILLIP LOPATE

Nothing is more common in a personal essay than the letter *I*. It is a perfectly good word, one no writer should be ashamed to use— especially in an essay, a form so dependent on the particulars of character and voice. The problem with *I* is not that it is in bad taste but that fledgling personal essayists and memoirists may think they have conveyed more than they actually have with that one syllable. In their minds, that *I* swarms with a lush, sticky past and an almost fatal specificity, whereas the reader encountering it for the first time in a new piece of writing sees only a slender telephone pole standing in the sentence, trying to catch a few signals to send on.

Even the barest *I* holds a whisper of promised engagement but doesn't give a clear picture of who is speaking. To give that picture you must build yourself into a character. Here I use the word *character* much the same way the fiction writer would. E. M. Forster, in *Aspects of the Novel*, drew a famous distinction between flat and round characters, between those fictional personages seen from the outside, acting with predictable consistency, and those whose teeming inner lives readers come to know. We turn ourselves into characters every day, of course. At the job interview, the cocktail party, and the family Thanksgiving dinner, we may turn ourselves into three different characters. Turning yourself into a character in your writing requires the understanding that you can never project your whole self. You must be able to pick yourself apart.

The first step is to acquire some distance from yourself. If you are panicked by any examination of your flaws, you will not get very far in the writing of personal essays. You need to be able to see yourself from the ceiling, know how you are coming across in social situations, and accurately assess when you charm and when you seem pushy, mousy, or ridiculous. You must begin to take inventory of yourself so that you can present that self to the reader as a specific, legible character.

Start with your quirks—the idiosyncrasies, stubborn tics, and anti-social mannerisms that set you apart from others. To establish credibility, resist coming across as absolutely average. Who wants to read about the regular Joe? Many beginning essayists try so hard to be likable and nice, to fit in, that the reader—craving stronger stuff, a tone of authority—gets bored. Restraining one's expressiveness, smoothing one's edges, or sparing everyone's feelings will not work on the page. Literature is not a place for conformists. As writers we must maximize our small differences and project them theatrically, the way actors work with singularities of physical appearance or vocal texture. We must *dramatize* ourselves, positioning the traits we possess under the most clearly focused, sharply defined light. Cut away the inessentials and highlight just those features of your personality that lead to the most intense contradictions.

A personal essay needs conflict, just as a story does. Good essayists know how to select a topic, neither too ambitious nor too slight, that will generate enough heat to sustain the essay's exploration of it. If the topic is too small, the essay runs out of steam. Too large, and it drowns in the details. Still, what stands in the way of most personal essays is not technique but the emotional preparedness to be honest and to expose one's inner nature. A successful essay includes both personal disclosure and analysis. In my own essays, I try to convey thought infused with feeling—a feelingful thought as well as a thoughtful feeling. I try to merge heart and mind.

I like to remind myself of the tonal extremes available to us as writers. Literary models can be a great help. We can rant as much as Dostoevsky's Underground Man, whine—with self-aware humor—the way Joan Didion sometimes does, or be as passionate as James Baldwin or as sane and thoughtful as E. B. White.

Mining our quirks is only a first step toward becoming a character on the page. As a personal essayist you cannot assume that your readers will know a thing about your background, regardless of how many times you have explained it in previous essays. You must become deft, inserting that information swiftly and casually. In one essay you may decide to make a big thing of your religious training and very little of your family background, and in another, just the opposite. In each case it is a good idea to tell the reader a bit of both because it helps build you into a character.

Once you have sketched yourself for the reader—as a person of a certain age, sex, ethnic and religious background, social class, and region, possessing a set of quirks, foibles, strengths, and peculiarities—are you yet a character? Maybe not. You must solidify your relationship with the reader by springing vividly into his or her mind so that everything your *I* says and does on the page seems oddly, piquantly characteristic. Readers must sense from the first paragraph that you are going keep them engaged and amused.

Here we come to one of the main stumbling blocks of the personal essay genre: self-hatred. Most people don't much like themselves in spite of being decent enough human beings. Why this self-dislike should be so prevalent is a matter that would require the best sociological and psychoanalytic minds to elucidate. From my vantage point as a writer, teacher, and anthologist of personal essays, all I can say is that an odor of self-disgust mars many personal essays. It is just as unsatisfactory to constantly underrate yourself as it is to give yourself too much credit. At the same time, the narrator should not be smug but curious about him- or herself. Michel de Montaigne, the father of the essay, was the greatest exemplar of such self-curiosity. It is a discipline that can be learned and practiced even by people such as myself who have at times a strong self-dislike. I may be very tired of myself in everyday life, but once I start narrating a situation or set of ideas on the page, I begin to see my *I* in comic life; I maneuver him so that he will best amuse the reader. My *I* character is not me entirely but a character drawn from aspects of myself, a sort of literary Jerry Lewis.

As an essayist you must get into the habit of inviting your most far-fetched, mischievous notions rather than censoring them. They may point to elements of truth that are otherwise inaccessible. For example, when I wrote my essay "Against Joie de Vivre," I wanted to see how far I could get in taking a curmudgeonly stance against the pursuit of happiness even though I knew on some level that it was an indefensible position.

This brings up another aspect of making oneself into a character. I am sometimes more contrary on the page than I am in real life. I like to go out in nature, for example, but you wouldn't know that from my writings. I am a much more private person in real life. In fact, I don't tell people things as readily as I put them into my essays. As Montaigne once said, "Things that I would never tell anyone, you can go down to the bookstore and find out." We create in our writing a kind of ideal relationship with the reader, who will be our loving, understanding mother, while our interactions in the real world would be very different.

Once you have your fully developed, round, *I* character on the page, you must give that person something to do. It is fine to be privy to all of *I*'s ruminations and cerebral nuances, but consciousness can only take us so far in character illumination. If you are writing an essay with narrative and chronology, let the *I* character step beyond the role of observer and be implicated in the overall action. There is something off-putting about essays in which the *I* character is right and all the others wrong. By showing our complicity in the world's stock of sorrow we convince the reader of our reality and even gain his sympathy. How much more complicated and alive is George Orwell's younger self in "Such Were the Joys" for having admitted that he snitched on his classmates? Or James Baldwin in *Notes of a Native Son* for acknowledging how close he came to the edge with his rages about racism?

The process of turning oneself into a character is not self-absorbed navel gazing but a potential release from narcissism: You have achieved sufficient distance to begin to see yourself from the outside. Doing so can be liberating.

First Person Singular: Sometimes, It Is About You

DENEEN L. BROWN

An inscription in the lobby of the *Washington Post* offices advises reporters to pursue the truth as closely as possible. It challenges reporters to afflict the comfortable and comfort the afflicted. Each day as I walk into the building, I look at that inscription and think about that mission: comforting the afflicted and afflicting the comfortable.

What does that mean?

It means piecing together the threads of humanity that make us one, taking what is considered different and making it commonplace. It means, above all, writing about people, their lives, their humanity—no matter who they are, where they live, how much money they make, or what social class they are in (or think they are in). It means treating both people and stories with dignity. It means reaching for human themes in narratives and writing stories from those themes: loss, grief, love, loneliness, joy, pain, sorrow, faith, peace, despair. Sometimes it means telling our own stories if we can't find anyone willing to, not just be interviewed, but reveal the story's *truth*. To get to the truth in a story you have to go deep—deeper than any surface interview. Deeper, sometimes, than the subject knows he or she can go. Sometimes you must tell your *own* story.

I used to cover a beat called "the Black middle class" in an affluent county near Washington, D.C., that had a majority Black population. I kept telling my editors that I wanted to write about a person who had made it out of poverty and crossed over into the so-called upper-middle class.

As people rise through class structures, they are often called upon to help by the people they left behind. I, as a reporter, wanted to ask: What are the obligations of those who are no longer poor? What are their responsibilities to the family they left behind?

My editor thought it was a great story idea. The theme had been touched on during the Clarence Thomas hearings when reporters mentioned that he had a sister on welfare. The theme had been documented in books and in film, including the movie *Soul Food*.

I tried to report on this theme in Washington, D.C. I called all my sources. They said, "Yes, that's happening." I would ask, "Can I interview you about it?" And they would say, "No, not me."

I had a persistent editor who really wanted that story and finally suggested that I write about my own experience. I wrote the story about my family, and it ended up in the Sunday magazine. The story began this way:

Nini, my sister, is on the other end of the phone. She is hesitating. I can tell immediately that she needs something.

"You know I wouldn't ask you if I didn't need it." Her voice is unsure. She pauses. She doesn't want to beg.

"But," she begins to say, and I know exactly what she will say before she says it. The *but* is the key. The *but* hangs there somewhere between yesterday and tomorrow, somewhere in between where I live in Maryland and where she lives in the Midwest, somewhere between my middle-classness and her working poverty. Somewhere between two sisters, one who made it to the other side of being poor and one who's stuck in its cesspool.

After the story was published, I received many phone calls from people telling me they cried after they had read it. I also got calls from people who did not want that story told.

It was a complicated situation for me. I wrote the story because I felt it needed to be told. My sisters read the story and agreed to its publication. Each sister reacted in a different way. One felt validated by her story appearing in print. For another sister the story eventually became cathartic. And another didn't seem to mind at all.

My mother loved the story. "DeNeen," she said, "you didn't put everything in there. How come you left so much out?"

When you write about your own experiences, prepare yourself for strong reactions from those you write about, from your colleagues, and from your readers. I often tell people, "You may have read the story, but you know only as much as I revealed." People bring their own thoughts, feelings, and beliefs to the stories you write. That's okay. People's judgments can be difficult to deal with, but they are inevitable.

As journalists, our job is to help reshape the way one group of people thinks about another. We must dig deeper than stereotypes. We must get down on our knees or climb up on a chair or walk in the shoes of the people we write about. Sometimes we do that through immersion journalism. Sometimes we have to do it by writing about ourselves.

Columns: Intimate Public Conversations

DONNA BRITT

Writing a column is an intimate act—probably the most intimate one you can perform in a newspaper. It's a conversation. I am never happier than when I'm having a conversation with someone and we are both fully engaged in it. I approach column writing the same way. People hunger for connection. Most of us are curious about the rest of the world, about other people and their stories.

When I was very young, perhaps six years old, I decided that getting to know people was very important. I lived in Indiana, so I watched the civil rights movement on television. I wasn't in the thick of it. After watching for weeks, it hit me: *If I were there, I would be one of the people with dogs attacking them, with their churches being bombed.* My six-year-old self thought, "I'm a nice girl. I do my chores, and I get good grades. If those people only knew me, they wouldn't do those things. And if they only knew the people on TV, they wouldn't do those mean things to them."

That thought, or the adult version of it, still motivates me. I write intimate columns because I want people to *know* me. I still believe that if people know one another, they won't decide whether to like one another based on gender or race or religion.

I worked as a city desk reporter before I became a columnist. The Anita Hill hearing happened during my first year at the *Washington Post.* It mesmerized everyone I knew. Nothing that I read about it dealt with the anger that I was feeling, the anger that a lot of women were feeling. I *had* to write something. I wrote an essay that generated a huge response. After that, I started writing more first-person pieces. Still, when the Metro editor asked me to become a columnist, it amazed me, because I didn't think of myself as a columnist.

I write about sexism, racism, and violence—issues that many people would rather not deal with but have strong opinions about. In each column I have a couple of paragraphs, at most, to convince my reader: *You don't already know everything you need to know about this.* Given that, it's really important to start off with a bang, to engage the reader immediately.

One way I engage readers is by giving other people the right to their own experiences, observations, and even flaws. I acknowledge other people's points of view; I give those who disagree with me a little space in what I write.

Because column writing is like having a conversation, writing becomes listening. I'm aware—perhaps *too* aware—that many of my readers will disagree with what I write. Some haven't challenged themselves on important issues; I feel compelled to challenge them. I'm constantly addressing them as I write, and I hear them whispering in my ear.

For a column to be an intimate conversation, you must reveal yourself. The revelation will happen whether or not you intend it, so you might as well do it purposefully. I reveal myself in all kinds of ways and on topics not usually seen in the newspaper. For some reason a lot of things, such as God and spirituality, aren't considered valid newspaper copy. I refuse to follow arbitrary, unwritten rules about what can go in the newspaper. I write about my spiritual life, and I get tremendous response whenever I do. I'm not so inherently interesting, I'm just really honest. I'm honest about difficult things, including messed-up things that Black people do or how feminism can be stupid. Nothing is so sacred that I can't tell the truth about it.

I don't believe there are boring people or boring stories. Invariably, when someone climbs a building and shoots seventeen people, his neighbors will say, "He was the quietest person, he was almost boring." That's not a boring person, but an *undiscovered* person.

Just as there are no boring people, there are no trivial topics. Even things like fashion are connected to critical issues. There was a time when every piece of women's clothing had shoulder pads—just as women were struggling to establish themselves as a force in the business world. *Everything* has meaning.

I don't believe that local, national, and international issues are separate. All issues involve people; everything is personal. In late September 2000 a photograph of a Palestinian father trying to shield his son from bullets circulated in newspapers around the world. The man crouched with his little boy crying next to him. The caption read that minutes after the photograph was taken, the boy was dead and his father wounded. How many news stories have we read about Palestinian or Israeli children dead? But after I stared at that photo, that one little boy was *my* boy. I wrote a column about that—not about the politics but about people.

Unlike many columnists, I bring other people's voices into my column. It's one thing for me, a forty-something mother of three, to talk about Monica Lewinsky. It's another to include the words of a twenty-two-year-old intern who was appalled by her behavior. Letting your readers listen to other voices, not just your own, is an important part of intimate column writing.

I constantly question myself and my feelings. This makes me a better columnist and a more unpredictable voice in the newspaper. The only things that remain constant are my two goals: to let people know who I am and to smuggle optimism into the newspaper.

Writing About History

JILL LEPORE

British historian Lawrence Stone heralded the revival of narrative in academic history writing in 1979—not coincidentally the year the first Pulitzer Prize was awarded for feature writing. Story was back. This revival represented a serious departure from most historical writing in the twentieth century, which was rather hostile to storytelling.

Twenty-five years later, most historians have few intellectual objections to rattling good history as long as the story is told in the service of an argument. Often it isn't. Some popular histories tell a small story but fail to use it to interpret larger historical dynamics. The worst popular histories rip people out of the past and insert them into the social and political present. While the authors lovingly re-create descriptions of period clothes, hairstyles, houses, and the minutiae of daily life, they seem to assume that historically specific ideas about things like sovereignty, progress, and childhood remain consistent over time. In writing history, journalists ought to watch for two potential pitfalls.

First, avoid quaintness. There wasn't anything quaint about the pilgrims. The past wasn't simpler than the present. People were not kinder or dumber or gentler than they are now. At the same time, don't lapse into a progressive interpretation of history. Things don't always get better over time.

The second pitfall is what historians call presentism. The central point of the story can't be to explain to the reader why we are the way we are today. From a scholarly point of view, that contributes nothing to our understanding of either the present or the past. Understanding the past is undeniably important to understanding our current lives, but it can't be the only reason to look backward. Think hard about what sorts of questions you would ask about the historical event you're investigating if you weren't driven by contemporary concerns. For example, if you want to understand the origins of contemporary ideas about race, the past is crucial to that story. Thinking too much about the present will lead you to ask the wrong questions about the past. Take the past on its own terms, not on ours.

Writing narrative about history is much like writing other sorts of narrative: Immerse yourself in the subject's world and then immerse your reader in that world. Remember that the past is less familiar to you and to your readers. Writing about a kid who sings Scott Joplin tunes for fifty cents on the street corner is one thing; writing about a vagabond in sixteenth-century France is quite another.

Reporting historical events brings a special set of challenges. The most obvious limitation is that you can't interview your subjects. Still, many sources are available that can help you get at the interior of past lives. In recent years, historians' primary sources have broadened significantly. Letters and diaries are the most obvious records, but they are just the beginning. Other things can help you understand a community: census data, probate records, tax records, maps, city directories, receipt books, trade cards. Massive data banks of historical material are now available online, although a good deal of the material requires subscription. Talk your way into a university library to use its online resources. These sources can be extremely specific. For example, there is a database of all the runaway servant and slave advertisements that ran in Virginia newspapers in the eighteenth century. Online clearinghouses such as History Matters (www.historymatters. org) can direct you to the best sources.

When I begin researching any historical topic, my first inclination is to look at primary documents. My second impulse is to look at what historians have already written on the subject. I rarely use early newspapers; they aren't reliable sources of factual information. Their value lies in reporting people's understanding of the events, not in describing the events themselves.

It's cliché to say the past is a foreign country, but like most clichés, it's rooted in truth. As with a trip you might take to a foreign country, you will have a much better time if you research your destination before you set out on the journey. Even with historical subjects, firsthand reporting is key. Visit the places where your subjects lived. Try to see how the landscape looked when they lived there. Find and touch things that those people used. Talk to museum curators and beg them for permission not only to look at artifacts but also to touch them, to hold them. Knock on the door of a tiny local historical society, and you'll find a treasure inside.

When you shift from reporting to writing, some familiar narrative tools can help you with historical subjects. The ladder of abstraction is an important one. For journalists the opposite end of the ladder of abstraction from Bessie the cow is the idea of private property. For historians there is an even higher level of abstraction: a dry debate about the history of the idea of private property. To write successfully about history, you need to move up the ladder to a level of abstraction beyond Bessie's current relevance.

Unlike structural and scientific history, which are analytical, narrative history is largely descriptive. From the point of view of most historians, to call a piece of writing *descriptive* is the worst sort of damnation. Still, narrative history doesn't lack interpretation. Writing a story with strong historical interpretation is hard to do, and it is especially hard to do artfully. Many narrative histories tack endlessly back and forth between story and argument. It is enough to cause reader seasickness. The challenge is to write a seamless narrative that integrates story and context—no small order. For inspiration read Jonathan Spence's *The Question of Hu* or Carlo Ginzburg's *The Cheese and the Worms: The Cosmos of a Sixteenth-Century Miller*. Then pack your bags and head for the archives.

Adventures in History

MELISSA FAY GREENE

While writing my book *The Temple Bombing*, I sent drafts to the main character's widow. The book was about Rabbi Jacob Rothschild, who had stood at the helm of one of the South's prominent synagogues during the civil rights era. A friend of Martin Luther King Jr., Rabbi Rothschild became a real firebrand. Though I never met him, I kind of fell in love with him through his writings and sermons. His widow, Janice Rothschild Blumberg, was very much alive—an elegant, even haughty woman with black hair drawn severely into a bun.

I sent her the excerpts of the book that were about her husband to check my accuracy. We fell into a sort of unfortunate rhythm. I would send a piece to her, a couple of days would pass, and then she would call me. This was the unfortunate part: She would always start by asking, "Melissa, are you writing *non*fiction?" "Yes, Janice," I would say. "This is nonfiction. What do I have wrong?" She then would recite her list of corrections.

I wrote a long section about the rabbi's first visit to the Deep South. He arrived in Atlanta on a hot July day in 1946. I knew it was hot because I looked it up. I knew from letters archived at the Emory University library that a dentist had picked him up. I found myself spending too much time on the rabbi's arrival in Atlanta. Today, the Hartsfield-Jackson International Airport is enormous, but at that time it was a little brick building sitting out in a field. A large African-American woman dressed as a mammy sat on a bale of hay and welcomed visitors. While moving the rabbi slowly, page after page, through the airport, I could introduce African-American and Southern history and the story of Jim Crow. Finally, by about page 312, Rabbi Rothschild exited the airport. Here I presented the book's most lyrical passage, involving a "hot wind blowing across a thousand acres of cropland from the sizzling Atlantic beyond." I boxed up the pages, sent them to Janice, and then didn't hear back.

"I've really nailed it this time," I thought. "She's overwhelmed."

Then she called. "Melissa, is this *non*fiction?" she asked.

"Yes, Janice."

"Melissa, he took the train."

It was a serious error, an anachronism. I had extrapolated backward from my present-day world. In 1946, people didn't fly anywhere unless it was an emergency.

No one asked us to be keepers of the flame of history; we've taken it on ourselves. When we choose to write nonfiction, our first commitment is not to be readable or to educate or to curry favor with our readers. It is to be as accurate as possible.

Narrative Investigative Writing

KATHERINE BOO

Most newspaper people in this country maintain a sort of species difference between narrative and investigative reporting. Narrative writing must be soft and explanatory, while investigative reporting in pursuit of social change must be bullet-pointed and just the facts. This surprises and even saddens me. The best narrative isn't soft, and the best investigative reporting isn't only steel-plated facts.

The best narrative pursues both readers and social change relentlessly. Getting the laser-accurate level of detail needed to meet these challenges requires hard-nosed, uncompromising reporting.

Here is a short example by Anne Hull. She wrote this for the *St. Petersburg Times* in a piece nominated for a 2000 Pulitzer Prize. The passage describes one of the heroines of her story about Mexican guest workers in North Carolina: "She was 35, barely five feet tall in her sandals. Her pans of tamales had gradually found their way to her hips. For a mother of eight she was unusually mild mannered. A hen would fall asleep in her hand as she drew the hatchet back to chop its neck."

In four sentences, just fifty words, Anne included an astonishing number of facts and images: the woman's height, age, body shape, number of children, footwear, her family's diet, their food source, and even a fleeting glimpse of life in her rural hometown. She also fit in, crucially, the woman's gentle, decisive, and unflinching demeanor. In those fifty words Anne created more of a feel for this woman than many writers do in an entire story. This economy works so well because Anne knows exactly what the reader needs to know about the character: her combination of gentleness and ruthlessness, the qualities that make it possible for a mother of eight to leave her home and work at intensive, degrading labor in another country. The narrative works because Anne has done the hard analysis implicit in those fifty words. This is, at its core, investigative reporting.

This sort of reporting requires both looking for facts and rooting out fiction. When I'm diving into someone's life, maintaining my peripheral vision is one of the most important things I can do. Sometimes, after talking to someone for five hours, I'll suddenly think, "This person is full of shit. This stuff didn't happen."

When I'm out in a community, I don't expect to find answers. I'm looking for questions. When I started reporting for the series I wrote on neglect in Washington, D.C., group homes, I saw profoundly needy men in a house where the electricity had been cut off. My question was: What would it be like to depend on the government—not for your driver's license or for street repair but for your very survival twenty-four hours a day? That question, which sprang from my reporting, *began* my research.

Sometimes these questions come to me because someone tells me a story that is different from the one I'm reporting. Sometimes, in the course of riding the bus, sitting in the Laundromat, or just being in a world that isn't my own, I find a story much more meaningful than the one I thought I was reporting. I'll find a story that social welfare advocates or government officials don't know about, the story that most wants to be told.

Here are three ways to improve your narrative investigative writing.

Remember that your story's villains are your guides as much as the story's victims.

Let the villains of your story know about the goods you have on them—early on and in detail. Don't sandbag them. Don't do the closeout interview six hours before your story runs. The real stories often don't come from the so-called victims; they come from the perpetrators. Go to your bad guy early and often. If he feels that his livelihood or his way of life is threatened by what you write, he may want to see his side of the story in print. Or he may want to blame someone else. His side of the story may lead you to a more powerful culprit higher up. This approach will also help keep you out of libel jail. More important, it exposes not just individual bad actors but dysfunctional government and business regulation.

Admit when you don't know. Admit the troubling things you do know.

Acknowledge that the heroic mother of your story is goldbricking at work. Don't omit that the grieving mother of the retarded man who died hadn't visited her son in ten years. If you give your readers characters who are as complex and flawed as they truly are, your readers are more likely to trust you on matters more important than character: the crucial policy issue that your narrative elucidates.

When your story goes to print, graphics are your great ally.

Put the details of your spreadsheet or your computer analysis in a graphic box. Leave your text for the storytelling. In that storytelling, embrace complexity.

Good investigative writing always comes from the search for problems, from rooting out corruption. Still, it can't solve the problems by itself—even when rendered as fine narrative. I have no doubt that five years after my series about abuse in group homes, the situation will be almost as bad as before. Reporters must keep following the story. That sort of daily accountability journalism *must* follow investigative journalism.

Public Radio: Community Storytelling

JAY ALLISON

Radio gets inside us. Lacking ear lids, listeners are defenseless, vulnerable to ambush. Radio documentary makers have this tactical advantage over our colleagues in print, film, television, and photography. Our tool is the aural story, the most primitive and powerful. Invisibility is our friend. Prejudice is suspended while our audience sits blind, receiving our story.

Radio journalists understand that radio is inherently narrative. Radio occupies time; our audience can't put it down and come back later. Radio journalists must hold on to listeners, so we have to perform. Print journalists who move to public radio should know that they are signing up to be performers. We have to create our own stage and then populate it with characters. The first character is the radio journalist—the audience's eyes. The relationship between radio journalist and listener lies near the heart of public radio journalism. It lies close to some utopian ideal: We use the airwaves to share our stories as we try to better understand one another, try not to be afraid of one another, try to come a little closer together.

When doing a radio piece, there is an indelible moment when everything shifts: Topic and subject transform into story. You can almost feel that click. Before it was just information, text without subtext.

Noncommercial public radio isn't regular media or even regular journalism. We have a calling, a mission that exists outside the marketplace, squarely in the public realm. We are expected to defy the bottom line in favor of giving voice to those who are not often heard. We can serve that mission through traditional reporting and documentary, but we also help citizens speak for themselves and speak directly to one another.

I got involved with public radio because someone at National Public Radio lent me a tape recorder and microphone. It was the mid-1970s, and NPR was just inventing itself—always a good time to join an enterprise. I used the recorder as a passport into every part of life that seemed interesting to me. I could find out anything I wanted.

Amazing. At the beginning I was simply a citizen armed with the tools of production and a means of distribution—an independent journalist being born. By apprenticing at news shows, reading everything I could get my hands on, and prodding my elders with questions, I learned the trade on the fly. Over the next twenty-five years I made hundreds of radio features, documentaries, and series.

For much of that time I also lent out tape recorders and tools to others, encouraging citizen voices on the air, repaying and replaying my own start. In an age of corporate consolidation on one side and a lot of bogus Internet journalism on the other, it is more important than ever to bring a range of voices to the airwaves. The public radio journalist can assume a shepherding role.

I sent out my first batch of tape recorders in the 1980s for the series "Life Stories," which sought stories best told by the source. I showed the storytellers who crossed my path how to use the recording gear and then helped them edit their pieces. I often invited them to mix their recordings in my home studio. These storytellers included the son of concentration camp survivors who accompanied his parents on their visit to the Holocaust Museum, hoping they would talk to him about their experiences for the first time in his life. There was a young woman who wanted to revisit the scenes and characters of her hospitalization and near death from anorexia ten years earlier. She needed the passport of the recorder to enter her own past. Stories like these are better lived and narrated by the main characters.

Radio is well suited to the "diary" form, because it is inherently intimate and confidential. It lends itself to scribbled notes, fragments, and whispered entries at night. The technical inexperience of the diarist doesn't show as clearly as it does in video or even in print, so it doesn't get in the way. As the eventual producer/editor, you are there, but you disappear. You must be facilitator, fact-checker, and ethicist, but not director. You allow the listener an authentic, direct, empathetic encounter with the teller.

In 2001, we founded a new public radio station in Massachusetts, for Cape Cod, Martha's Vineyard, and Nantucket. We wanted it to sound like the cape and the islands, not like everywhere else. A place defines itself by its stories. We chose to broadcast our citizens' stories on and off all day, unexpectedly. Portraits, oral histories, poems, anecdotes, memories, and overheard fragments of life pop up during national shows, around the clock. They are short bursts of life as experienced or remembered by all of us who live there, the thread in the fabric of our broadcast day.

The effect is startling, unexpected. While listening to world news there is a pause and then an unheralded speaker—a local elder or high school kid or sandwich maker or scientist—comes on. The voices of our neighbors, surprising us, are given equal weight with events on the world stage.

A radio station is a set of characters, people who come and sit there and talk to you. For our Cape public radio station we wanted something even wider than that. We lent out tape recorders. We called people and said, "Who should we talk to?" "Who are the tellers?" "Who are the community scholars, the citizen historians?" We gathered up the stories and the histories. We have hundreds and hundreds; we play them all day long. They are thirty seconds or one minute long. They don't have titles; they just drop in. It's neighborly. All we have in common is our place. It happens to be our little place by the sea, but it could be anywhere on the planet. Listeners have said that these little breaks in the national programming don't just con- tribute to community, they actually *build* it. We live in a geographi- cally fragmented place—a cape and islands. Each region feels itself to be more "special" than the others. Yet the radio signal extends across them all, disrespecting the boundaries.

We have feuds and jealousies, political divisions, and parochial ig- norance. Is it so different from anywhere else? These stories, almost miraculously, tend to break down those divisions. When a story be- gins, those of us listening don't know where the teller is from, so we listen without judgment. Then we discover that the teller isn't from our island. The contradiction may lead, helplessly, to acceptance. Eventually, we may even come to think of *their* stories as *our* stories.

PART IV

CONSTRUCTING A STRUCTURE

Introduction

MARK KRAMER AND WENDY CALL

No one, not even the greatest writers, creates good first drafts. "I have to write crap before I can write anything that is not crap," says Walt Harrington, who has been writing well for thirty years. "Writing is thinking. It is an extension of the reporting process." A first draft might have promising sentences or paragraphs, a brilliant conceptualization, a few surprising turns of phrase, or a sturdy framework. All that, however, will probably be barely visible, entangled in the general messiness of half-formed ideas. Those promising elements will reveal themselves as the writer begins to tease apart the mess with the next draft and the one after that.

Still, as you read through a flawed first draft, remember that the hardest work is behind you. You have moved closer to defining the topic and developed strategies for explaining it. You have picked a research site (or several) and spent a day or a week or several years there. You have reviewed your notes and ideas as well as done your homework at the library or the courthouse. You have stared down the blank page and begun building something on it.

Good writing is far too complex to get right in one draft or two or five. Good writers are most often plain ol' writers who go the extra mile and then a few more.

High-quality articles, essays, books, and documentaries put words and scenes to work systematically. They present events, ideas, and characters in an order that clarifies them, carefully guiding the reader's reactions. Structure is the deliberate and purposeful sequence of the reader's experience. The strength and tone of your voice determine how enjoyable that experience will be—even in the most conventional news story. The most mundane tale, imparted by an inspired storyteller, captivates.

DeNeen L. Brown, a *Washington Post* writer, says, "An editor once said to me, 'Come on, you aren't writing a novel. Hit the button; send in the story.' Well, why not think of it as a novel?" This section of *Telling True Stories* explores everyday applications of novelistic structure: narrative stance, dialogue, strong beginnings, and satisfying endings.

What Narrative Writers Can Learn from Screenwriters

NORA EPHRON

A lot of college graduates approach me about becoming screenwriters. I tell them, "Do not become a screenwriter, become a journalist," because journalists go into worlds that are not their own. Kids who go to Hollywood write coming-of-age stories for their first scripts, about what happened to them when they were sixteen. Then they write the summer camp script. At the age of twenty-three they haven't produced anything, and that's the end of the career. By the time I became a screenwriter, I knew a few things, because I had worked as a journalist. When I wrote *Silkwood,* I knew what a union negotiation looked like because I had been in on several of them.

I have also learned things through screenwriting that would have been good to know when I worked as a journalist. As a young journalist I thought that stories were simply *what happened.* As a screenwriter I realized that we *create* stories by imposing narrative on the events that happen around us.

Structure is the key to narrative. These are the crucial questions any storyteller must answer: *Where does it begin? Where does the beginning start to end and the middle begin? Where does the middle start to end and the end begin?* In film school you learn these three questions as the classic three-act structure. This structure is practically a religion among filmmakers. Learning it is more instinctive among journalists.

I started working at the *New York Post* in 1963 when there were seven daily newspapers in New York. No one would talk to reporters from the *Post*. We were the least among the papers, so we had to report much harder than anybody else. I often found myself writing long pieces about people who wouldn't give me five minutes on the phone. I had to talk to fifteen or twenty people who had known them since college or had made a movie with them or had run for office against them. Very early in my life as a reporter I learned to collect a lot of material.

The *Post* was an afternoon paper. Writing for an audience that had read a morning paper, I had to find what we called the "overnight angle" on the story. When we covered the same news events that the *Times* covered, we had to turn them into features; that meant developing a strong writing voice. I had been working as a journalist for nearly eight years before I could easily write in the voice that I turned out to have. The skills that I learned at the *Post* became enormously helpful when I moved into narrative journalism and then into screenwriting.

There is more justice in the print world than there is in the movie business. If you write something for print and it's any good, it will probably get printed somewhere. That's not true with movie scripts. People ask writers, "Do you have anything in your trunk?" I used to think, "Of course I have nothing in my trunk. I'm a writer. What I write gets published." But by the time I started writing screenplays, I had a *big* trunk.

When we began writing the screenplay for *Silkwood*, a lot had already been written about Karen Silkwood. There was a ton of daily journalism, narrative journalism, and even a couple of books. I didn't find any of it interesting, in part because Karen was a mixed bag, and all that writing didn't reflect that. Liberal journalists completely whitewashed her, while right-wing journalists turned her into a sort of devil. That made our movie very difficult to write.

All the regular questions that face writers also faced us. Where does the story begin, where is the middle, and where is the end? Each of those things is entirely up to the writer. They are the hardest decisions for any writer to make about any story, whether fiction or nonfiction. If you make the right decision about structure, many other things become absolutely clear. On some level, the rest is easy.

As we wrote *Silkwood*, we realized that we had to condense the period before Karen's death. We knew the movie would end with the automobile accident that killed her even though parts of her story continued long after her death. Since Meryl Streep was playing

Karen, we couldn't eliminate our lead character before the end of the movie. After we made that decision, it was clear that the movie had to begin before plutonium plant worker Karen became whistle-blower Karen Silkwood.

We had one other major problem, one that always faces screenwriters. What do you do in the middle of the movie? In the middle of any movie complications ensue and the whammies mount up. In the middle of *Silkwood*, Karen becomes a political human being. Well, that's boring to watch. How could we show this process without turning off the audience?

The answer was to make the movie very domestic, about three people in a house. Martin Scorsese says the dream movie scene is three people in a room. We had that: Karen, her roommate, and her boyfriend, Drew Stevens. These three people, all going in different directions, gave us a huge amount of material to play against the story that we wanted to tell: *A young woman becomes political.*

Because I started out as a journalist, I believe that if you just keep reporting, eventually you will come to know the structure that your story should have. A certain moment will come when you have figured out how to start, what to put in the middle, and what can wait until the end.

My move from print to film was gradual. Every nine months I took three months off from screenwriting and worked on a novel. After three years I had written my novel, *Heartburn*, and one of my scripts had been made into a film. *Silkwood* and *Heartburn* both came out in 1983. Twenty years later it is a lot easier to see *Silkwood* than it is to find a copy of *Heartburn*.

Too few journalists become screenwriters. I say to all the would-be screenwriters: *Become journalists.* And I'll say to working journalists: *Do not stay journalists. Become screenwriters.*

To Begin the Beginning

DENEEN L. BROWN

The hardest thing about the beginning is the blank screen. Writing is like scraping off a piece of yourself; people can see beneath your skin. I sit at my computer with a container of Slim-Fast bars on my left, a box of Godiva chocolates on my right, and books surrounding me. Many of those books are short story collections. The screen stares and the cursor blinks nothingness, taunting me. It says, "Ready, set, *go!* What are you going to write this time?"

I sit down to write, but I want to rise above the story, as if I am going to tell the story to someone sitting in front of me. I summon a voice strong enough to say, *Sit down and listen to me.* The beginning is important, because you are establishing a relationship with the reader. You are asking to be invited in for a while. Tom Wolfe wrote in his introduction to *The New Journalism,* "Why should the reader be expected to just lie flat and let these people come tromping through as if his mind were a subway turnstile?"

Beginning to read a story should feel like embarking on a journey, starting toward a destination. The writer must decide what larger meaning the story represents and lead the reader to that. Is it about fear? Is it about shame? Pain? Love? Betrayal? Hate? Faith?

As I consider how to begin, I ask myself: What is the story about? What's the theme? What can I use to place a character quickly in a scene? How can I tempt the reader? How can I allow a reader to enter the subject's thoughts, share her feelings?

I wrote a story about a woman who went to an abortion clinic the very day that John Salvi attacked it, so she couldn't get her abortion. Later, she sued the state for the cost of raising her child. I spent a couple of days with her, and then went back to the newsroom and talked with my editor. He said, "What is this story about?" I said, "Well, it's about this woman who went to the clinic . . . and now she is suing the state." He repeated, "What is the story *about*?" And I repeated, "Well, it's about this woman . . ."

"No," he said. "It's about *choice.*" I thought about that. In the end, every scene of my story focused on the central theme of choice.

Here are other questions to ask yourself as you begin: What would you write if you were not afraid of your editor? If you didn't care whether the story appeared on the front page of the newspaper or was published at all? If you were telling the story to your mother on a long-distance telephone call? If you had enough space to run with the full dialogue of your characters, letting in the truth of how people really speak? The full truth of what you saw?

Where would you begin if you were an omniscient narrator? As journalists, we must give ourselves permission to be reporters *and* writers. We must write our stories as natural storytellers would, letting the fingers fly across the keyboard, writing what the muse tells us to write.

Don't even stop for punctuation, just let the words fly, because you know that particular story better than anyone else in the country. You have tracked down every detail and read all the documents.

Each sentence in your story should build on the one before, tugging the reader through the material until she is hooked. I often begin with the tensest moment I've encountered in my reporting. I start the story on a pinpoint but then spread out. Start with a tight shot and then pan wide. Films often begin with the most intimate moment; then the camera pulls back. I begin with the specific and then explain the story. Not only must your story have a beginning, middle, and end, but each scene needs its own beginning, middle, and end.

I once sent a story to my editor, Phil Dixon, and he returned it to me, saying, "This could run on the Metro page or even the front page. But you haven't evoked the soul of the place." I walked away from him thinking, "If it's good enough to go on the front page, then put it in the newspaper and let me move on." I had no idea what he was talking about. I sent him several other beginnings for the story, and he kept returning them, saying, "No, this isn't it."

I finally came to believe that he meant: Don't just tell me what so-and-so said and what so-and-so *felt.* Tell me what so-and-so *meant* to say and *why* she said it, and what had brought her to this point in her life that would *make* her say it. He meant: *Create multidimensional stories and characters. Go deep.*

Thinking about Phil Dixon's phrase, *evoke the soul of a place,* led me to the idea that good stories are like good songs. Like Aretha Franklin songs, they ebb and they flow. Like James Brown, they repeat themselves; they grunt and grind, rise and fall. Sometimes they just scream. The beginning of the story is the first note of the song. Finally, that story Dixon had rejected so many times was published with this beginning:

> Jessica Bradford knows five people who have been killed. It could happen to her, she says, so she has told her family that if she should get shot before her sixth-grade prom, she wants to be buried in her prom dress.
>
> Jessica is 11 years old. She has known since she was in fifth grade what she wanted to wear at her funeral. "I think my prom dress is going to be the prettiest dress of all," Jessica said. "When I die, I want to be dressy for my family."
>
> In the last five years, 224 children younger than 18 have been killed in the District [of Columbia] either as targets of shootings

or as bystanders. The carnage has been taken in by children who live close to the gunfire, such as Jessica, and by some children removed from it.

As they've mastered Nintendo, double Dutch and long division, some children have sized up their surroundings and concluded that death is close at hand. So, like Jessica, they have begun planning their funerals.

Each one of us has a storytelling voice deep inside. We've been listening to stories since we were knee-high, and we know how stories should be told. In her book *Negotiating with the Dead: A Writer on Writing*, novelist Margaret Atwood writes, "The story is in the dark. That is why inspiration is thought of as coming in flashes. Going into a narrative—into the narrative process—is a dark road. You can't see your way ahead. . . . The well of inspiration is a hole that leads downward." Go deep into the darkness and find the story.

Narrative Distance

JACK HART

Narrative distance describes the stance of the writer as the story's narrator. Also called *psychic distance*, it's a concept I learned from John Gardner's *The Art of Fiction: Notes on Craft for Young Writers*. The book is aimed at fiction writers, but it also applies to what we do. Whether or not the writer realizes it, he or she is choosing a narrative distance—deciding how close to stand to the action—in each scene. Changing this distance is analogous to a documentary filmmaker mixing close-ups and long shots.

Mid-range narrative distance is like watching from a hanging balloon. The writer describes the scene from about ten feet away and eight feet off the floor. For example: *She stood, walked across the living room, and pushed the door open. Snow was falling.*

We can get a little closer, moving onto the protagonist's shoulder: *She pulled her feet under her, pushed both hands against the cushion, and rose from the couch. She glided through the living room into the foyer and pushed on the door. It creaked open, wind hissed, and snow blew across the porch at a steep angle.* In this case we're next to her ear, experiencing something close to what she experiences.

Finally, there is the internal view, describing the scene as though you are inside the head of the protagonist, looking through the protagonist's eyes: *The brocade of the couch upholstery pushed into her palms as she lifted herself off the couch. She glided over the soft give of the Persian carpet and the foyer's cool tile. She grabbed the icy brass doorknob and twisted. The door creaked open. Wind whipped her hair across her eyes. Snowflakes burned on her cheeks.* The reader feels the experience almost as the protagonist did.

We are trained as journalists to describe action secondhand, through quotes and observation. Skilled narrative writers put the reader there and let her witness it, have the experience, feel it. That's much more powerful than a secondhand version of reality.

Hearing Our Subjects' Voices: Quotes and Dialogue

KELLEY BENHAM

Looking back at the stories I especially admired while growing up, I'm struck by how sparsely and carefully writers like Rick Bragg used quotes and dialogue. That's my first rule about including a subject's exact words: Do it sparingly. Using fewer quotes makes me a more disciplined and thoughtful writer. It forces me to think harder about my job and take better control of the story.

I wrote a profile of a Colombian man who had come to the United States after having been kidnapped and robbed. He had been a famous magician in his home country; here he worked at Wal-Mart. He spoke very little English, so he used one of his tools—a deck of cards—to explain the situation in Colombia to me. I wrote:

He takes out his cards.

Here is the seven of diamonds, on the table. It represents land. Say, a farm in a small Colombian village, with a peasant family living on it.

The paramilitaries—he picks up another card—want the land so they can plant coca. Cesar puts that card on top of the first. The guerrillas want it for their own drug crops. He piles on another card. The drug cartels want it. Another card.

What happens to the people on the farm? They are buried under the pile.

Maybe the paramilitaries take the family's oldest son and threaten to kill the whole family if he resists. Then the guerrillas get word that the family supports the paramilitaries.

And then?

"*Muerte*," Cesar says. "*Muerte.* Understand?"

That single word, in Spanish, was more powerful than paragraphs filtered through a translator.

Getting strong quotes from people who speak often with the media can be even harder. Sound bites by the famous aren't useful in narrative writing. I look for the less-crafted things they say. During the 2004 elections campaign, I had ten minutes to interview Elizabeth Edwards, the wife of Democratic vice-presidential candidate John Edwards. I started the profile this way:

Emma Claire has lost a tooth. That was Monday, her mother thinks. Today it is Wednesday. Twelve days until the election. Four days since she saw her kids.

"No," she says. "It must have been Sunday. She called and I was between things and I talked to Jack. . . ."

Jack is 4. Emma Claire is 6. Their mother, Elizabeth Edwards, is 55. She is trying to nudge the direction of the free world, and be their mom. She's between one thing and another thing. She has 15 minutes until the next thing. Twelve days until the election. Ten days to Halloween. Three days until she sees her children again.

"I talked to Jack," she is saying. "He said, 'I don't miss you.'"

"I said, 'That's too bad, because I miss you.'"

Jack told her, "Well, I miss you a little bit."

The best quotes, of course, aren't stand-alone quotes at all, but dialogue. I try to include dialogue even in stories about the city council. Dialogue is easier for people to read than straight narrative, because that's how we listen to the world and how we communicate. Dialogue opens up a bit of space on the page, gives the story some breathing room.

I sometimes use dialogue even if it doesn't exactly fit into the narrative. I wrote a piece about a man who owned a $17,000 lawn mower and a quarter-acre yard. I used several short snatches of dialogue as section breaks. Here's one of them:

> Kimberly: "I made the mistake of mowing one time. Like to have caused a divorce."
> Mike, to Kimberly: "But tell her what speed setting you had it on the entire bloody time."
> Kimberly:
> Mike: "Slow."
> Slow!

I like using quotes or bits of dialogue the way you might use the punch line of a joke. I want to give the subject's voice the best platform possible.

Even without direct quotations, I can let my subjects' voices through. In some of my stories, much of the text not in quotes comes from the subjects. I drop the quotation marks, but rather than rewrite it, I just tighten it. I try to remain as close as possible to the spirit of the subject's speech patterns.

Sometimes, when the people I'm writing about can say it better than I can, I just let them. I once interviewed an elderly saxophone player who had played in marching bands for almost ninety years. I interviewed her the first year of her life that she *wouldn't* march. She told me her life story—ninety-six years' worth. For the most part I just let her talk. I interrupted occasionally to move ahead to the next part of the story.

> "I was taking voice lessons in Chicago. I didn't have a voice, but I was taking voice lessons with a little French lady named Madame LeBrun. I always said when I got to be 25 I'd get married.
>
> "Well, here I was 25 and nobody in sight. I went to Madame LeBrun and I told her my story and I said, 'What should I do?' And she said, 'Well, I'll get you a job at the café on Wabash Avenue. You watch the door and whoever you're going to marry will walk in the door.' I believed her and I got my job and I watched the door. One day in comes this little guy in a little green felt hat and I thought, that's him. And I went back to her and I said, 'I found him. What do I do next?'"
>
> She married him.

I almost couldn't get a word in edgewise while interviewing her. If I had quoted her in a three-word chunk, it would have been dishonest.

In a college poetry class we crafted a poem from bits of found language: dialogue, books, cereal boxes. It was a surprising and joyful way to write. The rhythms of the little snippets played off each other and rolled across the page. People's voices are like found poetry— raw, uncrafted, imperfect. Still, we do them the greatest justice when we choose carefully and get out of the way.

Hearing Our Subjects' Voices: Keeping It Real and True

DEBRA DICKERSON

The *Washington Post* published a big spread about my first book, *An American Story,* and about me. It was extremely positive but included one quote meant to illustrate—as the writer noted—my immaturity.

The problem was, the writer had misinterpreted what I had said. During the interview in a café, I looked out the window and a woman walked by. She wore a *very* hip dress with the most hideous shoes. There was no way that someone with the sense of style to choose that dress had intended to wear those shoes with it. I wondered to myself, "Did she just have a fight with someone?" I was thinking of a time that I fought with my boyfriend and then left in a huff. When I got home, I realized I had put my dress on inside-out. As I was thinking all of this, I said out loud, "Nice dress." I looked down, stared at her feet, and said, "The shoes don't match."

He printed what I had said as if I were judging her. Actually, I was empathizing with her.

Being the subject of profiles has been useful to me as a journalist because it has given me a better sense of what our subjects go through. One thing I have learned is that the most important thing about using quotes and dialogue—about *all* journalism, really—is to bring a strong sense of humility to the work. A journalist might think she knows the meaning of the words coming out of a person's mouth but be completely wrong.

When we publish a quote or a bit of dialogue, we're telling the reader, "This is exactly what the person said." This is obvious but bears keeping in mind. Accuracy is essential. When I come to a conclusion about a subject, especially if it's a negative one, I return to that conclusion four or five times. If I've pegged someone as an arrogant jerk, I want to be sure the person really *is* one. I give the person many opportunities to repeat the offending behavior.

On the other hand, newspapers and magazines often publish quotes that are not what the person actually said. I have seen journalists unconsciously correct the English of professional people but not working-class or poor people. A journalist must make a conscious decision about correcting a person's grammar. I don't think that quotes should be sanded smooth; quotation marks mean that what is enclosed in them is verbatim. I face this issue a lot because I write about regular people in the community, and *real people talk real.* I'm using poor English here because that's how most of my subjects talk.

I wrote an article for *U.S. News & World Report* several years ago about the relationship between working-class Blacks and the Vietnamese immigrants who run the nail salons in their neighborhoods. I rendered their English the way they spoke it, angering many in the Vietnamese community. I used a translator for most of the interviews, but some of the things they said in English were more powerful as they actually said them. I don't regret my decision.

Letting people's voices come through, without having the reader think the person sounds ignorant, is an ongoing struggle. It is not just a question of craft, it's a question of our readers' assumptions and biases. The problem isn't necessarily people using nonstandard English. The problem is other people—the readers—judging them incorrectly because of that. The stories that my subjects live are amazing ones. Their humanity shines through the dangling participles.

On the other hand, we often have to write about people who aren't necessarily so amazing. One way to get people to say interesting things is to ask dumb questions. I ask really dumb questions. I let people talk as long as they want. If they don't talk, I sometimes remain silent. Silence makes people uncomfortable and people will keep talking to fill the space. Often, I'll play devil's advocate. When I was working on a story about a crack dealer, I spent a lot of time riding around his neighborhood with him. We passed some people who looked homeless. To test him I said, "Gee, look at those people. Why don't they clean themselves up?" He became very angry, telling me, "You're not better than those people!" After that he became sad. Little by little the true story of his circumstances came out. Making people angry is a good way to get to the truth. I'm willing to be yelled at or disliked in the interest of the story. The real story, framed accurately and rendered honestly, is what counts.

A Story Structure

JON FRANKLIN

Narrative is chronology: This happens, that happens, the other thing happens, and then something else happens. All of our lives are narrative—usually a rather confusing version of it. Story is something else: taking select parts of a narrative, separating them from everything else, and arranging them so they have meaning. Meaning is intrinsic to storytelling.

That is one reason it's so difficult for those of us educated in newsrooms to understand storytelling. We're trained *not* to insert meaning in our news stories. But we mistake meaning for opinion. Journalism as we currently know it is relentlessly cognitive. We use facts; we prove things. Journalism has very little to do with meaning.

Narrative writers can bring meaning to journalism. The successful narrative writer presumes that he or she can find meaning in real life and can report on it.

Until the death of the *Saturday Evening Post* in 1969, many people made their living writing short stories. With the demise of the general interest magazine, that livelihood all but vanished. No fewer writers are born today than fifty years ago, though. All the would-be writers had to go somewhere. Many of us were forced into journalism.

Like a lot of other writers, I soon grew frustrated by the limitations of journalism. I wanted to write stories. I found myself thinking that all good stories—fiction or nonfiction—must have some things in common. If so, we should be able to understand them and, with that understanding, more predictably find other good stories. I went hunting. I found that texts about writing published between 1900 and 1960, the age of the short story and realistic novel, talked a lot about what made stories powerful. They all focused on character and plot.

Anton Chekhov laid out the anatomy of story, defining a story by its points of change, or plot points. The first point of change, at the end of the beginning, is the *character complication*. It is the point when the main character runs into something that complicates his or her life. The character complication comes where a nutgraf would go in a traditional newspaper narrative and can be interchangeable with it.

The *complication* isn't necessarily a *conflict*; it is merely something that forces the character to exert effort. It is often a conflict in the literature of Western cultures, but less so in the literature of African cultures.

In nearly all stories, the characters go through some transformation. The reporter may have trouble discerning it at first. If it isn't there, the reporter probably doesn't have a story. The key is to find that significant point of change.

My university students often write about people dying of cancer. I encourage this, actually, because too often no one wants to talk to dying people, although they really want to discuss what they are experiencing. My students often assume that the complication of their stories is the cancer. If terminal cancer is the complication, then death must be the ending. So, what's the meaning? That's hard to say.

Let's go back and look at the story again. Maybe the complication is something else. Most people who are dying of cancer receive their diagnosis and are afraid; they deny; they fight. In the end, they make peace with their cancer. The point of insight becomes the conquering of fear, not the diagnosis of cancer. By "point of insight" I mean the moment when the story turns toward the resolution, when the main character (and/or the reader) finally grasps the true nature of the problem and knows what must be done about it. The meaning: There are fates we can't change, but we can deal with them in ways that allow us to retain our dignity and our sense of control.

In most good stories the characters decide their own destinies. In the real world that often doesn't happen. In that way stories are not like real life. Good stories show how people survive.

All stories have three layers. The top layer is what actually happens— the narrative. The next layer is how those events make the main character feel. If the writer succeeds in getting the reader to suspend disbelief and see through the character's eyes, then the character's and the reader's feelings will be joined. There is another layer below the factual and the emotional. It is the rhythm of the piece and evokes the story's universal theme: love endures, wisdom prevails, children mature, war destroys, prejudice perverts.

The preeminent neuroanatomist of the mid-twentieth century,

Paul MacLean, coined the phrase *triune brain*. His idea was that each person has three brains: One understands rhythm, one understands emotion, and the third is cognitive. The cognitive brain is programmable; it speaks English or Chinese or logic. But to really communicate deeply, a writer must use the languages of all three brains. That is why rhythms are so important to storytelling.

Storytelling can be symphonic. John Steinbeck wrote that he wanted *The Grapes of Wrath* to sound like Igor Stravinsky's *Firebird Suite*. Ernest Hemingway was a little more brutal. He chose Bach. If you take the first chapter of *Farewell to Arms* and read it aloud to the first movement of the Brandenburg Concerto, Hemingway's words seem to match the music perfectly.

The narrative writer may choose to speak at these three levels very consciously, but the effect on the reader is usually unconscious. Readers read very fast, seeing none of the layers. They simply feel it, as you feel a highway while traveling over it.

Rhythm exists in story from the sentence level right up to the sectional level. A lot of my writing is in blank verse. You don't need to know the names of the tropes; you just need to listen for them.

Looking at how the human brain developed—to make an extremely long story very short—it evolved to resolve complications. We like stories because we think in stories; it's how we derive meaning from the world. When you read a hard news story about something that interests you, you already know the context. That is to say, you know the narrative behind the piece of news. The human mind looks at the evidence—new information and past experience—and figures out scenarios, possible narratives. This is why structure reveals meaning and why we like stories that have structure.

Summary vs. Dramatic Narrative

JACK HART

Most narrative pieces shift between summary and dramatic narrative. The summary provides the links between scenes, which are usually written in dramatic narrative. Standard news stories are written in summary narrative. But true storytelling requires mastery of dramatic narrative. Traditional journalists, because they have limited experience with dramatic narrative, often have a tough time distinguishing between the two. One of the reporters at my newspaper, who had been struggling to grasp the distinction between summary and dramatic narrative, finally saw the light. "Aha!" he said. "I get it. You're either *in* story, or you're *out* of story." *Exactly!*

The following chart shows the main distinctions between the two forms:

Summary Narrative	Dramatic Narrative
Emphasizes the abstract	Emphasizes concrete detail
Collapses time	Readers experience action as if it were happening in real time
Employs direct quotes	Employs dialogue, characters talking to one another
Organized topically	Organized scenically
Omniscient point of view	Specific point of view
Writer hovers above the scene	Clear narrative stance
	Writer is inside the scene
Deals with outcomes rather than process	Deals with process, gives specific description
Higher on the ladder of abstraction	Lower on the ladder of abstraction
Composed of digression, backstory, and explication	Composed of the story's main line of action

Weaving Story and Idea

NICHOLAS LEMANN

Narrative nonfiction that is mere yarn-spinning won't ever rise to greatness. As practitioners of narrative nonfiction, we often seem to lack a full sense of the importance of ideas in our work. We need to develop a common set of techniques for combining ideas and narrative.

Tom Wolfe's anthology *The New Journalism* came out when I was a young lad starting out in journalism. I almost devoured it. Wolfe's wonderful introduction to the book had even more impact on me than the articles he anthologized. His introductory essay challenged the standards for journalistic criticism. At that time the aesthetics of journalism's literary and visual techniques were almost entirely missing from the grim-faced business of media criticism. But here came Wolfe with a joyous, funny, infectiously ambitious idea about the possibilities of journalism as an art form—poised on the brink of supplanting the novel as the richest and most vital form of published writing.

As important as that essay was to me, a couple of points of dissatisfaction with it have rattled around in my mind in the years since. Both relate to the weaving of *story* and *idea* in narrative writing.

First, Wolfe's thrillingly detailed playbook of techniques for new journalism doesn't fully describe what Wolfe does in his own journalistic work. Yes, Wolfe uses status details about dress and decor and accent, nailing everything to precise locations on a socioeconomic map. Yes, he uses set scenes. Yes, he writes from the characters' points of view. Yes, he includes a lot of dialogue. But those things are not all that he does.

He doesn't fully own up to the fact that he is not just a reporter and a narrativist, but also an intellectual. In his last and greatest narrative nonfiction work, *The Right Stuff*, he uses techniques that he doesn't really acknowledge: A master hypothesis drives the entire work, while he proposes constructs and rubrics throughout the book that drive and shape the story.

Wolfe begins the book with an elaborate, hilarious series of scenes about the lives of fighter pilots in the 1950s, establishing the eponymous "right stuff" as a master concept for the work. The "right stuff" is on the idea track. It is absolutely necessary, and it has to come first. Otherwise, you lose the wonderful joke of the early astronauts' humiliation, even as they are being publicly lionized as heroes over being put into space in capsules that they didn't actually pilot. This humiliation—more idea than event—permits the role of the press in the story to be treated as farce, to memorable effect.

In addition to offering us precise status details, Wolfe offers us a wonderful anthropology and psychology of fighter pilots, bureaucrats, politicians, and the press. *The Right Stuff* is an elaborately disguised public policy analysis of a government agency, the National Aeronautics and Space Administration. The book argues that space travel was probably a mistake, having been undertaken for cultural, political, and publicity reasons—not scientific ones. The subsequent tragedies involving the space shuttles have made Wolfe's analysis seem prescient.

Wolfe, like most other writers who amount to anything, works actively with ideas as well as techniques. It is theoretically possible for long-form narrative journalists to select a topic that has no idea content but is merely—to use the technical term of our profession—*one hell of a damn story*. Even those stories, when rendered exceptionally well, include some larger issue or implication. All those nonfiction narrative books that have subtitles containing the phrase "that changed America" or "that changed the world" commit themselves to advancing a thesis.

My book *The Big Test* has a very precise idea plot. The big question of the book is this: *By creating a newer lead that will be chosen by supposedly scientific and scrupulously fair means, can you then create a group that the rest of society will follow, hence building a harmonious democratic society?* The answer is *no, you can't.* That's the idea plot of the book.

The events of *The Big Test*'s narrative track advance the idea track. The story of California's Proposition 209 on affirmative action puts into play all the elements of the idea track. I was highly conscious of the interplay of the story track and the idea track both as I reported and as I wrote the book. I used little charts and graphs that showed each plot point and the development of the idea that accompanied it. I chose narrative plot points that efficiently advanced the idea plot.

To develop a strong idea track, the writer gains strong command of the material. Ambitious narrative journalists must do literature reviews. This process gets the writer up to speed on the subject and identifies the compass points in the debate. Journalists often argue that the academic literature pertaining to their subjects is incomprehensible and of no use to them or their readers. Our job as journalists, however, is to encounter the unfamiliar and learn to understand it. Understanding academic discourse is just another reporting problem solved the same way we solve all the others: with persistence, by finding guides, and so on.

If the material is incomprehensible, that's good news. A journalist who encounters something interesting—as usually happens in this process—gets to be the first person to tell the nonspecialist world about it.

In the mid-twentieth century, many historians, sociologists, and anthropologists thought of themselves as people who wrote for the general public. They commanded a very large public audience. Over the second half of the twentieth century, academics in those fields abandoned that role. Their conversations became much more self-directed, technical, and hard for outsiders to understand.

A journalist's literature review can end up completely invisible to the reader. Still, it is an important tool for avoiding a common pitfall: being unconscious of the assumptions, frames of reference, and master narratives that work their way into the writing.

For example, political writers often operate on the assumption that interest groups are a maligned force in politics. In a nonfiction narrative about politics, therefore, the politician who heeds interest groups is a bad guy, while the one who ignores them is a good guy. Why? James Madison didn't think interest groups were so bad. Most political scientists would laugh at the idea that interest groups can be extracted from politics. Writers should at least be aware of arguments against the conventional wisdom before plunging ahead.

Once the writer is fully familiar with the subject, the next step is analogous to matching up the sound track and the visual track while making a movie. The audience notices the novelistic aspects of narrative nonfiction: the movement of the characters through a series of dramatic events in memorable settings. That's the equivalent of a film's visual track. The film's sound track is vitally important and requires elaborate working out. Still, it doesn't entirely penetrate the audience's conscious awareness. The narrative nonfiction equivalent of the film sound track is an *idea plot*: an ordered succession of arguments that moves forward in sync with the narrative plot. The terms from journalism that best convey this process are *signposts, billboards*, and *nutgrafs*. In all these places the writer stops the narrative and signals the meaning or where the narrative is headed next. The more the writer thinks about the movement of the idea track in the narrative *while reporting*, the less clunky the execution.

At a few key places in the narrative there should be what I call "marriage moments," places where the idea track and the narrative track intersect. During a movie scene in which the main character picks up the guitar, the audience becomes much more aware of the sound track because it is temporarily in one-to-one correspondence with the visual track. That is a marriage moment.

In journalism, marriage moments often arise when authority figures make decisions that shape the story's direction. These individuals make their decisions on the basis of material in the idea track. In works of narrative nonfiction, judges, welfare caseworkers, and parole officers often make for good marriage moments.

Marriage moments fasten the idea track more firmly to the narrative track. Narrativists tend to focus heavily on developing their reporting and writing capabilities just to spin a dramatic yarn. This is a mistake. The marriage of narrative and analysis is the fundamental project of journalism.

Once you get past the realm of the purely entertaining or sensational, nearly all journalism is a promise to explain the world via narrative. Stories and characters have a powerful hold on the human mind. We translate the world into narrative form. That is why story, rather than datum, is the basic unit of journalism. Purely analytic work or purely narrative work is conceptually cleaner than the blending of the two. Narrative married to idea is complicated, difficult, and somewhat messy. So what? Life is, too. If it weren't, there wouldn't be any need for journalism.

Endings
BRUCE DESILVA

Every story must arrive at a destination; the purpose of a story is to lead your readers to it. The ending is your final chance to nail the point of the story to the readers' memory so it will echo there for days. Among those who write for a living, newspaper writers are the only ones who do not seem to understand this fact.

Screenwriters know that if a movie doesn't have a good ending, people will leave the theater feeling like they wasted their money. Novelists know that you can't write a good book without a good ending. Speechwriters always try to end on a high note. And everyone knows that when you write a love letter or a letter asking for a raise or a letter of complaint to the phone company, the tone and substance of the last line is crucial.

But most newspaper stories dribble pitifully to an end. This is the enduring legacy of the inverted pyramid—a form that makes good endings impossible. The inverted pyramid orders information from most important to least important, robbing stories of their drama and leaving nothing to reward readers who stay with it to the last line.

It is important to recognize that the inverted pyramid never had anything to do with writing or readers or the news. Those of us who have studied the history of the form trace its emergence to the invention of the telegraph. Reporters covering far-flung news about, say, a sinking ship or a Civil War battle now had a speedy way to transmit their stories to their newspapers, but they found that they could not always rely on it. Sometimes the line would fail; sometimes their messages would be preempted by urgent official business. So they learned to transmit their information in bursts, with the most important facts first.

This proved to be the perfect form to accommodate the manufacturing process in every newspaper's back shop. Stories were written and edited on paper and then sent to typographers, who set them in lead type. This type had to fit into a designated space on a newspaper page, but often it was too long. The only practical way to cut lead type was to trim it from the bottom.

We don't send our stories by telegraph anymore, and it has been more than thirty years since U.S. newspapers used lead type. Today, most are fully digital, so stories can be trimmed anywhere with the stroke of a key. Furthermore, stories for online use don't have to be trimmed to fit a preexisting hole at all. The only appropriate use for the inverted pyramid today is briefs, but old habits die hard. The best journalists know this, but the form persists. Many editors still routinely cut from the bottom. If you are stuck with such an editor, keep writing good endings while you look for another job.

Your ending must do four things: signal to the reader that the piece is over, reinforce your central point, resonate in your reader's mind after he or she has turned the page, and arrive on time. The very best endings often do something else: They offer a twist that readers don't see coming but that nevertheless strikes them as exactly right.

There are many ways to do this well. A good ending can be

- a vividly drawn scene
- a memorable anecdote that clarifies the main point of the story
- a telling detail that symbolizes something larger than itself or suggests how the story might move forward into the future
- a compellingly crafted conclusion in which the writer addresses the reader directly and says, "This is my point."

Sometimes you may want to bring the story full circle, ending with an idea or words echoing the beginning. Symmetry appeals to readers. Occasionally, you may want to end with a quote that is superbly put, but don't do this often. After all, you are the writer; you should be able to say it better. It's *your* story; why give the last word to someone else?

This advice applies to all stories, but narrative writing has an additional requirement. Every narrative tale—from *The Iliad* to the latest Pulitzer Prize–winning newspaper serial—has the same underlying structure you have read about elsewhere in this book: A central character encounters a problem, struggles with it, and, in the end, overcomes it or is defeated by it or is changed in some way. If the story, as it unfolds in life, lacks one of these elements, you should not attempt to write it as a narrative.

In narrative, the resolution of the problem is your ending. Once you arrive at it, find the nearest exit. Readers devour narratives to discover how the problem will be resolved. Once they know, they stop reading—so you had better stop writing.

Here are some examples of effective endings from stories written by Associated Press reporters.

At the beginning of "What Price the News?" a first-person story by Ian Stewart, he is drifting in and out of consciousness. Something terrible has happened to him, but he doesn't know what. Ian had been shot in the head and his friend killed covering the war in Sierra Leone. The story follows Ian as he struggles to understand what happened and to overcome this terrible injury. It also explores the macho world of foreign correspondents and the importance of getting news of remote wars to the public. But Ian ends his story this way:

> Miles, David and I were naïve to hope our reporting could make people care about a little war in Africa. In fact, Freetown might never have made your daily newspaper had it not been for the death of one Western journalist and wounding of another. Will I continue to work as a journalist when I am well enough? Yes. And most likely I'll go back overseas. Will I risk my life for a story again? No, not even if the world cares the next time.

This ending works because you don't see it coming, and yet at the same time you realize: Of *course* this is how he feels.

In "A Town Is Born," Ted Anthony describes how the denizens of an unincorporated patch of New Mexican desert go about forming a local government. Near the beginning he presents readers with a nutgraf: "In a few hours they would become fathers. The new arrival would be rambunctious, assertive and self-determined, ready to make the kind of glorious mess that only democracy can."

The bulk of the story is details: How much land should be included in the town? How should they set the tax rate? Do they need a road grader? At the end, Ted nails his point home this way:

> For now, they're simply crafting their own community: negotiating workaday squabbles, liking and disliking each other, dealing with constituents, hop scotching forward, and doing it themselves. Everything is theirs, even the mistakes. Big ideas on a small canvas, laws in action. People deciding together how they want life to be. The glorious mess that is American democracy, alive and kicking, just off Interstate 40 on a plateau under the vast New Mexico sky.

Here, Ted directly tells the reader the story's point. He also pulls the camera back, away from the tight shots of the road grader and the tax rate. Suddenly, you're on a plateau under the vast sky, viewing the historical and constitutional context in which this story unfolds.

In "Mysterious Killer," Matt Crenson and Joseph P. Verrengia chronicle New York City's 1999 West Nile epidemic. The story begins with dead birds mysteriously falling out of trees. Before long, human beings are dying, too. Epidemiologists race to discover the cause. By the end of the story they've identified the exotic virus carried by mosquitoes breeding in kiddie pools, birdbaths, and abandoned tires. And suddenly the outbreak stops, not because of human action but because the mosquito season ends. The story concludes this way:

> In the New York City neighborhood where it all began, barbecues and kiddie pools have been put away for the season, and many of the old tires have been carted away. But here and there, tires missed during the cleanup, or discarded since, lay in the grass, ready to become mosquito nurseries with the first spring rain.

The ending is an ominous peek into the future. Think of it as the Godzilla ending: The monster has been destroyed, everyone is celebrating, and then the camera pans to the monster's egg at the bottom of the sea.

For a story called "In Case We Die," Tim Sullivan and Raf Casert traveled to Conakry, Guinea, and Brussels, Belgium, to re-create the lives of two fourteen-year-old boys who died in the wheel well of a jet airplane during a desperate attempt to escape the poverty of their country. On one of their bodies Belgian authorities found an envelope bearing the words: "In case we die." Inside was an eloquent plea for the world to help the children of Africa.

Tim and Raf described the boys' lives in Africa, their plans to escape, their ill-fated journey, and the outpouring of emotion their case initially caused in Belgium, a country still torn with guilt about its colonial past. They ended the tale this way:

> Now the boys' letter rests inside dossier number 4693.123506/99 of the Belgian State Judiciary. And on another continent in a public cemetery, two graves ten feet apart mark the end of the journey for two boys who had a message for the world. The small mounds of dirt in the Conakry graveyard are edged with rocks and rotting chunks of palm trees. Staked to each grave is a small metal marker. Both are blank.

This is not the ending we would have hoped for. We would have wanted these boys' deaths to have meant something. But in the end, the boys are forgotten, the poignant point made starkly with two small details: the letter filed away in the bowls of a bureaucracy and the unmarked graves.

In "God and Country," Richard Ostling and Julia Lieblich explain why the same conflicts over church and state go on generation after generation in America. The piece, datelined Ecru, Mississippi, starts this way:

> Long after the high school football game ended, Lisa Herdahl and Pat Mounce sat on wet bleachers talking intently under a shared umbrella. The two 36-year-old mothers were discussing something they cared deeply about: the prayers broadcast over the intercom of their children's schools in the Pontotoc School District. Herdahl opposed the prayers and was taking the county's school district to court. Mounce had organized the town to fight back.

The story explores the enduring debate over the sixteen words about freedom of religion in the U.S. Constitution. It is a story of conflict—until the very end:

> Americans disagree, and perhaps always will, over matters of church and state. But the debate is never over the fundamental right to religious freedom embodied in those 16 words from two

centuries ago. What Americans argue about is how best to practice it. Unlike so many people throughout the world even today, Americans do not settle their religious differences with blood. They debate them in legislative chambers and mannered courtrooms, or even while sharing an umbrella.

The story takes an unexpected turn as the writers suddenly pull back, putting the debate in a global context. They accomplish this by returning to the umbrella, a metaphor for the Constitution that shelters Americans from violent religious strife.

One final piece of advice: When your story is a narrative, write the ending first. Remember, the ending is your destination. It is a lot easier to write the rest of the piece when you already know where you are going.

PART V

BUILDING QUALITY
INTO THE WORK

Introduction

MARK KRAMER AND WENDY CALL

Quality writing is the sum of myriad parts: action, characters, scenes, voice, insight, research, and narrative structure. We can parse these elements and peer at their workings and interactions. Experienced writers can describe—more often in someone else's work—effective common practice. This section of the anthology gathers insights gleaned from the twelve writers' three-hundred-plus collective years of word-working.

We might have called this section "Revising." Strong characters, compelling scenes, controlled passage of time, complex ideas, and the discovery of deep truth all emerge only as writers work through draft after draft. Each one of those drafts embodies hundreds of subtle insights and a few large ones. That cleaned-up, more efficient copy instructs the writer how to make a next set of improvements.

The process is hardly arbitrary, as the writers of this section demonstrate. A learnable set of skills allows writers to develop a compelling narrator's voice, build strong scenes, describe the world as it is seen by a main character, and offer important insights—without imposing them on readers. The writer is the liaison between subject and reader. As translator and author Ilan Stavans says,

> All nonfiction writers, whether they like it or not, are translators. The translator is the *perfect* journalist. The best journalism endeavors to convey an essential idea or story to an audience that knows very little about it, and that requires translation. To do this successfully, the writer must filter the idea through the prism of his eye, and his mind, and his writing style.

Voice and structure are interconnected. Redrafting strengthens the connections. Every text has a voice—a personage who accompanies the reader. From the reader's perspective, that personage is the writer's personality. From the writer's perspective, it is a personality carefully crafted through the writing. An effective writing voice does much more than provide good company. It offers authority, savvy, and order; it guides the reader on a journey, navigating the most engaging route toward a thematic destination. That travel route, the story's structure, determines the reader's experience. A strong relationship between reader and writer creates a meaningful trip. If you establish yourself as a trustworthy and genial host, you can take your reader—and your story—anywhere.

Good, clean sentences are fundamental to a strong writer's voice. Once you have achieved control over your sentences and paragraphs, you can torque a phrase into an unusual shape, offer a knowing side comment, leap forward and backward in time, digress from the main story line, and meander back to it. Readers will gladly follow a voice they trust almost anywhere.

That voice might sound genial and easygoing, but that derives from disciplined work. Writing is a craft for the thoughtful fanatic. This section offers fuel for that fanaticism.

Character

JON FRANKLIN

The most powerful thing literature can do is move people to suspend disbelief: Readers forget that they are on the train or at the doctor's office or babysitting, and enter the story. Readers enter most stories through the main character. That character can be hero or antihero, but must be sympathetic—or at the very least understandable to the reader. Narrative journalists use the word *character* in various ways, and the word's definition has changed over the centuries.

Medieval European writers portrayed a struggle between God and the devil over the human soul. God, these writers asserted, put human beings on earth for a short time, and the devil tried to tempt them with the "illusion" that post-Enlightenment writers consider "reality." In medieval times, reality was internal, and illusion was external. During the Enlightenment, internal and external switched places. Now, our demons are inside, and reality is outside.

Victorians generally defined *character* as morality. People had good character or bad character, and those judgments were based on family background; experience didn't count for much. The Victorians were just beginning to discover genetics, which led to the awful notion of eugenic determination of character. Eugenics led, in turn, to the backlash of behaviorism, the idea that character is determined by environment. We are just coming out of that phase now.

These days, narrative writers need to tell readers how a character's inner world stacks up against the outside reality he or she faces. It is a challenge because the character created on the page must come from reporting, from observing externalities. Most often, the first thing that attracts a writer to a story is a plot element, some action that has occurred. The character, the person responsible for (or affected by) the action, is secondary. If the writer thinks more deeply about character, and especially the relationship between plot and character, the story becomes much richer.

It requires quite a leap from standard journalistic reporting for a writer to say: *I can understand another human being, my character, well enough to put the reader inside that person's mind.* This level of understanding requires rigorous reporting. It is hard work, but there is a process for it. The psychological interview (see "The Psychological Interview" on page 34) is an important part of that process.

While the writer must draw a true portrait of the character, it can't ever be a complete one; no writer can capture a whole person. Every person is involved in many parallel, consecutive stories. I am a writer, teacher, gardener, father, dog owner, and husband. A story about me couldn't possibly include all those elements. The reporter usually ends up choosing just one facet of a person's life. In a story about a music teacher and her mentorship of one student, her personal life doesn't matter. If the story is about her life as a barfly six nights a week, then mentoring of the student probably doesn't figure in the story. A writer chooses what matters.

New writers sometimes make the mistake of trying to create a character on the page by drawing on details of the person's surroundings. Few readers would care that there's a golf trophy in a subject's office unless they also learn its significance. Description alone isn't helpful. A reporter who doesn't understand a subject has no way of knowing what the details of the surroundings mean. To put it another way, information that explains *motive* goes into the piece. Everything else stays out. The *why*, the character's motive, is secondary information. It is part of the backstory.

Stories, by definition, are chronological; events happen over time. Narrative without chronology is a disaster, but this doesn't mean the author must start at the beginning and move straight through to the end. Character-centered stories often start most effectively when the character is close to a decisive action; then they move back in time to explain how the person came to that point.

The writer's goal is to understand how the character looks at the world and understand the character's responses to events. After the reporter has come to know the character well enough, he or she should be able to predict that person's reactions to things.

Test yourself. If you learn something new about the subject's experience from another source, try to predict the subject's reaction to it. Ask the subject about the event. If your prediction was wrong, you haven't finished your reporting. You may be able to show the reader how the world looks through the character's eyes. A story with such strong, skillfully drawn characters may be enough to invite the reader to suspend disbelief.

Details Matter

WALT HARRINGTON

I once visited Mobile, Alabama, to do a story about a fundamentalist Christian family that had brought a lawsuit to ban public school textbooks that were allegedly "secular humanist." I was dispatched by the *Washington Post Magazine* to answer the question: *What kind of family would bring a lawsuit to get books banned in America*?

It turned out that the answer was *a lovely family*. After I arrived at their middle-class home and started chatting with them, I realized that right away. I didn't know how to begin my interview, so I asked for a tour of their house. Mrs. Webster, a sweet woman, walked me through the house, full of tacky teddy bears and knickknacks. "Boy, these people have bad taste," I thought.

Then she made comments like "This really ugly teddy bear was a gift from the thirteen-year-old girl who moved in with us after her mother kicked her out when she was two months pregnant. She stayed with us, and we took care of her through the pregnancy. And this silly little knickknack is from the eighty-four-year-old woman who my husband takes to the pool twice a week. He carries her out of her wheelchair and into the swimming pool so she can have some exercise."

Everything in the house related to deeds they had done for others. They hadn't collected any of the things to prove their good taste. In fact, the meaning of the objects had nothing to do with the Websters' taste. Their meaning was *these are good people*.

Details do hold meaning, but sometimes not the sort we expect. Tom Wolfe defined status details as the items around people that define their social circumstance. Such details make the subject's interior world clearer to us. Yet the meaning of such details isn't always inherent in the objects themselves but is in their importance to our subjects. None can simply be taken at face value. Had I not asked, I never would have discovered the real meaning of the "status details" in the Websters' home.

Developing Character

STANLEY NELSON

Developing complex characters is difficult in any storytelling medium, but it might be even more challenging in film than in print. We're so accustomed to seeing simple characters on screen: old Hollywood movies where good guys and bad guys are immediately obvious from their clothes and from the background music. Film school students watch *Citizen Kane* over and over again—even now, more than sixty years after it was produced—because it doesn't fit that rubric. I watched that film as a student and also wondered: *Is Kane good? Or is he bad?* Kane's extremely complex character gives the film its depth.

Character development is especially challenging in documentary film because characters are most often presented as heroes, and less often as demons. It's important to hint at richer character, but let audience members decide for themselves. Saying too much—especially in the film's narration—ruins the audience's sense of *discovery*. The experience of watching a film should be making a series of discoveries. This process keeps viewers engaged. This is particularly important when making television documentaries, to combat the Remote Factor—with the push of a button the viewer can abandon your story.

In my documentary about Emmett Till, originally titled *Chicago Boy*, I tried to give the film an air of objectivity. I didn't want the narration to deliver the message: *Those dastardly men kidnapped and killed Emmett Till.* We relied on the people interviewed in the film to say that.

In addition to presenting Emmett Till and his attackers, the film established two other characters: the city of Chicago and the region of the Mississippi delta. In the story these two characters converged on a collision course—in the person of Emmett Till, who traveled from one to the other. Emmett had been raised to understand Chicago's cultural norms. Taking that understanding to the Delta killed him; he was murdered after he allegedly whistled at a white woman. Our film asked: *Well, why not whistle?* In Chicago that act didn't carry the same implications that it did in Mississippi.

Every word of a film's narration is considered and reconsidered, because there must be so few of them. The entire script of *Chicago Boy*'s narration ran only twenty pages. Every single word had to carry significant information. We noted that the train trip from Chicago to Mississippi took sixteen hours—to emphasize the vast gulf between these two places and to develop them as characters.

To foster the audience's sense of discovery, we planted clues throughout the film, quietly foreshadowing important story elements. For example, Emmett Till's body was so badly mutilated that he was identified by a ring he was wearing. The men who committed the murder were acquitted after the defense claimed that the boy's family and the NAACP had dug up another body, placed Emmett's ring on it, and thrown the body in the river. The ring is introduced early in the film; the audience later discovers its importance.

Characterizing historical figures brings particular challenges: You can't speak to the subject, and your audience members may believe they already know who the person was. Our film *Marcus Garvey: Look for Me in the Whirlwind* included a beginning teaser that laid out our perspective on Garvey. He was an extraordinarily complicated character, both good and bad—the kind of guy who would not only shoot himself in the foot but borrow your gun to do it. Still, Garvey remains an icon for people in the African-American community, especially in countries such as Jamaica.

Here is some of the narration from the beginning of the film, setting up both the film's purpose and Marcus Garvey's character:

On the morning of August 3, 1920, forty-six-year-old Jacob Mills shined his boots, polished his sword, and headed to Harlem to take part in one of the biggest parades in New York's history. . . . Mills was one of a hundred thousand Black people marching under the red, black, and green flag of the Universal Negro Improvement Association. The world had never seen anything like it. It was all the work of one man, Marcus Garvey.

The film starts with that emblematic event, and then the narration pulls back to note the overall context:

At the age of thirty-four, Garvey claimed millions of followers worldwide. His controversial goal to create an independent Black nation made him one of the most powerful people in America and one of the most hated. The federal government targeted him as a threat to national security. Rival Black leaders denounced him as a lunatic and a traitor to the race. But Garvey may have been his own worst enemy.

Next, the narrative jumps back to a scene from Garvey's youth that shaped his identity. Robert Hill, an academic at the African Studies Center of the University of California, Los Angeles, says in an interview:

He started something that became bigger than Garvey himself. He, more than any other figure in the twentieth century, symbolizes the turning of the perception of Black people into something positive. Garvey's father was a professional mason, and among the things that he did was create tombs for people in the St. Ann's Bay Graveyard. He took Garvey with him to the graveyard one day, and they were digging this grave, and his father had Garvey go down inside the grave. But then he pulled the ladder up and left the child in the bottom of the grave. Garvey said that he cried out, and his father wouldn't let him get back up out of the grave; he wanted to teach him a lesson.

The narrator continues: "Alone in the grave, young Marcus Garvey learned that he could rely on no one but himself. It was a lesson he would carry for the rest of his life."

From there the film steps back to Garvey's birth. In the teaser for the film, we give the audience a good reason to stick around through the entire film, but we allow the audience to discover the characters for themselves. To develop a character—whether a kid whose trip to the wrong place triggered social change or an important historical figure—we do two things: explore the subject's complexity, and present that complexity through a series of revelations.

Reconstructing Scenes
ADAM HOCHSCHILD

Authors have written plays in scenes for thousands of years, and short stories and novels in scenes for hundreds of years. Narrative journalists have to write that way, too, because life unfolds in scenes. We can render two types of scenes: those we observed, and those we must reconstruct from what others observed.

The advent of film has pushed literature toward greater reliance on scenes, has made it more cinematic. Great novels of the nineteenth century such as George Eliot's *Middlemarch* include some wonderful scenes but also a lot of authorial exposition. Chapters often begin with a long disquisition on the novel's themes. Compare that structure with a twentieth-century, post-moving-picture novel like F. Scott Fitzgerald's *The Great Gatsby*, a cinematic novel in which one scene moves swiftly to the next. Competing with television and film has probably been good for nonfiction writers. I fear those media might overtake us at some point, yet they force us to work harder to make the reader *see* the events in our narratives.

Strong scenes, whether observed or reconstructed by the author, must include several key elements.

1. Accuracy. All the details must be completely accurate. Either you saw the ghost come down the corridor, or you must have an eyewitness account of it, if not several.

2. Atmosphere. For your readers to experience the scene, you must do more than describe how things looked. Sounds, smells, temperature, and even the textures of objects are all important.

3. Dialogue. The people in your scenes must talk to one another and interact with one another, or the narrative will feel lifeless. Think about telling a friend about something that happened. How many times do you say, "He said to me, and then I said to him . . ."? We tell stories this way because life sometimes unfolds this way; we talk to people all day long. Dialogue is how we get to know people, fall in love, tell someone off—in short, do everything that matters in life. If you are reporting a story, you can hear what's said when the opera diva argues with her voice coach or the pharmaceutical lobbyist sidles up to the congressperson. If you try to use accurate dialogue to show what was said when Washington crossed the Delaware, you may have a harder time. People's memoirs often include this information. Sometimes you can achieve the dramatic effect of dialogue by quoting people's letters. You can get a complete record of legislative sessions or trials—often sources of high drama—going back two hundred years.

4. Emotion. You must know what people were feeling about the events depicted in your scenes. If you were there, how did you feel about what you saw? When you interview participants about an event, you must ask them what happened and how they felt at the time.

I wrote a narrative nonfiction book, *Bury the Chains*, about England's antislavery movement in the late 1700s. In the space of about five years, a remarkable group of people turned public opinion strongly against slavery. One key moment in this monumental change occurred in May 1787. Twelve men assembled in a Quaker bookstore and printing shop located in what is now London's financial district and planned their strategy.

This dramatic moment was crucial to my book. The only surviving direct record of the meeting is a one-page handwritten summary. It simply noted the date, list of attendees, and resolutions they had unanimously adopted: that the slave trade was unjust and should be stopped, that they would open a bank account, and that a certain number of people would constitute a quorum for future meetings.

How could I bring this important moment alive? I used several different types of information: documents and newspapers, personal experience, memoirs, and biographies.

I found extensive biographical information about two of the men who attended the meeting. I can describe what another man looked like from a portrait. I learned that a fourth person in the group, the printer-bookseller, had stopped every morning on his way to work at a coffee shop just around the corner. These little details made a difference.

For other aspects of this book I read lots of newspapers from that time. In one I noticed an advertisement for dancing and fencing lessons offered next door to the bookshop—an additional detail. When scouring background material, it is a good idea to have a well-developed wish list but also to be open to unexpected finds.

I visited the location of that Quaker bookstore: a courtyard off Lombard Street in London. The small building has been replaced by Barclays Bank's twenty-two-story headquarters. Just across the courtyard, though, a pub has survived that was there in 1787—a detail I could actually observe.

I found in my reading that a few years before that 1787 meeting, workers had discovered a huge trove of two-thousand-year-old pieces of pottery, Roman Empire coins, and so forth while excavating the street that runs near this courtyard. It is not conventional scene-building material, but that detail gave me a springboard to mention another great empire also based on slavery and to emphasize just how long slavery had been part of human experience, and how audacious it was to think of ending it.

The bookstore was just around the corner from the British Empire's central post office. I found a journalist's description of the scene as the afternoon mail was dispatched. Dozens of delivery coaches raced out of the post office courtyard, carrying the mail to all parts of the kingdom. The meeting minutes say that it began at five in the afternoon, so I know there must have been sounds of galloping horses and postmen blowing their horns.

What other details of sight, sound, and smell could I find? Though no description of that particular bookstore and printing shop survives, there are depictions of similar ones in London at that time. Bookselling, publishing, and printing usually took place under the same roof. The printer and his family lived upstairs, and their cows and pigs often lived out back. From this information I could set the scene: books displayed for sale in the front of the room, and the huge printing press in the middle.

I studied eighteenth-century printing presses to add to my description of the scene. Large sheets from the flatbed presses hung on wooden racks overhead, and buckets of human urine would have stood around the room. In these very unlikely surroundings, the British antislavery movement was born.

Not all of these details are in the excerpt of my book that appears here (see page 135). Still, I was able to make use of almost all of them somewhere in the narrative because—happily for storytelling purposes—a huge amount of the story happened in a very small geographic area. The antislavery campaigners, some of the leading slave merchants, and various other players in this great drama lived and worked within a few minutes' walk of one another. The coffee shop where slave ship captains collected their mail, for instance, was just around the corner from the Quaker bookstore.

Whenever you vividly reconstruct a scene you weren't present for, you want to be sure that readers know you're not making anything up. Readers should know that every important detail you use must have a source. Sometimes you can do that unobtrusively in the text itself, by making clear who later recalled that it was a dark and stormy night or that the Duke was scowling. When writing books you have the luxury of source notes. The first few books I wrote were without source notes, but my more recent books have included them. I've become more and more a partisan of source notes. If your writing includes a lot of vivid detail and the book reads like a novel, readers may assume that you're inventing things. It's important to show that you aren't, that every crucial detail—especially every quote—has a source.

A Reconstructed Scene

ADAM HOCHSCHILD

"Went to town on my mare to attend a committee of the Slave Trade now instituted," confided Dillwyn to his diary as he headed for the first meeting, on the afternoon of May 22, 1787 at James Phillips's bookstore and printing shop. Phillips's neighbors in George Yard included a Mr. Mussard, who gave dancing and fencing lessons, and a pub, the George and Vulture. From descriptions of similar establishments at this time we can imagine the printing shop itself. Type would be sitting in slanted wooden trays with compartments for the different letters; the compositors who lined it up into rows, letter by letter, would be working, as the day ended, by the light of tallow candles whose smoke, over the decades, would blacken the ceiling. The printers, operating a flatbed press by hand, would take the large sheets from the press, each with many pages printed on it, and use a special pole-like instrument to hang them up on dozens of overhead lines for the ink to dry. Around the sides of the room, stacks of dried sheets, the latest antislavery book or Quaker tract, would await folding and binding. And finally, the most distinctive thing about an eighteenth-century printing shop was its smell. To ink the type as it sat on the bed of the press, printers used a wool-stuffed leather pad with a wooden handle. Because of its high ammonia content, the most convenient solvent to rinse off the ink residue that built up on these pads was printers' urine. The pads soaked in buckets of this, then strewn on the slightly sloping floor, where printers stepped on them as they worked, to wring them out and let the liquid drain away.

These were the unlikely surroundings in which twelve men gathered, the Quakers in their broad-brimmed, high-crowned black hats. The minutes of the occasion, only one page long, are in Clarkson's clear and flowing handwriting. They begin with a simple declaration: "At a Meeting held for the Purpose of taking the Slave Trade into Consideration, it was resolved that the said Trade was both impolitick and unjust."

An excerpt from Bury the Chains: Prophets and Rebels in the Fight to Free an Empire's Slaves *by Adam Hochschild.*

Setting the Scene

MARK KRAMER

Set scenes in narrative writing, whether fiction or nonfiction, should foster the reader's sense of immediacy. It is kinesthetic: You write, "She had a mishap," and readers feel nothing. But if you write, "She stepped out into nothing and pitched downstairs," readers feel it in their stomachs. You write, "She smells roses," and readers do, too. You write, "She blinked in the bright light," and we squint. Set scenes implicate the reader in the action. Strong scene-setting includes several features beyond specifying action, dialogue, and detail; here are a few of them.

Camera and Microphone Control

Purposefully or not, the author sets out the camera and microphone—might as well put them where they help most. They are often set in one spot, but they can move—say, to the shoulder of a main character. The author may reset the range but must do it with care and intention, as filmmakers do. For example, you can move from the inside to the outside of a house, but it won't do to mix these locations in the same shot. Slow motion and fast motion are possible, too, as are blinding whiteouts.

Sense of Volume

Try to array details and events so that readers experience the location in three dimensions. You can write, "Out past the window, a tree waved in the wind," or "She spoke from across a room."

Austere Timing

Start your scenes at the last possible instant, cutting out all action tangential to the main point, and end them as soon after the action as possible. Such clean use of scene-setting usually happens in the final drafts of writing, because the writer must have a precise sense of the work's flow and destination.

Emotional Weight

Scenes can convey and authenticate irrational, emotional, and nuanced information more efficiently than can explanation. As a writer you should explore the power of sharing complexity with your readers. Opening up readers' comprehension in this way is liberating. Set scenes also convey a level of accuracy ("stuff" *does* happen) that scene-free writing can only point toward.

When I need to include a scene that I didn't observe but must glean from interviews, I say to the people I'm interviewing: "Listen, the next fifteen minutes of our conversation will be hard work, not normal conversation. I want you to work with me, please, as though we are two carpenters. I need parts to assemble." They aren't haplessly yammering while I take things down but become complicit helpers in building the scene. They create the story *with* me. I interview helpful sources first, to get the basics of what happened, and then move on to adversarial sources.

The best scenes grow from fine-grained research. Even observed scenes are often partial reconstructions, including information and detail you don't catch at the time of the events.

The final section of my book *Three Farms* focuses on a twenty-thousand-acre parcel of a huge corporate farm in California. Though I knew the farm, I was kept under a rather tight watch. I had even bought new farm-executive-like clothes for my interviews so I would blend in with the agricultural executives. I thought perhaps I was passing, but I later found out that the farm manager had told his staff, "Watch out for Kramer. He has communist shoes." I had worn beat-up old shoes in a land of polished wingtips. I learned my lesson: Now I just act like myself no matter who I'm interviewing.

I secured closest access to a mid-level executive, meaning the one who made the hundred-thousand-dollar decisions, not million-dollar ones. After about a year of visiting this farm, there was a financial shake-up, and nearly all of the workers I had followed were fired. I called my insightful editor, Richard Todd at the *Atlantic Monthly*, which was publishing part of the book. "This is a disaster," I told him. He replied, "Is there a liquor store nearby?"

"You want me to drown my sorrows?" I asked.

"No, I want you to buy champagne and celebrate. You'll see."

I wrote up that section of the book, about thirty thousand words, and then flew back to California. I invited five of the former field executives to a meeting and carried in a case of beer. For five hours, stopping and starting, I read them my draft of the entire section about their farm. They corrected every inaccuracy, explained what I had misunderstood, and deepened the scenes with more information. They gave me a great gift.

I had seen a field of carrots being plowed under but hadn't made it past front-office double-talk about the reason for it. It turned out that someone had forgotten to press an executive button on a harvest decision, and the carrots had grown three inches too long for super-market carrot bags. The farm accountant had calculated that it was cheaper to plow under those hundred million carrots than to trim them all to the appropriate length.

I'd also written an elaborate scene of pruning valuable almond and pistachio trees. They must be tended and irrigated for years before yielding. My new advisors told me the pruning had been done wrong, ruining the trees' yield. And I described a pesticide-spraying scene but hadn't known it was too much of the wrong chemical, a $300,000 mistake.

These scenes ended up observed *and* re-created, and were much better for it.

Optimal preparation for scene writing begins with reporting specifically to gather the scene-building materials. Re-created and recollected scenes, done with honor and craftsmanship, work wonders. But the strongest, fullest, and most delicately built scenes follow field reporting that is attentive to sensory data, idiosyncratic quotes, pacing, personality, mood, and odd but telling detail. Then you have everything, and through cunning selection you can build scenes that are efficient, strong, and simple.

Handling Time

BRUCE DESILVA

Chronology is one of the basic ways that we orient ourselves in the world and in the stories that we tell. In all narrative writing, readers need to sense time passing but must not get lost in time. If readers suddenly don't know whether a week or a year has passed, they stop reading. Too often, writers keep the clock ticking and the calendar moving in clunky ways, such as beginning each section with a time stamp. This works well only when time is intrinsic to the story—as in a recounting of the space shuttle disaster. Dropping time markers in unobtrusively works better.

In "Storm Gods and Heroes," a serial narrative about a Coast Guard rescue at sea, Associated Press writer Todd Lewan slipped in a time marker this way: "Kalt's going over the checklist in his mind when Le Feuvre's voice crackles over the intercom. 'We're launching, boys, hang on.' They are on the scene 49 minutes later, in complete darkness."

Writers often convey the passage of time by invoking the physical world. Shadows move across the floor in a room; the morning sunlight comes through one window, by afternoon, through another window; the room grows dark. A story that occurs over several months or a year can include other markers: dry leaves falling, the opening of the baseball season.

Speeding and slowing time is just as important as marking it. This technique is best explained by example. Tim Dahlberg, an AP correspondent, wrote about a horrific crime and the police work required to solve it:

At first they thought it was a baby doll burned and blackened, covered still by bits of red, white, and blue baby outfit. It sat upright with stiff arms outstretched, as if it were reaching to the heavens.

And Alan Kessler saw it first, amid a busted-up TV and some other trash in a ravine outside the sprawling Orem Ranch. He rode by and was almost up the other side of the ravine when his son, J. B., riding behind him, cried out.

"Dad it's a baby."

"It's just a doll," replied Kessler. "You've got to get across the pasture to round up calves."

"No, no. It's a baby."

Late afternoon, the sun cast long shadows as Kessler got off his horse and with the ranch hand Robert Green, approached the tiny figure. Unbelieving, he watched as Green took a pen from his pocket and touched its shiny, blackened face. The skin gave and fluids leaked out.

Kessler rode to the ranch to call the sheriff.

It was October 9, 1990, and nearly six years would pass before the world would come to know the baby's name and how she came to this desolate place.

The piece begins slowly, the reader riding down the ravine with the men. Once the reader understands what the men have found, the writer speeds time, moving to the next key moment in the story. The writing shifts from dramatic narrative, with dialogue and visual detail, to expository narrative simply imparting information.

Sequencing: Text as Line

TOM FRENCH

Sequence is intrinsic to text. A person looking at a photograph or a painting receives the information within a frame. The eye might move to different parts of the rectangle, but all the information is presented at the same time. Readers, on the other hand, receive information sequentially. The act of narrative writing is arranging the elements of each sentence, each paragraph, each section, along a line. The skillful writer arranges a line that the reader can follow easily.

This line, the reader's sequential experience, is narrative's basic element. Many of the writing rules we learn are intended to maintain the line's integrity. Take, for example, *Use adjectives or adverbs sparingly*. Too many of them clutter that line, distracting the reader from the action expressed by the subject, verb, and object. Many of the questions a writer asks herself as she constructs a story are sequence questions on a larger scale. *How do I introduce the primary characters? In what order? How can I be sure people will remember who the characters are? How do I plant a plot element early in the story? How do I build a scene? How do I create surprise?*

Here are seven principles about sequence to keep in mind as you strive to maintain a clean line.

Principle #1: Study the natural sequence first.

All action, whether it unfolds over five minutes, a day, or several years, has a natural sequence. With every story, a daily article or a long series, I ask myself: *What was the* natural *sequence of events?* I study how the event unfolded chronologically. I usually don't end up writing the story in that order, but I must know how everything happened before I can determine how best to present it.

Usually, you can't just re-create the natural sequence on the page. Even if you are writing an obviously chronological story, such as "a day in the life of the mayor," you aren't going to tell every moment of her day. You will choose particular moments and then transition from one to the next, emphasizing some more than others.

The further you get from the natural sequence as you write, the more artifice you must use to keep your narrative moving. Transitions are often difficult to write because they represent deviations from the natural sequence. New writers sometimes think they must tell a story out of its natural sequence to make it more interesting. Most of the time the natural sequence is very interesting. Sometimes it's the perfect way to tell the story.

Principle #2: Report and write along a clear, simple line.

In the excerpt below, from an article titled "Give and Take on the Road to Somewhere," writer David Finkel describes what happened after a farmer drove a tractor into a Kosovo refugee camp to give out food. It appeared in the *Washington Post* on April 6, 1999.

> Out goes more bread, out go bottles of water. Out go cartons of milk. "Milk for my child," a woman calls out. Now someone tries to climb into the cart, and once he does other people try, and now people seem to be everywhere at once, trying to climb into the cart, onto the tractor, onto the tires, working their way toward the food however they can. They are slipping. They are

falling against one another. They are screaming. They are push-
ing. A week earlier they were in their homes and now they are so
desperate for food that the people bringing it are swinging bot-
tles of water at them to try to bring them under control.

But they can't bring them under control.

"For children, for children," a woman is shouting, arms out,
trying to reach the cart. She is wearing earrings, a headband and
a sweater, and when she can't reach the cart she brings her hands
to her head and covers her ears because behind her is her daughter, perhaps 8, holding on to her, getting crushed, screaming.

And behind her is another girl, 10 perhaps, wearing a pink
jacket decorated with drawings of cats and stars and flowers and,
now, mud.

Look at the last sentence's sequence. Finkel designed the whole
sentence to lead up to that last word: *mud*. The line allows the reader
to see the girl as he did.

He tells the whole story chronologically, along one straight,
chronological line, except for one small loop in time: "A week earlier
they were in their homes." He loops back to give the reader key information: These people had only recently become refugees. Loops
are digressions for the action line that allow you to include essential
background information. The key is not placing too much information
in the loop; boil down what the reader must know to its very essence.

Principle #3: Zoom in.

The refugee situation in Kosovo affected hundreds of thousands.
Finkel deliberately zooms in on one small event within the huge crisis: one farmer giving food to one group of refugees.

Deciding which portion of the larger sequence to describe is an
essential part of sequencing. The writer can't tell everything without
making the story massive, rambling, and untenable. In the example
of Finkel's story, if he had wanted to tell everything, he would have
had to start with centuries of history and then decades of those
refugees' lives. Instead, he took one tiny piece of the sequence, a
farmer bringing food on one day, and told the story in real time.
I would guess that the entire story unfolded in less than one hour.
Finkel's decision to zoom in so tightly gives the story its power.

Principle #4: Open strong, build to better.

Good stories have rising action. If you give away your best material
at the beginning of the story, you can't create tension. The funda-

mental purpose of a narrative's first paragraph is to make the reader continue to the second paragraph. And the purpose of that paragraph is to make him read the third paragraph.

Even in daily newspaper stories, I don't think about a lede, I think about an opening section. It is not useful to think about just your first paragraph, because you don't want the reader to stop at the end of it. The entire opening section must offer an experience that propels the reader forward through your story. Whatever you convey, it will be pointless unless the reader stays with you to the end. To make that happen, your story must get better as it goes. Open with something good. Build toward something even better.

Every sequence has a beginning, middle, and end. We're taught in journalism school that the beginning is the most important part of the sequence. For narrative writing, the ending is most important; the beginning is the second most important.

David Finkel says that when he constructs a story, he decides on his ending and then commences the story as close to that as possible. That allows him to zoom in and keep the sequence tight.

Principle #5: Set the table.

To learn about sequencing, study jokes—the form of storytelling most reliant upon it. To tell a successful joke you must line up each part of it precisely. The punch line falls flat if the teller hasn't successfully sequenced all the crucial elements. In every form of storytelling— books, movies, and even song lyrics—the teller must figure out how to transmit all the crucial information, so the audience makes sense of what follows.

Think of that old writing dictum from Chekhov: *If you show a gun in the first act, it has to go off.* To put it another way: If the story involves a gun going off in Act 2, you had better have introduced it in Act 1. Readers are very savvy, so you must introduce that gun as gracefully as possible. We must set the table before we serve the meal.

In the excerpt below, from my *St. Petersburg Times* series "13" about middle school students, I set up a later conflict between the character Danielle and her parents.

In the pre-dawn darkness, Danielle Heffern's alarm goes off again. She heads into the bathroom, washes her face and brushes her teeth, gets dressed. As usual, she puts on the blue Mickey Mouse sweatshirt. The house is quiet. No one else is up yet.

Every morning her routine is the same. She makes her own

breakfast, packs a lunch for school, heads for her bus. But this morning is different. Danielle doesn't feel like packing a lunch. She wants to buy something; she is thinking about the cheese pizza they sell at the Booker T cafeteria. Last night, she asked her parents if she could have some money. But they said no.

Danielle heads down the hall. She is walking through the family room when she notices some spare change on the end table. She counts the coins: $1.55.

She picks up the money and puts it in her purse. She gets her backpack and leaves the house, locking the door behind her.

This scene set up the situation and leaves the reader wondering: *Will her parents find out? How will they respond?* It is a tiny conflict but powerful enough to draw the reader through the story.

Principle #6: Slow down.

After you have built tension in your story, slow down to maintain it. As the world around us moves faster and faster, this technique becomes even more powerful. If you build your scene properly, the reader will hold still and look carefully at anything you wish.

Learning how and when to speed up and to slow down is key. It's something of a paradox: Speed up when explaining boring (but essential) information, and when the action is moving rapidly—your very best material—slow down. You slow down so the reader can enter the scene and process what is happening. You speed up because you have a lot of ground to cover.

How do you slow down? Allow more space on the page. Use more paragraph breaks. Find natural pauses inside the scene. You might be inclined to skip over them, but they can help you slow down the pace. A story that I worked on about a murder included a police chase. The police started shooting out the tires of the escape car. As the car began to spin, the music on the car's CD player stopped. I included that pause in the music to draw out that suspense-filled moment.

Principle #7: Learn to crescendo.

At the end of your story or the end of every section of a longer story, your narrative must crescendo. It doesn't have to be a loud moment; quiet moments are often more powerful.

Here is another example from David Finkel, a daily story that he wrote while at the *St. Petersburg Times*, on the day that Ted Bundy was executed. The story was about the parents of one of Bundy's victims, Margaret Bowman. Here are the last several paragraphs:

The TV went off. In the quiet, Jack Bowman regained his composure and then headed outside. He wanted the day to go by easily and the night to go easily, too. He wanted to sleep soundly. He wanted to awaken and sense that Ted Bundy was already beginning to be old news. He wanted the vengeful signs of strangers to be thrown in the trash and their firecrackers put away. He wanted to finally get to the point where at last he could think about everything that had happened.

Tuesday, for a short time, he tried.

"Tell me your feelings about the execution," someone said to him.

"I wanted him punished," Jack Bowman said. "This was not hard for me."

"Tell me about Margaret," he was asked.

He began to cry. He shut his eyes. "I don't think I can."

Writing narrative is like rendering a complex piece of music on the page. The writer hears it and then must reproduce it. For the reader to really hear it, too, each note—each component of your story—must be struck in a way that develops the reader's experience of the text.

Writing Complicated Stories

LOUISE KIERNAN

People sometimes ask me, "Are you an investigative reporter, or a features reporter, or an explanatory reporter?" I never know how to answer. Why ask at all? Categorizing journalism is in part why many investigative stories are dull, feature stories can be superficial, and explanatory stories explain so little. For complicated stories, we need to combine all three. This blending is both my central goal and biggest challenge as a reporter.

In June 2000, I wrote a front-page story for the *Chicago Tribune* about a woman named Ana Flores, who was killed by a piece of glass that fell from a building. The story, a Pulitzer finalist, begins this with image: "The glass falls like a shadow, swift and silent, a dark blur swooping through the wet sky."

The image of the shadow didn't come from observation or creative license, but from a police report, which I also used to track down and interview witnesses. That document and others enabled me to tell a story that would have been otherwise impossible. Ana Flores, the protagonist, was dead, and several people involved in the story didn't want to talk to me because they were responsible for the accident that killed her. Documents were key to that project.

Narrative reporters sometimes consider public documents dry, statistical, and boring. That couldn't be further from the truth. In 2003, I completed a two-part series about postpartum depression, including profiles of two women who had committed suicide as a result of that illness. The medical examiner's autopsy reports included one of the women's suicide notes: a dozen pages she had written to explain why she was about to jump from a twelfth-story hotel window. One of those notes was to the front-desk clerk:

> Dear Tim,
>   I'm sorry to have used your kindness this way. You knew something wasn't quite right, but your kind heart took pity on me and let me stay in the hotel. I hope this doesn't get you into trouble. You really are a fabulous clerk, very good at what you do. Tell your boss this wasn't your fault.
>   Melanie

That note, scribbled on a piece of Days Inn stationery, told me a great deal about Melanie Stokes. And I found it in a public file.

When I begin to work on a story, I list all the public and private documents that might exist. Public documents are the more familiar ones: court records, police reports, government studies, and so forth. All reporters should know how to file Freedom of Information Act requests and search court records. (See www.ire.org and www.poynter.org for helpful advice.) Practice finding records at your local courthouse—go down there and look yourself up. Private documents are the ones that people make and keep for themselves: journals, a child's baby book, high school yearbook inscriptions, letters home from summer camp. All these documents can help tell a story, even in short, daily pieces. When you write the classic "teacher of the year" story, ask to see lesson plans and graded papers, or watch a woman working her way off welfare fill out a job application.

Often, what people write is more compelling than what they tell you. Ana Flores, the woman killed by the falling piece of glass, was walking to a job fair when the accident happened. She had practiced filling out an application on a piece of paper her best friend kept as a memento, painstakingly writing out in English, "Cleaning, cooking, take care of old lady, I am willing to perform." Those phrases served as shorthand for her struggle to make a life for herself in Chicago, after emigrating from Mexico.

Complicated stories demand careful use of detail, but some narrative stories include too many details, describing how every last thing looks and smells and sounds. Every detail you select should help communicate your story's theme.

Within the framework of your story, use your characters' experiences to explain broader concepts. Do the same thing with numbers—use only those that are key to the story and characters. In a story about the experiences of an elderly man who had come to Chicago as part of the Great Migration, the only migration statistic I used was the percentage of African Americans who had left his Arkansas county at the same time he did. That statistic was the one closest to his experience.

Imagery helps explain complicated concepts. In the falling-glass story, I had to explain thermal stress, the physics of the window cracking and breaking loose. One expert compared what happened with plunging a hot glass into a sink of cold water, so that's how I described it in the story. Experts can help you tell the technical aspects of your story. People with passions, whether for comic books or nuclear fission, tend to be good teachers. The imagery they have developed for explaining things to their students can be useful to the writer.

Writing about complex topics requires absolute mastery of the material. By the end of your reporting, you should feel that you know as much about the subject as the people you interview. That mastery allows you to write clear, strong, *readable* sentences. It's the iceberg effect: one-eighth of your work is above the surface, in the story. The seven-eighths that the reader can't see form your story's foundation. Trust your reporting. Embed it in your story.

In Ana Flores's story, I wrote: "No one knows exactly how much time the glass took to fall—twenty-five seconds at most, perhaps as few as five. It may have floated flat as a table for a time or tumbled like a leaf, but gravity eventually pulled it into an angled or vertical position so it cut down like a knife."

To write that paragraph, I talked with two physics professors and two glass experts. There are calculations about gravity in that paragraph. While I was tempted to point out how hard I worked to get that information, I knew those sentences should stand on their own.

By the time I wrote those sentences, I *knew* the glass had fallen like a knife, that it had fallen like a shadow.

So, perhaps I *do* know how to answer that question about whether I am a features, investigative, or explanatory reporter: "Yes."

How I Get to the Point

WALT HARRINGTON

To report and write good narrative it is important to develop a clear process that takes you from beginning to end: exhaustive researching, choosing a strong main character, thinking the story through, and reporting the story, scene, and theme. I have found that if I stick to that process and don't take shortcuts, I always end up with what I need for the story. It might not be the story that I started out looking for, but it will be a story.

Back when I wrote for the *Washington Post Sunday Magazine,* I put myself on a schedule. I would finish reporting on Wednesday and then schedule a week to turn out the piece. I started by placing two large notepads in front of me. Then I reread *all* the material I had collected: every document, letter, and note. On one pad I listed possible themes, jotting them down as I read the material. I would list as many as ten possibilities and then use just two or three. On the other pad I listed all the facts, details, quotes, and scenes I was likely to include in the story.

I usually completed that process late on Thursday and then filed away all the boxes of notes. On Friday morning I sat down, closed my eyes, and waited for something to come to mind. It can be scary at first, but you come to trust that it will happen. About 80 percent of the time the strongest scene or image from all my reporting appeared. That scene usually ended up as my lede. If nothing came to mind, I tried again, and again. If no single scene came to mind, I knew that my lede wouldn't be a scene, and I began to think of strong declarative sentences that captured the essence of a subject.

Once I had my lede, I moved on to the foreshadowing in the piece—a sort of nutgraf that clarifies the story for the reader. After writing the first three hundred or so words of an eight-thousand-word piece, I stopped writing, and at that late stage, with the project clearly centered, I finally jotted down an outline of the entire piece.

As I did that outline, I asked myself: *What are my strongest scenes? What ideas will I work with? What would make a good ending? What threads should I pull through the entire story?*

I put my trust in the process, and it always allowed me to turn in a solid draft by the following Wednesday.

The Emotional Core of the Story

TOM WOLFE

Philip Roth was the hottest young novelist in America in 1970—he had won the National Book Award with his first book, *Goodbye, Columbus*, in 1960 and had just lit up the sky with *Portnoy's Complaint* in 1969—when he uttered what I call Roth's Lament: *We now live in an age in which the imagination of the novelist lies helpless before what he knows he's going to read in tomorrow morning's newspaper.*

I imagine anyone, writer or otherwise, can sympathize with that. Just think of the story of Paris Hilton. I'm sure some novelist could have dreamed up a plot in which a beautiful young blond heiress with a lower lip like a slice of mango is caught on a pornographic videotape. But the rest of the novel would no doubt be about . . . the extortionists, who are demanding five million dollars for the tape, and so she enlists a couple of young computer hackers to invade her father's investment accounts and extract the five million dollars, but then the hackers demand a 20 percent cut as their commission, which would be a cool million, and she panics, and then—

And I suppose some novelist could have dreamed up a plot in which a beautiful young blond heiress with a sly fructose smile and no immediately detectable acting or show business ability gets a ten-million-dollar contract to star on a television show and goes on to turn herself into a national franchise with a line of clothes, perfumes, and handbags?

But I don't think there is a novelist living who could have dreamed up the actual story line, which is that Paris Hilton got her millions . . . *because* she made the pornographic tape. Otherwise she would have remained just another ripely labial random boldface name in the gossip columns.

I wrote only nonfiction for the first fifty-four years of my life, then wrote a few novels, and I can tell you that the problem with fiction today is that fiction has to be plausible. And plausible is not the first word that comes to mind to describe an age like this. . . . The newspaper will soon be extinct . . . High school students in New York stage cell-phone rights demonstrations protesting a new regulation that would ban cell phones in the schools, thereby making it impossible for them to watch movies during classes or text-message each other during tests . . . In 1992, a man named Francis Fukuyama published a book entitled *The End of History* about how all the world agreed that Western liberal democracy had created a utopia and was hailed as a seer and prophet. Nine years later a bunch of terrorists nobody ever heard of cranked history back up again and made him look like a fool. In an age like this, to update Philip Roth, the "serious literary novel" is now headed for—I started to say "extinction," but that is not exactly what is happening. Instead, that precious lap dog with all its ineffable wafts of sensibility is heading up to a snow-capped peak where poetry, a genre that reigned supreme until the mid-nineteenth century, now lives. It's cold up there. Everyone praises them because that's a lot more pleasant than visiting them.

The upshot is that two varieties of the species *Nonfiction narrative* now reign in American literature. One is the autobiography, whose popularity has never waned in the 444 years since Benvenuto Cellini's *Confessions*. Orwell once characterized autobiography as the most outrageous form of fiction, because autobiographers seemed perfectly comfortable retailing their sins and crimes, their swindles, drug abuses, betrayals, debauches, their pelvic saddle convulsions and loin spasms, even rape, murder, looting and pillaging, since all give off whiffs of excitement and bravado—whereas, said Orwell, they never mention "the humiliations that make up seventy-five percent of life." Yet some of Orwell's own most powerful books, notably *Down and Out in Paris and London* and *Homage to Catalonia*, as well as many of his great essays, such as "Shooting an Elephant" and "Why I Write," are autobiographical. Not even the occasional exposure of fiction masquerading as autobiography, starting with Defoe's *Robinson Crusoe*, is likely to diminish the genre for long.

The other is nonfiction using the technical devices of the novel and the short story, the specific devices that give fiction its absorbing or gripping quality, that make the reader feel present in the scene described and even inside the skin of a particular character. They are exactly four in number: (1) scene-by-scene construction, i.e., presenting the narrative in a series of scenes and resorting to ordinary historical narration as little as possible; (2) the use of copious dialogue—the (experimentally demonstrated) easiest form of prose to read and the quickest to reveal character; (3) the careful notation of status details, the details that reveal one's social rank or aspirations, everything from dress and furniture to the infinite status clues of speech, how one talks to superiors or inferiors, to the strong, to the weak, to the sophisticated, to the naïve—and with what sort of accent and vocabulary; (4) point of view, in the Henry Jamesian sense of putting the reader inside the mind of someone other than the writer. Those were the devices used by writers in the so-called New Journalism movement that began in the 1960s. In 1973 I took the equivalent of a Trappist vow of silence so far as the subject of New Journalism was concerned. I was tired of arguing. I said it was a technical thing, the use of those four devices in an objective, accurate, i.e., properly journalistic fashion. But others claimed it meant "impressionistic" journalism, "subjective" journalism, New Left Journalism, "participatory" journalism—there was no end to it. But now that thirty-three years have elapsed, I suppose it's okay to offer a brief footnote. Besides, in those thirty-three years there has been the best possible outcome. Journalists no longer argue about New Journalism—I mean, how many decades can you keep arguing about something that calls itself "new"? Instead, a new generation of journalists, writing books and magazine articles, have simply appropriated the techniques however they please and are turning out brilliant work—in fact, the best of contemporary American literature, taken as a whole. I could mention many more names, but consider just these two and you will know what I mean immediately: Michael Lewis and Mark Bowden.

To this day newspaper editors resist the idea, but they desperately need to encourage their reporters to adopt the Lewis and Bowden approach. It is not that it produces pretty writing—although indeed it does. They need such reporters and writers to provide the emotional reality of the news, for it is the emotions, not the facts, that most engage and excite readers and in the end are the heart of most stories. Take the subject of crime, for a start. I have just learned, thanks to the Boston newspapers, that the mayor is upset because there are "gangbangers" on the streets wearing T-shirts that say STOP SNITCHING, conveying the message, "Talk to the police, and you're rat meat." The shirts are sold all over the place. The mayor wishes to confiscate them, and he seems to feel that selling them should be a crime, like selling cigarettes to a minor. In itself, that's a story—but what a great story awaits the reporter who gets to know these teenagers who wear the T-shirts and finds out what that means to them—and what it means in their neighborhoods at whom the warning is presumably aimed. We report crime in our newspapers but not its emotional heart.

On Long Island, there's an epidemic of break-ins while people are in their homes. The robbers want the owners there, so they can be forced to reveal where jewelry and money are hidden. Invariably the news reports tell you how much was stolen, and perhaps what sorts of arms the assailants carried. But that's not the story. The story is fear, on the part of the victims and sometimes the assailants—or their ecstatic yodels after successfully dominating and humiliating their victims. Such are the vital facts of crime. The underlying emotions reveal so much about life, and they should be developed in journalism and not just in novels.

You need to provide readers two things in this sort of journalism: a detailed picture of the social setting and at least some insight into the psychology of the principals. I think of the setting as a horizontal plane and the individual as a vertical plane. The line created by their intersection—there lies the story. In 1808, the German philosopher Georg Wilhelm Hegel coined the term *Zeitgeist*—in English, "the spirit of the age." His theory was that every historical epoch has a "moral tone"—his phrase—that presses down on the life of everyone, and no one can avoid it. I think it's true, and why, in fiction or nonfiction about big cities, for example, the city should be treated as a character because cities are positively feverish with moral tone.

About life beyond the great cities even our best reporters are often clueless. Last August, in Tennessee, I saw the Bristol 500, a NASCAR race. There's a little half-mile track, and grandstands going up almost vertically, seating 165,000, and it's all shaped like a megaphone. The seats are on the megaphone's inner surface and you feel that if you lean too far forward, you'll land on the track. Before the race, a number of people greeted the crowd, including the head of the National Rifle Association—no longer Charlton Heston, not a celebrity. He spoke all of forty-five seconds. The stands rose up as one person and cheered him. Obviously ownership of weapons bears a lot more civic virtue in NASCAR country than it does in Boston. Just before the race, a Protestant minister invoked the Lord's blessing on the event. He asked the Lord to look out for these brave drivers, and these loyal fans. He asked this of the Lord, "in the name of Thy Only Son, Christ Jesus." Anyone who introduced an event that way in San Francisco or New York City would risk arrest for a hate crime. New

York writers really must cross the Hudson River, and writers in Los Angeles really must go as far as the San Joaquin Valley. Most of the meaning of America lies in between the coasts, I'm afraid.

Recently I undertook what turned out to be a very happy task, writing an afterword for a new edition of *Maggie: A Girl of the Streets*, by Stephen Crane. Crane is best known as the author of *The Red Badge of Courage*, regarded even in Europe as the greatest portrayal in all of literature of the emotions of a soldier in combat. Crane was the twelfth of fourteen children, with six older brothers. His father was a preacher and his mother a White Ribboner. She wore a white ribbon indicating the passion of her opposition to the sale and consumption of alcohol. She could be hell on wheels, but she was always a terrific writer.

One of Crane's older brothers, Townsend, was a writer, a correspondent for the *New York Tribune* covering the Jersey Shore resort area. Stephen Crane, a slender, good-looking young man with tousled blond hair, had, as of 1891, been thrown out of four schools in the preceding four years. So he went to work with his brother, for the *Tribune*. In 1892, he covered a lecture by Jacob Riis. Riis was one of the first people to pull the covers back on conditions in American slums, in this case the Lower East Side of New York City. He exposed the conditions but never captured the speech or personalities—never got to the emotional heart. His main emotion was pity.

Stephen Crane read Jacob Riis and formed his own questions: What are they thinking? What is it like to be one of these people? Meanwhile his brother was away, and it became his chore to cover a march through Asbury Park, a New Jersey resort, of construction workers on a patriotic holiday. He described the marchers as slope-shouldered, humpbacked, slovenly drudges. The onlookers, he said, were even worse. He described them as typical Jersey Shore resort visitors, the kind of people who, when a dollar bill is held before their eyes, cease to recognize the rights of anyone else. The story got him fired.

So he went to live on the Lower East Side, rooming with three medical students. He decided he could get to know the Bowery by masquerading as a bum. Here's a slender, young, blond, almost pretty guy—but he got his Bowery bum costume together, letting those wisps of beard and long locks of hair get dirty and fall over his face. He slept in the flophouses, not once but repeatedly. He even brought visitors in to take a look. Nobody ever went back a second time. It was probably in the flophouses that he contracted the tuberculosis he died of at twenty-eight. But out of that experience came his extraordinary *Maggie: A Girl of the Streets*, which is fiction, but closely based on fact.

One of his roommates recalled the day Crane came home highly excited saying, "Have you ever seen a stone fight?" He'd seen some urchins in pitched battle, hurling rocks. The roommates glanced at one another and rolled their eyes as if to say, "Okaaaay . . . a stone fight." Crane's stone fight, however, led to one of the great first lines in American literature: "A very little boy stood on a pile of gravel defending the honor of Rum Alley."

Crane worked as a newspaper writer up until the verge of his death. His accomplishments in what was truly a new journalism 110 years ago should be part of the common knowledge of all newspaper editors, especially now that every newspaper editor in the United States is asking, "How can this newspaper be saved?" They should be asking, how can we get to the emotional heart of our stories? Yet only a few newspaper editors are considering any such thing—not knowing that it is the question of the hour, and that this is the eleventh hour.

Telling the Story, Telling the Truth

ALMA GUILLERMOPRIETO

When I began at the *Washington Post* as a reporter in Central America, I found myself working for a very professional organization, but one located inside the world's greatest military power and largest economy, which considered itself to be under threat by a ten-elevator country. I actually counted all the elevators in Nicaragua while I was living there. As a *Post* reporter working in Managua, I was expected to take this threat seriously and report on it.

As the locus of revolution shifted, I moved from Managua to San Salvador. I continued to report what seemed to me hard facts: massacres and mutilated bodies that appeared on San Salvador street corners at dawn. The evidence pointed to the Salvadoran government as the source of this horror. Since the United States supported the Salvadoran government in its fight against the guerrillas, that evidence was questioned in ways that sometimes made me feel as if I was losing my mind. *Post* editors repeatedly asked me to strike a neutral tone. Those editors were brave, intelligent, caring people, but the Reagan administration was setting the agenda.

Eventually, I wrote about a mass killing that turned out to be the largest massacre of the twentieth century in the Western Hemisphere. Salvadoran soldiers, who had been trained by U.S. advisors, shot, burned alive, or hacked to death eight hundred men, women, and children. The *Post* ran the story I wrote on the front page. The *New York Times* ran a story the same day. And then *nothing*—no follow-up stories, no editorial, no television coverage, no stories in other newspapers. A few ultra-right-wing Reagan administration officials responded by saying that the *Times* reporter and I couldn't be trusted.

For quite a few years liberal media outlets and activists revisited the question of whether the *Times* reporter and I had been hounded out of our respective newspapers because of those articles—as if *that* were what mattered. Twelve years later an Argentine team of forensic anthropologists excavated the site of the El Mozote massacre. They documented the deaths, bone by bone.

The years rolled by. Eventually, the U.S. government decided that maybe a ten-elevator country didn't pose such a threat, and that maybe the Salvadoran guerrillas wouldn't seem such a menace if they were allowed to participate in the political process. A decade after it all began, Central America vanished from the map. Just like that.

The Central Americans weren't any less poor. The victims hadn't come back to life. No justice had been done. Nevertheless, the U.S. public's attention was deemed exhausted on this particular subject. When was the last time you saw an article about El Salvador? And when you saw one, did you want to read it?

When Central America dropped off the U.S. media's map of the world, it was as if *I* had dropped into that void as well. I felt like the character from *One Hundred Years of Solitude* who survives a massacre of banana plantation workers. He spends the rest of his life saying, "There was this massacre," to which people respond, "You're crazy. That never happened." I never stopped being angry about that.

My driving desire as a writer is to make it impossible for the U.S. reader to ignore Latin America. I do that by telling stories. Stories are the opposite of hard news, the opposite of the easy anecdote.

While I worked for the *Post* in Central America, I was a victim of news addiction. I was always searching for the "big story." What creates news addiction? Why do people want to read newspapers and turn on the television to find out what's going on? I'd like to believe it's some basic, ethical desire to participate as a citizen of the world community. Too often, though, hard news doesn't give us the knowledge or ability to do that. Watching CNN out of the corner of one eye while answering e-mail and learning about an earthquake in Kabul or of Yasser Arafat's death in a sixty-second spot, while the text at the bottom of the screen reports the collapse of a stock market somewhere, is *not* participating in the world. It is the opposite: feeding the strangely comforting sensation that the world spins too fast to really think about anything.

This sort of news addiction assumes that hard news, as reported in the United States, is fundamentally linked to reality. In spite of my own former news addiction, I disagree. So-called pure news, just the facts, is now considered so pure that newspapers routinely *label* analysis as they label packs of cigarettes: *Warning: this article contains both hard facts* and *thought.*

In my writing, I purposefully blend information, observation, analysis, and my own reactions to the material. I tell stories, because stories allow us to think wholeheartedly, to truly understand. The greatest Latin American novelists, such as Gabriel García Márquez and Mario Vargas Llosa, began as journalists. That experience has contributed to a literary school of Latin American journalism that is better written and that contains much more emotional content than U.S. journalism.

To write for a U.S. audience about Latin America I have developed some operating principles. I rarely mention the United States. While reporting, I don't talk to State Department officials, ambassadors, or World Bank staffers. I pretend that Latin America is an independent entity, that we Latin Americans have the authority to talk about ourselves on our own terms. By doing this I present a more complete Latin America, one that doesn't rely on what a third party told me.

I do enormous amounts of reading before I begin reporting. If I can, I spend a month before I begin a trip, as well as my first week in a place, reading prodigiously.

Once I begin to write, I spend days and days working on a lede. I often trade on the reader's fascination with exoticism and the grotesque in my ledes. In the interest of getting people in the United States to read about Latin America, I'm willing to play that for all it's worth. Here is one example, from my book *The Heart That Bleeds*:

> Garbage has become an obsession for the inhabitants of Mexico City, spawning any number of fantastic stories, all of them true. There is, for example, the story of the open-air garbage dumps that spontaneously ignited one day in July, spreading fire and toxic fumes over acres of refuse stacked twenty yards high. There

is the story of the *cacique* who controlled more than half of the city's seventeen thousand-odd *pepenadores*, or garbage pickers, demanded sexual favors from the garbage pickers' daughters, and also took all his workers off to Acapulco on vacation once a year. There is the story of a sixty-square-mile garbage dump that the city government decided to turn into a park, complete with picnic tables—tables that have since been sinking gently into the settling layers of trash and loam.

And then there are the rats. One of the most memorable stories dates from the beginning of the decade when an evening paper announced above the fold that a giant mutant rat had been discovered floating dead in the sewage canal. The article said that the rat was the size of a Volkswagen and in the accompanying photo one could verify the caption's claim that the beast had the face of a bear, the hands of a man and the tail of a rat. Two days later, a morning paper explained that the corpse belonged to a lion owned by a three-flea traveling circus.

By being extremely specific in what I report, I don't just bring readers into a world of exotica and the grotesque, but into a world where human beings survive with dignity. Once I have hooked them I trust my reader to care about the same things I care about, the same things that my subjects care about.

Specificity is central to both my writing and my reporting. Focusing on details somehow lashes me to the story, as if it were a mast. I find that as long as I stay focused on detail, detail, *detail* while I'm reporting, I advance the story.

I write in the first person a lot. The "I" in my stories is the reader's proxy. My great ambition is to take readers out of their comfort zones and put them in positions of discomfort. I want them to see and smell and taste and touch and hear the things that I did in their place as the reporter.

While out reporting, I stage a little theater in my mind. Before choreographers begin rehearsals, they choose a group of dancers. By the end of the first rehearsal, one dancer will stand out. As a reporter I do the same sort of casting. By the end of the first week I have my leading cast selected. Later on, I figure out how much I can use the other, minor characters. I have been accused, rightly, of having a tendency to favor strong, impoverished, old peasant women who must go down miles to the river for their bucket of water every day and climb back up again—singing! It's true. Once that weakness was pointed out to me, I tried to work against it. When I write, I try not to indulge my weaknesses, but I also try to avoid playing to my strengths. It forces me to stretch and makes the story bigger.

Writers must give themselves that freedom to fail. As a dancer I learned that unless I jumped as hard and as high as I could until I fell, I hadn't found out how hard or high I could jump. Risk-taking and failure are important. When an editor says to me, "You know, that sentence is awful," I don't say, "Oh, my editor is so terrible." I say, "Oh, that sentence *is* awful. Let's take it out. It's only words."

On Voice

SUSAN ORLEAN

Developing a writer's voice is almost a process of unlearning, one analogous to children's painting. Young children often create fabulous paintings, only to be told after they start school that real houses don't look that way. At that point, most people lose their ability to be visually creative. Truly great painting retains some element of a child's emotional authenticity. Great writing does, too.

Self-analysis is crucial to developing a strong voice. *Who am I? Why do I write?* Your identity and your self-understanding become subliminal parts of your writer's voice—especially in long-form narrative writing. Imagine yourself telling friends about a story that excites you. Your friends follow the story even though it's not linear but circles back as you tell it. The way you tell a story over dinner is true to who you are, whether that is deeply analytical or extremely witty. At such moments you aren't self-conscious, and you aren't thinking about your editor.

You can't invent a voice. And you can't imitate someone else's voice, though trying to can be a good exercise. It can lead you to begin to understand the *mechanisms* that convey the voice. Read your stories out loud so you can *hear* how you tell stories. As you read, ask yourself: *Does it sound real? Would I have said it that way?* If the answer to either question is no, you have done something wrong. I find that sometimes when I give readings of my published work, I skip parts that seem boring to me. Then I wonder, would it have been better to edit that out in the first place? When you read aloud, extraneous material falls away.

Voice is—as the word itself tells us—the way a writer *talks*. You are *speaking* to your readers. Sometimes we think we have to come up with something clever, but cleverness for its own sake is rarely powerful.

Pace, the sense of timing in a piece, is linked to voice. Pace determines whether attempts at humor will succeed. Change your story's pace to change the mood. Long sentences can slow down the reader. Short sentences race the reader through a scene. As you read your piece aloud, you hear how your readers will make their way through it. Then you can control that movement.

Word choice is another element of voice. When you make an analogy, it's not just to give the reader an image but to advance a larger idea or theme. Once I had a fight with an editor because I wanted to describe a basketball player's feet as "banana-shaped." My editor argued that feet can't really be banana-shaped. And, further, thinking about bananas takes the reader away from the subject: a person playing basketball. "You're giving the reader a ticket to the tropics," he said. I spent hours trying to find the right image to replace *banana*. Suddenly, it came to me: *pontoon*. His feet were pontoon-shaped; he floated over the basketball court. Analogies like these don't usually come as I am reporting. I have to sit at my desk and really work at finding the strongest image possible.

Another aspect of voice is taking on your characters' voices. Sometimes, immersed in my reporting, I find myself thinking in the same rhythm as someone I'm writing about. This is part of my temperament; I tend to become caught up in other worlds. As long as I don't slide into mimicry, it can help a piece of writing. You don't want to hijack someone's voice but draw inspiration from it. It is often a sign that you have submerged yourself deeply in a story, inhabiting it. I wrote half of "The American Man at Age Ten" in the voice of a boy. I stepped in and out of that persona throughout the story.

Soon after I started writing, I realized that I was crafty and could come up with gimmicks to make my work look jazzy. As I matured as a writer and gained more confidence, I began losing what I had mistakenly understood to be my style. I returned to something simpler. One watershed moment was the realization that my writing voice had circled back to something natural, intuitive, and instinctive.

PART VI

❖

ETHICS

Introduction

MARK KRAMER AND WENDY CALL

This section is one of the longer ones in *Telling True Stories*. There is much to say about ethics, a subject often absent from books on the writing craft. Blame it on narrative journalists' high aspirations. The work of the narrative nonfiction writer is full of choices that demand a clear ethical sensibility. Out in the field, writers define topics not always confined to observable detail. They enter into protracted and personal relationships with sources. Back at the desk, they befriend and share confidences with readers. They offer a range of emotional, political, and scholarly discernments, seemingly on personal authority but also on behalf of the publications in which their stories appear. Meanwhile, by means of stylish writing, they lead readers toward specific feelings, insights, and conclusions.

At each of these stages the narrative writer must make choices that affect the trustworthiness of the text and, therefore, the genre. Is a topic choice built on bias or presupposition? Are relationships with sources consensual and untainted? Are readers presented with honest scenes and characters? Is background research reliable and complete?

It is hardly possible to write about the real world without taking a few steps onto a slippery slope. As writers who delve into other people's lives, we can't stand on the edge of that slope prissily avoiding it. We are *there*. To operate ethically we must begin by acknowledging that. Where one stands on that slope is influenced by one's employer, but it's ultimately a personal choice. This section addresses some basic ethical questions that narrative nonfiction writers face.

How do we work with subjects? The professional narrative journalist gathers material that may violate the subject's sense of privacy. While the norms and needs of friendship might govern your source's feelings and actions toward you, the norms and needs of professional journalism affect your actions. How do writers handle this dilemma?

How do we let readers know how we've gathered the information included in stories? Nonfiction writers in different fields and subgenres have different attitudes toward disclosing and explaining their sources. Academics, like journalists, write within a collective discipline predicated on shared honesty and open sourcing. Scholarly writers offer citations with gusto in brackets, footnotes, bibliographies, and appendices. In the past, journalists rarely included elaborate sourcing notes. Meticulous disclosure of sources has become more common in narrative nonfiction. Sonia Nazario's Pulitzer Prize–winning "Enrique's Journey" ran in the *Los Angeles Times* with seven thousand words of endnotes. Many readers let her know that they read them with care.

Meanwhile, the work of memoirists involves a host of ethical complications because of the elusive nature of recollection and the complex webs of familial emotion.

The great rewards of narrative writing are possible only when writers accept ethical responsibility. In this section of the anthology, eleven newspaper, magazine, book, and memoir writers explore how to do fine work that is also deeply ethical.

The Line Between Fact and Fiction

ROY PETER CLARK

Novelists reveal great truths about the human condition, as do poets, filmmakers, and painters. Artists, after all, build things that imitate the world. Fiction writers use fact to make their work believable. They return us to historical periods and places accurately chronicled and described: the battlefield at Gettysburg, the Museum of Natural History in New York City, a jazz club in Detroit. They use detail to make us see, to suspend disbelief.

For centuries writers of nonfiction have borrowed the novelist's tools to reveal truths that could be exposed and rendered in no better way. They place characters in scenes and settings, put them in dialogue, reveal limited points of view, and move in time through conflicts and toward resolutions.

Historically, nonfiction contained a lot of made-up stuff. It seems that fifty years ago many columnists, sportswriters, and crime reporters—to name the obvious categories—were licensed to invent. The term *piping*, making up quotes or inventing sources, came from the idea that the reporter was high from covering the police busts of opium dens.

Tom Rosenstiel, of the Pew Project for Excellence in Journalism, catalogs more recent confusion:

> The line between fact and fiction in America, between what is real and made up, is blurring. The move in journalism toward infotainment invites just such confusion, as news becomes entertainment and entertainment becomes news. Deals in which editor Tina Brown joins the forces of a news company, Hearst, with a movie studio, Miramax, to create a magazine that would blend reporting and script writing are only the latest headlines signaling the blending of cultures. . . .

The controversies continue. Edmund Morris creates fictional characters in his authorized biography of Ronald Reagan; CBS News uses digital technology to alter the sign of a competitor in Times Square; a purported memoir by Wyatt Earp's wife, published by a university press, turns out to contain fiction. Its author, Glenn G. Boyer, defends his book as a work of "creative nonfiction."

To make things more complicated, scholars have demonstrated the essential fictive nature of all memory. The way we remember things is not necessarily the way they were. This makes memoir, by definition, a form in which reality and imagination blur into a "fourth genre." The problems of memory also infect journalism when reporters, in describing the memories of sources and witnesses, wind up lending authority to a kind of fiction.

The postmodernist might think all this irrelevant, arguing that there are no facts, only points of view, only takes on reality influenced by our personal histories, our cultures, our race and gender, our social class. The best journalists can do in such a world is offer multiple frames through which events and issues can be seen. *Report the truth?* they ask. *Whose truth?*

Basic principles to help journalists navigate the waters between fact and fiction *do* exist. They can be drawn from the collective experience of many journalists, from our conversations, debates, and forums, from the work of writers such as John Hersey and Anna Quindlen, from stylebooks and codes of ethics, standards, and practices.

Hersey, author of *Hiroshima*, used a composite character in at least one early work, but by 1980 he expressed polite indignation that his work had become a model for the so-called new journalists. In a 1986 *Yale Review* essay, he questioned the writing strategies of Truman Capote, Norman Mailer, and Tom Wolfe. Some contemporary non-fiction authors defend invention in the name of reaching for some higher truth. Such claims are unjustifiable in any journalism.

Hersey admits that subjectivity and selectivity are necessary and inevitable in journalism. If you gather ten facts but wind up using nine, subjectivity sets in. This process of subtraction can lead to distortion. Context or history or nuance or qualification or alternative perspectives can drop out. While subtraction may distort the reality the journalist tries to represent, the result is still nonfiction. The addition of invented material, however, changes the nature of the beast. When we add a scene that did not occur or a quote that was never uttered, we cross the line into fiction. This distinction leads us to two cornerstone principles: *Do not add. Do not deceive.*

To make these cornerstone principles definitive, I have stated them in the simplest language. This may cause confusion by failing to exemplify these rules persuasively or by not offering reasonable exceptions. For example, by saying "Do not deceive," I'm talking about the promise the journalist makes to the audience. A different argument concerns whether journalists can use deception as an investigative strategy. There is honest disagreement about that, but even if you go undercover to dig for news, you have a duty not to fool the public about what you discovered.

Be unobtrusive. Work hard to gain access to people and events, to spend time, to hang around, to become such a part of the scenery that you can observe conditions in an unaltered state. This helps avoid the "observer effect," a principle drawn from physics, in which observing an event changes it.

Of course, some circumstances *require* journalists to call attention to themselves and their processes. Go ahead and loudly confront the greedy, the corrupt, the secret mongers. But remember, the more reporters intrude, the more they risk changing the behavior of those they investigate.

Stories should not only *be* true, they should *ring* true. Reporters know by experience that truth can be stranger than fiction, that if a man walks into a convenience store in St. Petersburg, Florida, and shoots the clerk in the head, the bullet can bounce off his head, ricochet off a ceiling beam, and puncture a box of cookies.

Avoid using anonymous sources except in cases where the source is especially vulnerable and the news is of great import. Whistleblowers who expose great wrongdoing might fall into this category. A person who migrated illegally into America may want to share his or her experience without fear of deportation. But the writer must make every effort to make the character real. An AIDS patient may want and deserve anonymity, but making public the name of his doctor and his clinic can help dispel any cloud of fiction.

Never put something in your story that hasn't checked out. The new media climate makes this exceedingly difficult. News cycles that used to change daily now change by the minute or even second. Cable news runs twenty-four hours a day, while more and more stories have been broken on the Internet in the middle of the night. The imperative to keep news up to the second grows stronger and stronger. Time frenzy is the enemy of clear judgment. Taking time allows for fact-checking and proportional coverage.

In a culture of media bravado, there is plenty of room for strategic humility. This virtue teaches us that Truth, with a capital T, is unattainable; that even though you can never get it, with hard work you can get *at* it. Humility leads to respect for differing points of view.

These principles have meaning only in the light of a large idea that is crucial to democratic life: *There is a world out there that is knowable.* The stories we create correspond to what exists in the world. The words between quotation marks correspond to what was spoken. The shoes in the photo were the ones worn by the man when the photo was taken, not added later.

A tradition of verisimilitude and reliable sourcing can be traced to the first American newspapers. A Boston newspaper called *Publick Occurrences* made this claim on September 25, 1690: "[N]othing shall be entered, but what we have reason to believe is true, repairing to the best fountains for our Information."

The principles *Do not add* and *Do not deceive* should apply to all nonfiction all the time, not just to the text of newspaper stories. Adding color to a black-and-white photo, unless the technique is obvious or labeled, is a deception. Digitally removing an element in a photo, or adding, shifting, or reproducing one, no matter how visually arresting, is a deception. This is different in kind from traditional photo cropping—although that, too, can be done irresponsibly.

In an effort to get at some difficult truths, reporters and writers have at times resorted to composite characters, conflation of time, interior monologues, and other unconventional practices. It may be helpful to test these techniques against the standards described here.

The use of composite characters, where the purpose is to deceive the reader into believing that several characters are one, is a technique of fiction that has no place in journalism or other works that purport to be nonfiction. An absolute prohibition against composites seems necessary, given a history of abuse of this method. Although considered one of the great nonfiction writers of his time, Joseph Mitchell would, late in life, label some of his past work fiction because it depended on composites.

Time and chronology are often difficult to manage in complicated stories. Time is sometimes imprecise, ambiguous, or irrelevant. But the conflation of time that deceives readers into thinking a month was a week, or a day an hour, is unacceptable in nonfiction. In his author's note to the best seller *Midnight in the Garden of Good and Evil,* John Berendt writes:

> Though this is a work of nonfiction, I have taken certain story-telling liberties, particularly having to do with the time of events. Where the narrative strays from strict nonfiction, my intention has been to remain faithful to the characters and to the essential drift of events as they really happened.

Nonfiction authors cannot have it both ways. Contrast Berendt's vague statement to the one G. Wayne Miller offers at the beginning of *King of Hearts,* a book about the pioneers of open-heart surgery:

> This is entirely a work of nonfiction; it contains no composite characters or scenes, and no names have been changed. Nothing has been invented. The author has used direct quotations only when he heard or saw (as in a letter) the words, and he paraphrased all other dialogues and statements—omitting quotation marks—once he was satisfied that these took place.

The interior monologue, in which the reporter seems to get into the head of a source, is a dangerous strategy but permissible in the most limited circumstances. It requires direct access to the source, who must be interviewed about his or her thoughts. Editors should always question writers about the sources of knowledge regarding what someone was thinking.

The more we venture into that territory, the more we need a good map and an accurate compass. John McPhee, as quoted by Norman Sims, summarizes the key imperatives:

> The nonfiction writer is communicating with the reader about real people in real places. So if those people talk, you say what those people said. You don't say what the writer decides they said. . . . [Y]ou don't get inside their heads and think for them. You can't interview the dead. You could make a list of the things you don't do. Where writers abridge that, they hitchhike on the credibility of writers who don't.

There should be a firm line, not a fuzzy one, between fiction and nonfiction. We can find many interesting exceptions, gray areas that would test all of these standards. Howard Berkes of National Public Radio once interviewed a man who stuttered badly. The story was not about speech impediments. "How would you feel," Berkes asked the man, "if I edited the tape to make you not stutter?" The man was delighted and the tape edited. Is this the creation of a fiction? A deception of the listener? Or is it the marriage of courtesy for the sources and concern for the audience?

I come to these issues not as the rider of too high a horse but as a struggling equestrian with some distinctively writerly aspirations. I want to test conventions. I want to create new forms. I want to merge nonfiction genres. I want to create stories that are the center of the day's conversation.

Hugh Kenner describes the language of journalism as "the artifice of seeming to be grounded outside language in what is called fact—the domain where a condemned man can be observed as he silently avoids a puddle and your prose will report the observation and no one will doubt it."

If you try something unconventional, let the public in on it. Gain on the truth. Be creative. Do your duty. Have some fun. Be humble.

Adapted from a longer essay by the author, previously published in the literary journal Creative Nonfiction *and at the Poynter Institute's Web site, titled "The Line Between Fact and Fiction."*

Toward an Ethical Code for Narrative Journalists

WALT HARRINGTON

Steven Bates, author of *If No News, Send Rumors: Anecdotes of American Journalism,* studies the ethical codes of professions. He notes that most professions have a specific client to whom its members owe allegiance: doctors to their patients, lawyers to their clients, anthropologists to their subjects. In a 1995 article in the journal *Media Ethics,* he asks, *Who is the journalist's client?* He looked at the ethical statements of the *Washington Post, New York Times,* and many other newspapers, and found that journalists have multiple constituencies.

We are bound by honest relationships with our sources and our subjects. Because narrative journalists write intimate portraits, that last group takes on great importance.

We also owe some allegiance to our employer who pays our salaries and defines the ethical standards we agree to work under. Most ethical codes in journalism declare our primary constituency to be our readers. We often translate that into something even larger— the so-called public or even the public interest, but a term as broad as "public interest" can be variously defined.

This much is clear: Ethics are crucial to journalism's legitimacy. In part this is because *journalists claim the right to determine their own ethical relationships.* The complexity of the journalist's ethical situation is only compounded in the case of narrative journalism. In some ways the work of immersion journalists resembles the work of anthropologists, but anthropology's ethical code is clearer. Their constituency is their subjects, first and always. Although journalists can't go quite that far, I believe narrative journalists should operate under an ethical code similar to that of anthropologists. We *do* owe something to our subjects.

There is a practical aspect to this assertion. Our subjects—unless they are public figures—can more easily sue us for what we write. They can withhold information or withdraw their permission to publish their stories right up to press time. For those practical reasons we must get their stories right.

Human considerations are even more important. When I approach potential subjects, I discuss the difference between "off the record" and "on the record" material. Everyone has the right to know what any politician knows: If he or she says it's off the record, we don't print it. Sometimes, later in the reporting process, I go back to the subject and ask if I can include off-the-record material. I have even read paragraphs to subjects so they know exactly how I would use the information. People are often afraid of *how* material might be used, not *whether* it is used. If the journalist is sensitive and thoughtful, people often give consent.

Still, you must sometimes give away material in a negotiation; no story includes everything. It is important to ask: Is this story honest? Is it a true story, not just a factual one? If I must withhold a piece of information from a story, I ask myself: If the readers learned about it, would they feel deceived?

I wrote a story about the family of a teenager who had committed suicide. I spent about a month with the family, two years after the son's death, going over and over the consequences of the suicide. I had planned to include all the family members in the story: mother, father, and three surviving siblings. But I discovered many things about the siblings' lives that they didn't want published. I realized that I couldn't write a true account of the siblings' reactions to the suicide and leave that material out. Their parents allowed me to include everything. They wanted their story published so that other families could learn from it. I revised my plan and focused on the parents; the siblings barely appeared. I believe it is an honest story. There is more to the larger story, but it wasn't part of the story I told.

I worked with several psychologists on that story. The psychiatrist of the deceased teen believed that what I might publish could cause another family member to consider suicide. That scared me, and I thought it would be safest to gauge the family's response before publication. Even though the *Washington Post* has a rule against showing a subject the story before publication, I went to the family with a copy of the story in hand and read the entire piece to them. (My admittedly flimsy defense to my editor would have been that I hadn't actually *shown* the family members the story. Had the family told me that the *Post* couldn't publish it, I would have had to tell my editors that I'd just wasted six weeks by breaking a *Post* rule.) I read the story to the family, and they started to cry. They hugged each other and me. I cried. They didn't want a single word changed.

I still believe I made the right ethical decision. In a sense, I was fact-checking. Journalists can always read back quotes and other attributed information to sources. In narrative stories, almost anything can be a fact that needs checking—including such statements as "She enjoyed the warm sun on her face."

Narrative journalism brings up special ethical considerations. We spend so much time with our subjects, and we are almost never prosecutorial in our interviewing of them. We want to be genuinely human to our subjects, because we want them to become genuinely human to us. Yet, in the end, we must write our story—one that is *not* the subject's version of his or her life but *our* version. Narrative writers must walk a delicate line to be certain that we are ethically honest with both subject *and* reader.

If you write narrative journalism and don't learn things about your subjects that shouldn't become public, you aren't a good reporter. If you don't struggle with this issue, perhaps you aren't a humane person. It is impossible to go intimately into people's lives without having to wrestle with what should be revealed.

Playing Fair with Subjects
ISABEL WILKERSON

Narrative writers must strike a careful balance: caring about our subjects without sacrificing our narratives, while caring about our narratives without sacrificing our subjects. Good journalism and empathy can go hand in hand. Empathy helps me understand my subjects better and immerse myself in their worlds.

I wrote a story titled "The Manful Life of Nicholas, 10," about a young boy with a man's obligations growing up on the South Side of Chicago. The story was part of a *New York Times* series exploring the interior lives of urban, at-risk children, amidst rising drug use and juvenile violence. The *Times* assigned ten reporters to spend whatever time it took to get inside the worlds of ten children. Each reporter was to suggest possible topics that each child represented. One of my suggestions was *family*, a maddeningly broad and ambiguous topic.

In my search for parents who would allow me to spend a lot of time with their children, I visited GED, job training, and court reporting classes. Wanting to attract as many candidates as possible, I made a very broad appeal to the participants in these adult education classes: "If you have children between the ages of nine and twelve, I'd like to talk with you for a story I'm writing about family, about how difficult it is to raise kids today in the city." I made my appeal over and over, "auditioning" several potential candidates over several weeks' time, but still hadn't found the right subject—one with a great story to tell who was willing to give me the necessary access. Finally, at a nursing training program—the very last place on my list—a woman walked in late. She hadn't heard my pitch to the group. My sign-up sheet came her way, and the woman next to her said, "You're supposed to sign it if you have a kid between the ages of nine and twelve." The woman signed, not knowing what it would mean: her life laid bare on the front page of the *New York Times.*

As it turned out, Angela Whitiker was the perfect parent for me to work with, and her son Nicholas was the perfect main character. She was open and frank about her life, articulate, and willing to give me complete access to her children. Her son Nicholas was a brooding, complex figure with a heavy weight on his shoulders, a kind of everychild in a harsh world.

I spent as much time as I could with Nicholas and his family, doing what ethnographers call "participant observation." Rather than ask questions, I joined whatever the family happened to be doing. My first day, I folded socks with them at a Laundromat.

Spending time doing mundane things builds trust and helps you get to know a subject better than merely asking questions. It also helps shift the subjects' notions of what a journalist does: show up, mine them for information, write down whatever they say in a notebook, and leave fifteen minutes later. I spent about a month with the family—little time for narrative journalism, but a very long time in the world of daily journalism.

We fell into a rhythm: I arrived at their home early and stayed as late as they would allow me. I attended fourth grade classes with Nicholas. After school, we usually went to McDonald's. I'm sometimes asked whether I changed the situation by taking the boys to eat, since they might not otherwise have eaten. Journalists use food to buy time with sources constantly; these boys deserved no less. Perhaps they deserved much more, because they gave so much of themselves to help me create so intimate a portrait. In the end, because McDonald's was their restaurant of choice, it was a very cheap date.

As reporters, we worry too much about doing something that might "change the story." We must admit that our very *presence* "changes the story." Having a reporter in your life is an unnatural occurrence, by definition altering it in the short term.

When you spend as much time with subjects as I do, the question of intervening is bound to come up. My standard is based on what I would do for any other person I encounter in my life. I'll help carry groceries or offer a lift to the store as long as it seems appropriate to the situation and doesn't fundamentally alter their life direction. We should do no less for our subjects than we would for any acquaintance.

Our job is to make our presence in our subjects' lives as comfortable and as normal as possible as quickly as we can. We must learn the subtle rules and hierarchy of the world we have stepped into, adjusting ourselves to it and finding a place in it by responding in natural and human ways.

How do you get close but not *too* close? How can you be empathetic yet not intervene when you know that a phone call or a check could solve a significant problem? At times like these I must embrace my role as a journalist and resist the urge to be counselor, social worker, or savior. I focus on the great gift of intimate detail that my subjects share with me and pour that into the story. I channel my empathy and compassion into the writing. That is the way journalists can have an impact, and perhaps a far greater one than we could by clumsily inserting ourselves into a momentary crisis.

Even the most difficult moments while reporting inform my writing, such as when I want to confront someone or sweep the children up into my car. I once observed Nicholas's mother strike him when he balked at handing over a trinket to a younger brother. As desperately as I wanted to intervene, I had to remember that I am a reporter, not a trained social worker. I could have done more harm than good by intervening. I had no expertise or authority or even a complete understanding of what I'd observed. I had to maintain my faith that a moving story could attract the interest of people who could truly help and also might spur Angela to action. To my relief and gratitude, both of those things happened.

To be authentic and truthful about intimate, even painful aspects of people's lives, we must be absolutely sure of the facts. Authenticity comes from a thorough understanding of a situation and subject. It is so easy to get it wrong. Authenticity comes from long conversations and then playing back to the person what you think you just heard. It is worth reminding yourself often that you're not advocating for the subject but helping the reader understand what it's like to *be* that person. Context is critical; mitigating circumstances must be explained. That context can only emerge from time spent. A passage at the end of "The Manful Life of Nicholas, 10" reads:

The children line up, all scarves and coats and legs. The boys bow their heads so their mother, late for class herself, can brush their hair one last time. There's a mad scramble for lost mittens, and then she sprays them. She shakes an aerosol can and sprays their coats, their heads, their tiny outstretched hands. She sprays them back and front, to protect them as they go off to school. Facing bullets and gang recruiters in a crazy, dangerous world. It is a special religious oil that smells like drugstore perfume, and the children shut their eyes tight as she sprays them long and furious, so they will come back to her alive and safe at day's end.

Had I not been there early that morning, I would never have known about this family ritual, which ultimately became the story's central moment, epitomizing the insidious normalization of violence in their lives. I observed this ritual very late in the reporting process, when I thought I was ready to shift from reporting to writing after having spent hours talking with them about how they protected themselves against violence. No one thought to bring up this ritual, perhaps because it was for them as normal as brushing their teeth each morning.

While the ritual was happening, I knew not to ask what they were doing. Only later in the day did I casually bring it up with Angela. *Why did she spray her children before they left the house?* Strange as the action seemed to me, I had to remember that if Angela and her family were to visit my world, they would also have found it strange. *Why does she spend so much time in front of her computer?* Angela and I were both African American but came from different worlds.

Our subjects give us so much more than they ever get back from us. We publish their stories and go on to win promotions, praise from colleagues, Pulitzer Prizes. Our subjects go on living their lives. Still, it is heartening to know that stories can change lives and perceptions. After Nicholas's story was published, a reader flew to Chicago from New York to buy the boys bunk beds. Someone else bought them a television. People sent them clothes and toys. An entire fourth grade class in Michigan wrote letters to Nicholas, as did President Clinton.

I received letters from all over, but the response that meant the most to me was a phone call from a man in Tacoma, Washington. He said, "I'm Greek American. I'm in my mid-sixties and I'm a dentist. I had to call you because after I read the story, I realized: She has written about *me*. I was the oldest of six children, and I had to be the father for everybody." That man's call showed me that I had succeeded in transcending the stereotypes and assumptions some readers have about people who seem different from them.

As narrative journalists we have a dual responsibility—to the reader and to the subject. It is not our primary job to help the people in our stories, but there is nothing wrong with showing our humanity and lending a hand where appropriate. More often than not, it is the only way to gain time and insight into their worlds, which is precisely what's required to write the truest and most authentic stories for our readers.

Securing Consent

TRACY KIDDER

Securing a subject's permission and cooperation, if that subject isn't a public figure, is one of the trickiest things I have to do as a writer. It is a matter of both law and ethics. I try to make sure that private individuals understand what I'm doing, and I try to give them some sense of what the consequences might be. It's a sort of Miranda warning: *Anything you say may be used against you in my book.*

I wrote *The Soul of a New Machine* when I was very young. I didn't know that you shouldn't be able to get inside a computer company, particularly down in the basement where they're designing the computers. That probably made it easier for me. I thought, "Well, they should let me in." And they did, without strings attached. I've since learned that that sort of access is extremely unusual.

These days, publishers often require authors to get signed releases from their subjects. Lawyers tell me these sorts of releases are of limited use in cases of invasion of privacy, a very vague area of the law, and of even less use in libel cases. The releases generally say something like this: *I can write anything I want to about you. I can steal your good name. And I'll give you a free copy of the book in which I do these things.* From what I understand, most courts don't think that's a valid contract. For those reasons I've stopped getting releases from the people who appear in my books. Nonetheless, releases can be a tool to help subjects truly consider what they are doing.

I do still talk extensively with subjects about the potential consequences of my writing about them. I try to answer all their questions. The issue of money almost always comes up. If it doesn't, I bring it up, telling them, "I can't pay you for this. This has to be something you're doing of your own free will." I approach subjects about this early on when I don't care whether they say yes or no. Of course I would like them to say yes, but it's good to know that I can walk away from the project at that point. I get those discussions out of the way right at the beginning when I have no investment.

Truth and Consequences

KATHERINE BOO

As a journalist I have more power than the people who appear in my stories. There's no way around that. Though it is disingenuous to suggest that there is some way to make it an equal relationship, it *can* be a respectful one. You can inform your subjects as fully and completely as possible about what you suspect will happen or what you fear might happen as a result of obtaining and publishing their story. I always tell subjects that there will be things in the article they hate or find embarrassing or wish they had never told me. There will be a photo that makes them look fat.

If you can help people understand that their stories actually mean something in the larger context of our society, it might inspire them to talk to you. It also better prepares them to accept the consequences of your writing about them.

I usually don't write about the people who approach me wanting to be subjects. I look for people who are still working through their problems, who don't have a moral for every story of their lives, who don't yet know whether there will be a happy ending. Those are the people whose stories should be told.

When you write about poor people, nobody may care more than you do about what happens as a result. Your institution's lawyers won't care, because poor people aren't going to sue. Your editors won't care as long as it's a good story. The moral imperative lies with the writer. You will make a thousand moral decisions in the course of reporting and writing each story.

> If you live in the same neighborhood as the people you write about, it's almost a matter of practicality. I want to walk down the street without feeling that there are dozens of people whom I've wronged. Sometimes my colleagues say to me, "I can't go in that neighborhood because I wrote this story . . ." If you can't face your subjects after the stories are published, then you should ask yourself whether you really told the truth.

Dealing with Danger: Protecting Your Subject and Your Story

SONIA NAZARIO

While doing immersion reporting, we witness people who are miserable, in pain, or in danger. When do we intervene? Where do we draw the line? It is important to plan for the worst. I spent eighteen months reporting and writing "Enrique's Journey," the saga of a Honduran boy's illegal journey to the United States. Enrique's mother had left him at home with her family when he was five years old. Eleven years later he decided to set off on his own, riding the freight trains north through Mexico to find his mother in North Carolina. I was able to spend the end of Enrique's journey with him, but I had to reconstruct much of the story. I rode on top of the freight trains with other immigrants, trying to see and feel and smell what Enrique had experienced along the way.

For this sort of narrative reporting about people in difficult situations, it is good to know as much as possible before going into the field. When I started my research, a government shelter director told me, "You're gonna get yourself killed doing this story." I knew that I had to work out worst-case scenarios.

Before going to Mexico, I looked at the train routes that I would follow. For months I visited INS (Immigration and Naturalization Service) jails, Los Angeles high schools, churches, and shelters along the United States–Mexico border—anywhere I could find kids who had made this trek. I tried to grasp the dangers at each point on the route. What specific places would I go? What hazards do children encounter in each of those places? I knew that the kids would face hunger, extreme heat and cold, thirst, menacing police, gangs, bandits, and even the train itself. They jump on and off the boxcars while the cars are moving; some kids have lost arms and legs. I tried to figure out in advance the social structures affecting the kids at each stage of the journey. Did they have access to food from churches? Medical help? Shelter?

Once I had a sense of the specific dangers, I had to decide how I would respond to each one. For example, on the Mexican side of the border the kids face bandits who knife them and steal their money. I also anticipated having to cross the Rio Grande with an immigrant child. Generally, after crossing the river at Nuevo Laredo, Texas, the immigrants walk through the desert for four days to San Antonio. The Rio Grande looks placid but has dangerous whirlpools. Hundreds of people have drowned there in recent years. To avoid the INS, migrants walk through the desert at night—when the rattlesnakes are out. Desert temperatures reach 110 to 120 degrees during the day, but at night it becomes extremely cold. It is physically impossible to carry enough water to avoid dehydration.

I was unwilling to take the risk of crossing the river without an inner tube, compass, cell phone, iodine pills, and emergency blanket. The question arose: Would I allow a child to use any of these things? The ethical issues were intertwined with legal issues. I learned that my crossing into the United States in an unapproved location—"entering without inspection," as the INS calls it—would be a possible misdemeanor. But if the INS thought that I was leading an undocumented child into the country, I could be charged with aiding and abetting illegal migration, a felony.

I tried to minimize the dangers to myself. A colleague helped me obtain a letter of introduction from the personal assistant to the president of Mexico. That helped keep the photographer and me out of jail a couple of times. I got permission from the train companies to ride on top of the trains.

I hashed out the issues ahead of time with my editors and a *Los Angeles Times* attorney. I decided my primary rule would be to intervene only if I felt that a child was in imminent danger. How would I determine whether a child was in imminent danger? Some cases would be clear; of course I would help a child who was drowning. In many other cases it would be more difficult to distinguish between misery and real imminent danger. Developing worst-case scenarios helped me prepare for those decisions ahead of time. The measure of imminent danger is a harsh standard, but there are good reasons for it.

Narrative stories must convey reality.

The reporter should try as much as is possible not to change the course of events. Sometimes the simple fact of my presence, without taking any action at all, changed things. While I was riding on top of the freight cars, the police who stopped the trains didn't beat up or rob the migrants as they usually do. It was clear that they had been forewarned of my presence.

When we intervene, we risk our subjects seeing us as something other than journalists.

I always told my subjects the rules up front: I couldn't help them. While reporting a story, if I were to intervene in the life of a subject, especially with the primary character, I wouldn't be able to use that person in my story.

I *did* help some children who I felt were in imminent danger. A twelve-year-old, Gaspar, who was at an immigration detention station in southern Mexico, had been abandoned by his smuggler. I knew that criminals often preyed on young children who had been re-turned to the Guatemalan border. Gaspar was desperate, crying and clawing me, begging for help. I called his uncle in Florida and gave the uncle's phone number to the immigration officials so they could arrange for Gaspar to be picked up by relatives in Guatemala and not abandoned at the border.

Reporters must decide for themselves where that line is. I did not help Enrique, my main character. He struggled for two weeks in Nuevo Laredo, just south of the United States–Mexico border, to get the money to call Honduras for his mother's phone number in North Carolina. The piece of paper with the number on it had been stolen from him. He was washing cars, eating once a day, and really strug-gling. The whole time, I had a cell phone in my pocket. I knew that my intervention would significantly change the story; I would have had to start all over with another main character. Most important to my decision, though, was that Enrique was not in imminent danger.

To avoid changing people's lives, we might have to withhold some information from our readers.

The editor's note that accompanied "Enrique's Journey" said, "The *Times*' decision in this instance to withhold his last name is in-tended to allow Enrique and his family to live their lives as they would have had they not provided information for this story."

While I was reporting this story and writing the initial drafts of it, I strongly favored using Enrique's full name. I had searched long and hard for a subject who would allow me to use a full name. I carried permission slips in English and Spanish for parents to sign, saying it was all right for me to interview and for the newspaper to photograph their child. Both Enrique and his mother had signed those forms.

There had been a case a few years earlier in North Carolina, where Enrique and his mother were living, in which the Raleigh *News & Observer* had identified an immigrant's workplace. Not long after, the INS showed up at the store and took that person into custody. I researched the specific INS director in North Carolina to assess whether he would try to find Enrique and his mother, Lourdes. I also tried to determine the odds that he would be successful. Nona Yates, a *Times* researcher, did computer searches using databases such as LexisNexis and ChoicePoint. She concluded it would be fairly easy to find Enrique if we used his full name. Because of all this, we decided against doing so.

We also pulled other details from the story that might have provided a roadmap for the INS: the specific town in Honduras that they were from and the kind of work that Lourdes did. At the same time we did many things to enhance the story's credibility with the reader. I had witnessed part of Enrique's journey, and I had interviewed other people who had witnessed other parts of it. I identified those people with their full names. I also included the full names of family members who didn't have the same last name as Enrique.

We even changed the order in which we revealed some parts of the story to strengthen readers' confidence. At the beginning of Chapter 2, Enrique was beaten while on top of a freight train. He had to hurl himself off the train to escape. He crawled under a mango tree and lost consciousness. He woke later and walked into the town. The townspeople saw him, stripped of his clothes and bloodied. The mayor, the mayor's chauffeur, and a doctor all helped him. I talked to all those people to corroborate Enrique's story. In an early draft I started Chapter 2 with a narrative account of the beating. My editor suggested starting with the testimonials of the very credible townspeople—whose full names I could use—who saw him after he was attacked.

In the weeks following the publication of "Enrique's Journey," I received at least one thousand phone calls and e-mails. Our goal was to educate people about the changing face of immigration, the harsh realities of the migrant's journey, and the deep poverty that pushes people to risk their lives to escape it. We also wanted readers to think about the huge number of INS agents that we have stationed at the border who are turning back eleven-year-old kids looking for their mothers.

Eighty-two percent of the immigrant nannies surveyed in a 1997 University of Southern California study had left at least one child behind in their home country. In a city like Los Angeles where immigrants are often demonized, humanizing them is an important part of a newspaper's civic mission.

Anyone doing this kind of reporting *will* witness harm. It is a necessary part of narrative reporting. We must weigh the harm to an individual child against the usefulness of witnessing reality and conveying it powerfully to readers. Stories like "Enrique's Journey" can motivate our readers to think more about the issues and to act on them. As narrative reporters we must aspire to write the most moving stories we can. That is our mandate. It is all we can do.

A Dilemma of Immersion Journalism

ANNE HULL

Several years ago I visited Kentucky to write about welfare reform. I traveled to a county where more than 60 percent of the residents received government assistance. Thirty-four percent were on welfare. Welfare benefits would soon end, and people there would face a whole new way of life.

I found a family to write about. It was the quintessential scene of poverty, of living on the edge. The couple, Gracie and Terry, lived with their two children up at the top of a holler. Everything was always breaking down. They improvised, doing some tobacco field work and other odd jobs, and subsisted mostly on a portfolio of government money—SSI for disability, welfare, and WIC. It wasn't nearly enough to live on.

I visited them for a total of three weeks. I spent a week with them, returned home to St. Petersburg, Florida, for a week, and then went back to Kentucky. At the time of my second trip, the end of the month, they were in dire straits.

Their baby, Jacqueline, had a fever. On the second day of my visit, she clearly needed medical care. Gracie fanned her while the photographer and I watched. They didn't have gas money to get to the doctor. Our rental car sat about two hundred feet away; they were looking at it. I could, of course, feel the ethical dilemma developing: *Should I offer to drive them to the hospital in my car?*

No. I decided to wait it out for as long as possible, not saying anything. I was there reporting a story about living on the edge. If I, an accidental visitor, solved their problem, then it would no longer be a true story. As a newspaper reporter, changing their situation didn't seem appropriate.

Time passed. The photographer and I kept waiting, even as it became increasingly obvious that the parents expected us to take them to the doctor. I started to think, "Why am I doing this job? This is horrible." I wanted to throw the notebook down, stop being the reporter, and take care of the baby. The photographer and I decided to wait just fifteen more minutes. The purpose of the story was to ask: *What happens when the government money shuts off? What will people do then?*

Terry went inside the trailer and got a shotgun. He went to a neighbor and pawned it for $20, getting the money to get the baby to the doctor.

Now, if I had taken the baby in my car, I would have solved their problem, but it was very important to witness how they maneuvered out of that tight situation. This wasn't a unique situation for them; something like that happened almost every month. That's the nature of living on the edge. As it turned out, the event with baby Jacqueline did not seem to damage my rapport with the family. If the baby had been in great danger, if it had become very clear that we *had* to go, I would have thrown down my notebook, of course, and driven them to the hospital.

There is no surefire way to inoculate yourself against this sort of dilemma. Still, at the very beginning of your work together, you must say to your subjects, "I'm just going to watch. As much as possible, I'd like to stay in the background." That doesn't always work, but it sets up a boundary. Newspapers operate under the strictest of codes. It's different from doing a book or another type of nonfiction where there's more give-and-take. Newspaper writers must set firmer boundaries. We can't pay people for stories or pitch in for their college scholarship funds or make cash contributions to ease their plight as long as we are writing about them. This makes us, as reporters, freer to examine and explore. We must stick to the basic framework, telling ourselves: *I am here to do a job.*

Ethics in Personal Writing

DEBRA DICKERSON

Writing for *The Record* of Harvard Law School launched my journalistic career. I took the events of the day, all the discourse and debate, and applied it to real people's lives. Many of the folks at Harvard Law didn't do that because they never spent time outside of their offices. From the beginning I wrote about my family—for example, the cacophony of devoting half my summer to working for a fancy law firm and the other half to helping my sister avoid eviction.

I graduated from Harvard Law School in July 1995. The day after I finished the bar exam, my sixteen-year-old nephew was shot. My worlds collided once again: I was turning down $100,000-a-year jobs, and my nephew was shot in the back for no reason at all. I went to North Carolina and spent all day, every day with my nephew. About two weeks after the shooting, in a pediatric rehabilitation ward, my nephew began to realize he wasn't going to walk again—the thing nobody had been saying. He had been a model patient, but he lost it, yelling and screaming, *Why? Why me?*

I couldn't leave the room; I had to stay with him. I pulled out my laptop because I had to put my pain somewhere. While sitting there that day, I wrote almost the complete article that ended up in *The New Republic* titled "Who Shot Johnny?" The second paragraph of the piece read:

> Talking with friends in front of his home, Johnny saw a car he thought he recognized. He waved boisterously—his trademark—throwing both arms in the air in a full-bodied, hip-hop Y. When he got no response, he and his friends sauntered down the walk to join a group loitering in front of an apartment building. The car followed. The driver got out, brandished a revolver and fired into the air. Everyone scattered. Then he took aim and shot my running nephew in the back. Johnny never lost consciousness. He lay in the road trying to understand what had happened to him, why he couldn't get up. Emotionlessly, he told the story again and again on demand, remaining apologetically firm against all

demands to divulge the missing details that would make sense of the shooting but obviously cast him in a bad light. Being Black, male and shot, he must, apparently, be gang- or drug-involved. Probably both. Witnesses corroborate his version of events.

I wrote a full draft in four hours; it felt as if it took years off my life. A week later I thought I was finished with the article. As I lay in bed one night, exhausted from being at the hospital all day, *boom*, the last two paragraphs came to me in a flash:

Alone lying in the road bleeding and paralyzed but hideously conscious, Johnny had lain helpless as he watched his would-be murderer come to stand over him and offer this prophecy: "Betch'ou won't be doin' no more waving. . . ."
    He's fine from the waist up. You just can't do anything right, can you?

A couple of years later I decided to figure out whether the person who had shot my nephew *could* do anything right. I got an assignment from *Talk* magazine and tracked him down. I had seen him at his arraignment—looking lost in his orange jumpsuit, a tiny little kitten of a person. I wanted to know how he had become the person who shot my nephew.

It sounds strange, but I think of the *Talk* magazine piece as a family story. Some of my nonwriter friends thought the idea of writing about the guy who had shot and paralyzed my nephew was horribly exploitative. They didn't understand how that could be a positive thing to do. To write about one's own life and the lives of family and friends is to accept that exploitation of self and others. To write about yourself and the people in your life is to accept that, in part, you are a bastard. You must face and come to understand your own demons.

Neither Dale Barringer, the person convicted of the shooting, nor my nephew had fathers in their lives. If Barringer had had others in his life, as my nephew did, he probably wouldn't have become the angry person that he did. He was eighteen when he went to jail. He had six children and was one of North Carolina's most notorious crack dealers.

I had to lie through my teeth to get the story. That's another aspect of being this kind of bastard. To track Dale down in prison, I couldn't say I was a journalist. I told his prison counselor that I was a friend of the family. When I finally met Dale, I did tell him I was a journalist but said I had picked him at random, to follow a young Black man through the criminal justice system.

As journalists we all know that people will tell you things they shouldn't. Dale Barringer had no ability to understand what was in his best interest. With what he told me, I could get years added to his prison sentence. But I work for the *reader*, not the police. I had to grapple with that. The lawyer and citizen in me felt duty-bound to set his full record straight, but since no one had ever done that in his favor, I decided that it all balanced out. The police could have found the information that I did with far less trouble, had they bothered.

I became a writer to deal with the complexities of my life. If I'd had the emotional and mental sophistication to deal with it from the beginning, I wouldn't have needed to become a writer. Growing up, I cherished an image of myself as having a horrible father. I have since realized what it must have been like to parent a daughter like me: a hypercritical child with a million questions. My father sacrificed everything to give me an education and opportunity, and I used it to try to make him feel stupid. At the time I felt he deserved it; I now realize that I was scared of him. I wasn't merely a passive victim; my father and I were doing a dance. I played a role in his life just as he played a role in mine. I couldn't write about him until I had faced that fact.

In my memoir, *An American Story*, I wrote in detail only about my mother, father, and brother. I obscured specific details about everyone else. I faced one complicated ethical question that every memoir writer faces: *Do you let people read drafts?* I almost never do. This time, though, I *did* give drafts of my memoir to my mother, brother, and the sister who is closest to me. I did this when the book was very close to being finished, saying to them, "Tell me what bothers you, and I'll think about it." I made no promises. What bothers people is never what you expect. You can devote two pages to describing someone's alcoholism, but what upsets the person is noting their dusty shoes.

One of my sisters didn't like the use of dialect. My family uses phrases like "Boy, you better git gone" and "I mighta would." If you render things the way people actually say them, you are accused of condescension. But I believe it's condescending only if you think there's something wrong with the way people talk. My mother speaks the way she was educated to speak; I wanted to render her words accurately.

I let my family read drafts because I had decided, for all sorts of reasons, that my allegiance to them trumped my allegiance to journalism. Of course, when I'm writing in the journalistic form, I accept journalism's conventions. As a writer my allegiance is complicated. I feel an allegiance to my people, to my country, to my craft, and to my family. It is very important for me to go back to the people that I have written about and face them, to be there and listen to what they have to say.

Taking Liberties: The Ethics
of the Truth

LOUNG UNG

I come from a culture where girls are supposed to speak softly and walk on the balls of their feet, rolling off their toes as if flying. Well, I wear boots and I stomp—like a cow dying from thirst, my mother used to tell me. I left Cambodia at the age of ten, a war refugee, to come to America. Twenty-five years later I still find myself falling into the role of the quiet Khmer girl when I go home to Cambodia. The men talk around the dinner table, and I keep my tongue still and show respect for my older brother—even though he says things I consider sexist.

My first book, *First They Killed My Father: A Daughter of Cambodia Remembers*, is evidence of the liberty I have as a Cambodian-American woman. Instead of staying silent about my experience, I laid open my tears and my heart. Some Khmer people told me: *Let the dead stay buried.* But the dead refused to disappear into the earth, forgotten, and so I wrote about them.

Lucky Child: A Daughter of Cambodia Reunites with the Sister She Left Behind, my second book, is the parallel story of two lives: my own and that of one of my sisters, Chou, who stayed in Cambodia. It covers the fifteen years we were separated, from the time I left in 1980 until I was able to return in 1995. Since that first visit, I've returned twenty-five times. There are universal truths as well as an understanding of our shared childhoods that bond us.

In the narrative of *Lucky Child*, I claim my sister's story as my own— an imaginative premise. I do that because her life *could* have been my life. On the day that our oldest brother, Meng, decided to leave Cambodia for the United States, we all knew that he could take only one sibling with him. He chose me. If he had chosen my older sister, I indeed would have had Chou's life: unable to read or write, wed in an arranged marriage at the age of eighteen, mother of five children, living in a village without electricity or running water.

I feared that *Lucky Child* would be a controversial book because of that dual narrative. As it turned out, it hasn't raised controversy at all. I think that is due in part to the book's detailed preface.

I wrote Chou's story from her point of view, as if I had witnessed it. *Lucky Child*'s preface explains my research process to the reader. It notes, in part, "As I was not there to witness Chou's life, this book is my best attempt to piece together her story from our numerous conversations, interviews with family members and neighbors, and our many literal and emotional walks down memory lane. . . . Here are our stories: mine as I remember it and hers as she told it to me."

I also included a caveat for my use of time in the book:

In America, I was helped by the many date books, journals, diaries, homework assignments, clocks, calendars and the sources that I kept to mark the passages of my life. In the village, Chou did not possess such items. Instead, time flows for her from one day to another, from one harvest season to the next, distinguished only by the rising sun, fallen stars, and the birth of a new generation of Ungs. And thus I was left with having to give the best "guesstimate" to the time and events that marked her life.

Lucky Child's preface also explains the multilayered translation process required to write the book. I translated not only Chou's Cambodian and Chinese words but also the Chinese-Cambodian culture in which she lives. I translated not simply into English but into book form. Cambodia's storytelling tradition is oral history, not published books.

Even the concept of individual authorship is understood differently in Cambodian culture. America is a deeply individualistic place: *I* did this; *I* saw this; *I* achieved this. I grew up thinking, "This is what my family has achieved," not "This is what I've achieved." Whatever I achieve is shared with my family. *Lucky Child* has been, from the outset, our collective achievement.

Some might be dismayed by my claiming my sister's story, but I believe her voice deserves to be heard. I made every effort to present it accurately, without invention, and explained the process to the book's readers. Immigrants to the United States used to hide their histories, lose their languages, and leave behind their heritage. Many worked hard at assimilation, until only traces of their former selves still showed. No more. As people come to the United States from around the world, they change our American literature.

Why should my sister's life be silent just because she doesn't read or write English or Cambodian or Chinese? My books are *memoir*, not reported journalism. Memoirs are *collections of memories*, not autobiography or biography. I write because I want my readers to take action. My ability to write these books—in fact, my very survival—is thanks to people who took action against the war in Southeast Asia. Journalists wrote about the refugee camps and inspired people in the United States to sponsor war orphans like me. I am thankful for that. Nonetheless, journalists have been telling our stories for a long time, and the people actually *living* those lives need to step into the role of storyteller. Cell phones, text messaging, and the Internet are changing things. The women of Cambodia—or of India or Guatemala— have not typically had access to the world, but now some of us do.

The Ethics of Attribution
ROY PETER CLARK

In the past few years the attribution and sourcing of narrative journalism have undergone rigorous scrutiny. Although most of the reporters who have lost their jobs for making things up never wrote narrative articles, the genre is now held to a higher standard for accuracy. Part of the scrutiny is driven by the politics of prizes, Pulitzer and other. The judges don't want to be embarrassed if a great story is exposed as a fraud.

The 1998 Pulitzer Prize–winning feature, a serial from the *St. Petersburg Times* called "Angels and Demons" by Thomas French, detailed a triple murder, one of the worst crimes in Florida's recent history. A mother and her two daughters from a farm community in Ohio were vacationing in Florida. They had made their way through Disney World and then to the Gulf of Mexico. They accepted a ride from a man on his boat. He raped them, tied cinderblocks around their necks, and threw them overboard. Thomas French's series describes the crime, law enforcement's long and tireless search for the killer, and that man's trial. Here is a scene from the women's funeral in Ohio.

> The pallbearers took up four rows of pews.
> Though it was mid-June, the day of the funeral was windy and cool, the sky overcast. Inside Zion Lutheran, an imposing Gothic structure with red-brick walls and green spires that stretched high above the surrounding farmland, the sanctuary was overflowing. So many people came to pay their respects, they were crowded into the church's basement and fellowship hall. Outside, the road was lined with vans and trucks of TV news crews. Not allowed within the church, reporters stood beside the road with their microphones, looking into the cameras. Driving by, Hal Rogers counted 12 news crews.
> . . . When Hal arrived at the church, the caskets were up front, each covered with flowers and adorned with a framed picture. There was Jo in her high school senior photo, looking like she had all the time in the world, and Michelle in her junior class photo, smiling a camera smile and wearing her glasses with the pink frames, and Christe in another school portrait. . . .
> The service got under way. The congregation sang "How Great Thou Art," and when it was time for the sermon, the pastor asked aloud the question that was on so many people's minds: How could God have let this happen? That night out on Tampa Bay, when Jo and Michelle and Christe were praying for their lives, where was the God? . . .
> "Don't you see?" [the pastor] said, his voice rising. "Don't you see how Jesus loved Joan and Michelle and Christe? Don't you see how Jesus loves you? How God must feel right now as he looks into our hearts and sees our pain and our sorrow and our grief?"
> The church was silent, but from outside came the sound of a sparrow chirping.

Thomas French was not present at the funeral. In fact, it had occurred a couple of years before he began covering the murder trial. Here are some of the things he did to re-create this scene: He visited Ohio and went to the church. He interviewed many people who attended the funeral. Several attendees gave him tours of the church, telling him where people sat, how they acted, what they wore, and how they responded to the pastor's words. He borrowed an audiotape of the service, which gave him the minister's precise words and intonation, the sounds of people crying, and the birds in the background. He asked a local bird expert to identify the bird songs.

Some might believe that he should have indicated in the text that he wasn't present but had an audio recording of the service. Or perhaps the story should have included an editor's box. The Web version does include this explanatory box:

> Staff Writer Thomas French gathered the information for this series from interviews with Hal Rogers and other family members, detectives and prosecutors, and others involved in this case. In addition, information was gathered in court proceedings and from more than 4,000 pages of police reports, court documents and other records. Some of the quotes and scenes were witnessed firsthand by the reporter or photographer or were taken from police reports or transcripts of official proceedings; others are by necessity based on people's recollections.

Others believe that such notes aren't needed. The point isn't whether the reporter was present; the point is whether the material is correct. Thomas French had to be sure that his writing conjured a funeral ceremony that mirrored reality. His editor needed to do some prosecutorial editing—an editor-writer session with such questions as *How can you be sure it was a sparrow? Have you checked this description against all available photographs?* Thomas and his editor also had to discuss how transparent the newspaper needed to be with its readership.

Why is narrative reporting held to such a high standard? The large majority of news articles are about reconstructed events. The sports section is probably the only part of the newspaper where reporters actually witness most of the events covered. Writers and editors are much more concerned than readers about the attribution of reconstructed events. As far as I know, none of the *St. Petersburg Times's* readers complained about the scene excerpted above.

Still, as standards rise, newspapers must rise to the occasion. "Methods blocks," small blocks of text that give the reader an overview of reporting methods, have become more common, providing brief metanarratives about the reporting for an article or series.

Web sites can also provide detailed sourcing. The Web site for *Black Hawk Down* (http://inquirer.philly.com/packages/somalia) not only provides sourcing notes, but also some of the original source material and documentation for readers who want to dig more deeply. That series ran for twenty-nine days in the *Philadelphia In-*

quirer. Even as Mark Bowden's series was being published, some of the soldiers and other subjects in the story used the Web site to follow the series and provide more information. They participated almost as parajournalists in that story's telling.

More elaborate attention to sourcing can deepen the relationship between writers and readers as well as give both readers and subjects a chance to understand the storytelling process more deeply.

What About Endnotes?

SONIA NAZARIO

I had strong reservations about including endnotes with "Enrique's Journey," my 2002 *Los Angeles Times* series. I thought using them would make the newspaper seem defensive. I also feared they might set a precedent for sourcing narrative stories in the future. I wondered, at a time when the space in the newspaper devoted to *news* is extremely limited, whether we really should devote so much space to endnotes. What is bulldozed out of the newspaper as a result?

As it turned out, readers appreciated the transparency of the endnotes. They liked seeing the sources of all the information in the series. Surprisingly, they used them to follow the reporting process. They read the endnotes to try to figure out what I had done—how I had ridden the trains in Mexico and who I had interviewed. I never would have guessed that people would read endnotes for that purpose.

NICHOLAS LEMANN

Books, unlike newspapers and magazines, often aren't edited or even vetted for accuracy. Nothing is fact-checked. Many journalists, upon writing their first book, are shocked to learn that fact, which is well-known within the industry. In my experience, most book publishers are surprised by that shock. A book publisher's job, essentially, is to package existing literary text and market it to the public. Though they might not say it publicly, book publishers seem to think of themselves as *purveyors* of literary material, not producers, assigners, or shapers of it. When it comes to verifying information and imposing standards, book publishers don't have anywhere near the resources that newspapers and magazines do.

At the same time, books offer our most memorable and very best narrative nonfiction. Because books are much more easily preserved than magazines or newspapers, the ethics of attribution become more complicated. Some sort of annotation, a system for indicating how the author obtained the material, is essential to the integrity of narrative nonfiction books. Still, footnotes often obstruct general-interest readers, serving as an invitation to stop reading. At the same time, the journalism-school model of always including attribution in the text can ruin the narrative. The best solution I've found is a Notes section at the end of the book. Endnotes allow you to include all the material that would be in conventional footnotes without disrupting the flow of the narrative. I encourage narrative writers to adopt this approach.

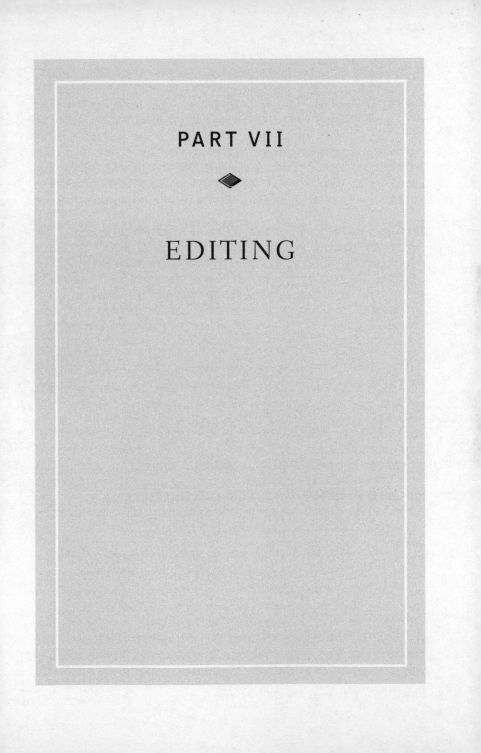

PART VII

EDITING

Introduction

MARK KRAMER AND WENDY CALL

Good writers craft every element of their work, down to the joints between the words. During this meticulous process it's nearly impossible to step back and experience the text as a new reader would. While writing, one needs that close-up understanding of words, adjacent ideas, characters' motivations, and the nuances of possible scenes. But to edit, one must come to the text fresh, mimic the sensibility of a first-time reader, and make the parts work together.

If writers need editors, readers need them, too. The editor is the reader's professional representative. She humbly enters the thicket of an engaged writer's process; she prunes even as she admires, and transplants to strengthen the overall design. Sometimes the toughest part of editing is continuing to trust the writer even while visiting the typical sprawl, disorder, and blundering of half-made work. Especially in newsrooms, where short deadlines and house conventions often limit writerly ambition, an editor's trust and patience are essential to a wholesome editing process.

Why do editor-writer relationships often feel so contentious? The group that gathers for the Nieman Seminar for Narrative Editors each spring devotes much time to this very question. Editors lament receiving stories tangled up like balls of yarn. Speaking for writers, Jon Franklin counters, "The first time most of us try most things, whether it's driving or riding a bicycle or love, it's a mess. Early on in my work as a writer, I gave an editor a draft, and he said it was a piece of garbage. It's not that it wasn't *true*, it's that it wasn't *helpful*. Good narrative writing demands a nurturing writer-editor relationship."

Editing narrative work differs, in kind, from other magazine and newspaper editing. The story's center often remains undefined much further into the process. The back-and-forth between writer(s) and editor(s) can take many more hours per page than other sorts of articles.

"Reviewing a draft with my editor is a tough-love session," says Anne Hull, award-winning narrative writer for the *Washington Post*. "I don't want to be loved unconditionally; I want to understand what's wrong with my draft so I can improve it." A great editor is a rare gift. In the absence of one, writers must serve as their own editors and protect their work from clumsy or inattentive editors.

A first-draft edit that cuts more than it keeps may signal an editor's misunderstanding of narrative structure—or it might signal great editorial work under way. As the clutter in any draft is carted off, you may discern within the remaining text some wonderful passages and sound structural elements. Several drafts and edits and declutterings later, one of writing's hard-earned but still magical moments often transpires: You suddenly have a vision for the entire structure. You have struggled to make it happen, but still it may seem to have just *appeared*, fully formed. However it happens, editing help is often a crucial part of conjuring the story's precise method, purpose, theme, and destination.

With this precision of understanding in mind, at last you can complete an authoritative final trimming: You know what is needed to advance the story and what is superfluous. After that, writer and editor can finally celebrate together—if they're still talking. In this section of *Telling True Stories*, five writers and three editors describe the editing process and offer suggestions for developing and maintaining effective working relationships.

On Style

EMILY HIESTAND

"All right, here goes, but I feel as if my petticoat is showing."

This was the endearing message I once received from a seasoned journalist at work on an essay for *Orion* magazine. I was her editor, the subject was urban nature, and the author's note was by way of agreeing to include more personal reflection and sensory detail. In her superb reporting, the writer was accustomed to muting her quirky observations on the world. But *Orion* values the personal voice, and one of the joys of my tenure there was giving journalists permission to cut loose in the expansive territory of the personal essay.

I wrote back: "Have fun; remember, personal isn't the same as private. Let's see what happens." Over the following weeks these things appeared in her narrative: the mottled sycamores of Central Park, circa 1955; the author's Uncle Abraham eating a homegrown tomato in a Brooklyn kitchen; fig trees wrapped in burlap against the winter cold; and an ode to puddingstone, a composite rock native to only Morocco and Boston (evidence of an ancient geological connection). Suffused with the warmth of memory, telling detail, and wit, the essay was wonderful company.

There are many ways to be good company for our readers. One is to offer the pleasures of stylish prose—language written with attention to texture and tone, imagery, music, and the resonance between words. The poet Derek Walcott tells students that their language should be as clear as water and so complete that readers can detect the *weather* of the poem. Like poets, prose stylists are alert to the ways that meaning can dwell *in* the particularities of language. Ultimately, prose style is the expression of a whole self (and like a self, resistant to dissection), but aspects of style can be named and explored. I offer the following thoughts with some trembling because on the matter of defining great style, even the master E. B. White must say, "Here we leave solid ground." Indeed, my first and most confident suggestion is: Keep Strunk & White's *The Elements of Style* ever close at hand.

Embody ideas in the nature of language.

Language is not a conveyor belt trundling a cargo of something else called "the idea" but is itself integral to the idea. Poets—those pure research scientists in the laboratory of language—might say that language is entirely the idea. But even in prose, whatever else our words mean to convey, the nature of the language is itself a mighty signal. Idiom, cadence, and the leanness or languor of language all work connotatively to communicate, often as strongly as an overt message. The links between ideas and language may emerge unconsciously; I noticed a stately, burnished sound—long lines and calm rhythms—showing up in an essay on the history of my watershed, and a sparkling feel in a story about neon automotive accessories. A writer's voice has a signature, of course, and tonal changes from one work to another are not a chameleon act. They are variations within a voice, representing our capacity to enter into various ideas imaginatively, to explore subjects via language.

Consider Henry James. Famously, one can be mesmerized for pages of a Jamesian narrative only to realize gradually that nothing is actually happening except, say, Isabel Archer has shifted her arm. But every possible psychological vibration in the room has been registered. As James explores the contours of consciousness, he unpacks the density and reverberations of even brief exchanges. After spending time in his company, we may notice more nuance in our own inner lives, too. Like his subject, James's language is complex: Sentences are convoluted and verbs delayed as passages of observation unspool. In this way, in his very style, James enlarges a reader's capacity for perception.

Restore worn-out words.

The poet George Starbuck often advised his students, "Work with words that make you wince." Starbuck wanted to see apprentice poets wrestling with cliché and other damaged language because one of the poet's duties is to restore words to a culture—to redeem lost and sullied words, and make them new. Just so, prose stylists are free to roam the whole continuum of vocabulary and speech, exploring formal, colloquial, and dated words as well as the specialized lingo of engineers, neurologists, and teenagers. The simple word over the fancy one, sure, but also consider the uncommon word that simply appeals to your ear. The most current meanings of words only skim the surface; as any time with the Oxford English Dictionary reveals, each word is a house of history.

Take an art class.

One enjoyable way to develop an eye for detail is to take an art class. Much of what artists learn in school is how to see: how to look at the world free of the abstracting preconceptions and the myriad simplifications that we form in order to navigate life. Visual assumptions are crucial shorthand (train, waitress, tooth), but they also become a cage that prevents fresh contact. To draw or sculpt something, however, we must call on the mind's eye to look again. Seen well, rust stains on a bridge are not ugly but a field of subtle color, like a brindled pelt or a Rothko painting—a visual insight that can flow directly into words. Similarly, even if we have no ambition to write poetry, many of the concerns of prosody—a syllable-by-syllable attention to sound, a feel for rhyme and breath—will also quicken prose.

Use concrete detail.

Surely we love writing that is alive with concrete detail because the mind develops in response to sensory experience and because our intelligence is so multifaceted. Writing that honors the senses—presenting sea smoke ghosting over a lake; a cool plum; the whir of a fan—engages not only the logical mind but also our visual, physical, and emotional intelligences. Sensory-rich writing awakens the full spectrum of consciousness and our myriad ways of knowing. It is also respectful of readers, at the core of the "Show, don't tell" mantra.

Compose the pace.

A narrative essay can bolt from the gate, amble into our affection, or move symphonically through passages of varying energies. The pace can be in alignment with the subject—moving glacially for the slowed-down time of grief—or can counter the subject. There are usually two forces at work in a piece of writing: a forward motion (this happens, then this) as well as a sense of dwelling in place. Dwelling is a way of dropping a plumb line for meaning and pleasure. Think of Thelonious Monk probing one corner of a musical phrase for dozens of bars before moving on. In narrative we like the reassurance of forward motion; if we feel we are in good hands, we also savor digression, linguistic riffs, and sustained immersion.

Experiment with form.

One glory of the essay is that it is not bound by a firm structure—like the plot points of the Hollywood screenplay or the inverted pyramid of traditional news. Instead, the essay is elastic, promising adventure and exploration. There are significant distinctions among the forms of literary nonfiction, but all of them combine the power of fact with the pleasure of style. Not only can an essay take various forms but a single work can incorporate aspects of, say, a short story, reportage, and biography. All of these forms, and others, are available to the narrative journalist.

By its nature a narrative implies order in the world. Very appealing. And yet the past is imperfectly known, the future uncertain. Biological order is based on dynamic change; the earth itself proceeds with the open-endedness of radical creativity, neither rule-bound nor chaotic, but creative within evolving forms. So we also need storytelling that experiments with structure and creates clearings for new ways of thinking and being. Perhaps narrative is at once daring and humble in the way that science is—offering provisional truths, saying in essence: *This is the best story we can tell now, based on limited knowledge.*

Cultivate your own style.

In Bertrand Tavernier's brooding 1986 film '*Round Midnight,* jazz great Dexter Gordon plays the role of saxophonist Dale Turner, a fictional character based on two real musicians, Bud Powell and Lester Young, and their years at the Blue Note. The center of gravity of this film may be the scene in which Gordon stands by his Paris hotel window talking to a young fan and aspiring musician. In a voice gravelly with age and hard living, Gordon shares the essence of style with the younger man: "You don't just go out and pick a style off a tree one day," he says, "The tree is already inside you. It is growing naturally inside you."

This isn't to say that there is nothing for us to learn. For our species, learning *is* natural. Note that the jazzman says the tree is "growing." Style and technique are not only tools for expression—for translating our moral, intellectual, and emotional responses into words—but are also tools for learning. The writer's lifelong engagement with craft and style is a remarkable time-honored way to discover what we think and what we care about—who we are.

A Writer and Editor Talk Shop

JAN WINBURN AND LISA POLLAK

In all editor-writer relationships there are times when one becomes the other's worst nightmare: when the writer keeps the editor late by blowing a deadline, when the editor asks the writer to do more reporting and rewriting—without changing the deadline, when the writer tries the editor's patience with last-minute changes. Forging a good editor-writer relationship is a constant process. When editors and writers work together as partners—with separate roles but focused on a mutual goal—the result is always better.

"From Citizen to Activist: The Conversion of Laura Brodie" was a typical story that we worked on together. It ran in the *Baltimore Sun*'s Sunday paper in November 2002. Our process was messy and the outcome far from perfect, but it offers an example of how we collaborate as writer and editor.

Jan Winburn, editor: In late September 2002, the *Sun* staff brainstormed ways the feature writers could write about impending war in

Iraq. I was interested in publishing something about the antiwar sentiment. I didn't want to focus on the usual suspects: graying peaceniks still fighting the fight. That story offered little discovery. I imagined a story about a newly minted activist, someone surprising who had just come to the cause. I often use working titles to help me focus a story idea. I called this story "The Unexpected Activist."

Lisa Pollak, writer: Of course, my first reaction to the assignment was panic. Where would I find the right person? I started with Internet searches and phone calls, identifying local and national groups working for peace. As I found potential subjects to profile, I discussed them with Jan. I rejected several candidates: people who weren't compelling personalities or speakers, or whose decision to protest wasn't that unexpected.

Winburn: We set a target publication date, October 26, 2002, the day of a large antiwar march in Washington, D.C., about four weeks away at the time.

Pollak: The clock was ticking. In his book *Writing for Story,* Jon Franklin notes that you can either spend 80 percent of your time looking for the right subject or 80 percent of your time trying to fix the story you end up with. I spent a lot of time chasing subjects, and Jan understood why. I wasn't pressured to start the heavy-duty reporting until we had found someone whose story surprised and intrigued us.

Finally, a staff member from the organization Peace Action put me in touch with Laura Brodie. She was a mother of three and the wife of an ex-Marine who worked at the Virginia Military Institute. She had called the Peace Action office wanting to know what she could do to stop the war. She had never been politically active before but had printed five hundred of her own buttons that read "No War in Iraq" and passed them out in her town. I called her, and she told me that she was organizing a forum on the war at the Virginia Military Institute.

Winburn: When Lisa told me this, I was excited.

Pollak: More important, Jan *told* me she was excited. A little encouragement goes a long way. It propelled me to start the next phase: figuring out how to report the story. I knew I would want to travel to Brodie's town to interview her, but for how many days? Who else should I speak to? What scenes might I be able to observe? What interviews needed to be done in person, and what could be done from the office after I returned? When I wanted her opinion, Jan was happy to offer it. She considered it part of her job to weigh in on these kinds of decisions long before there was copy to edit.

Each time I return from a big reporting trip, I spend about half an hour debriefing with Jan. As I talk, I'm listening to myself and learning what parts of the story are important to me. I did this after I returned from Laura Brodie's forum.

Winburn: At this point the editor's job is easy: *just listen*. I don't start with a barrage of questions. If I say anything at all, it is just to keep the writer talking. What surprises her? What mystery still propels her? What might the story's theme be? Sometimes I ask a writer to describe the story in six words. Then I ask if she can describe it in three words. What about one word? That focusing exercise moves the writer from content to meaning.

While Lisa talked, I took notes, and those notes become my road map—a window into the material and potential problems with it. Lisa was worried that she didn't have an intimate story, that she couldn't tell the story through Brodie's eyes. That didn't concern me. I heard Lisa telling me a story about process: an illustration, through one person's experience, of how a citizen becomes an activist.

Before Lisa left my office, I told her the piece would make a good Sunday story. I suggested that Lisa attend the October 26 march with Brodie so that we would be able to see Brodie in action at that event. The story could run the following Sunday.

Pollak: I wasn't sure this material was strong enough for a Sunday story, but Jan told me not to worry about it—we'd have a better sense after the march. I finished the reporting and started to write. But with the Sunday deadline just days away, I realized something wasn't right. The story was flat; it bored me. Some editors would have wanted me to ignore those instincts, to just shut up and get the thing done. They wouldn't have wanted to start editing in the middle of the process. But Jan saw this as part of her job. Even though giving your editor an unfinished draft can feel like going to work naked, I sent her a copy of what I'd written so far.

Winburn: That draft began, "This is the story of a button, a small, red button with four words in white letters. The first and only button that Laura Brodie has ever worn. The four white words are 'No War Against Iraq.'"

I found that lede interesting enough, but as I read on, I understood Lisa's concerns. She had taken a clever approach, but it was simplistic. As her editor I wanted to do more than say, "Yeah, you're right. It's not working." I had to determine *why* it didn't work. I went back to the notes from my debriefing sessions with Lisa. Her rough draft did include more thoughtful, surprising ideas about activism but took too long to reach them.

Now it was *my* turn to panic. Lisa had already tried all the approaches I could think to suggest. I told her, "Take a whole day and freewrite. Write as fast as you can. Don't look at your notes and don't censor yourself. Just write down all your impressions and the elements of the story that seem freshest to you."

Pollak: So that's what I did. And just a few minutes into doing that, I found myself writing about a moment that I'd observed at Laura Brodie's Virginia Military Institute forum. She had stood in front of a roomful of cadets and asked a Marine general whether he thought the war in Iraq was inevitable. He said that it was. Other activists in the audience were depressed by that answer; Brodie wasn't. She felt that she couldn't afford to be; she could never accept that the future was out of her control. That moment gave me the story's engine and its climax.

I sent a new draft to Jan. She sent back some ideas and even lines of text to help deepen parts of the story.

Winburn: I added some provisional sentences to get Lisa thinking. I probably wouldn't have made those suggestions to a writer I was working with for the first time. Lisa understood that I wasn't trying to intrude. I knew she would have to translate my suggestions into her voice.

In spite of all our efforts, we blew the deadline.

Pollak: And yet Jan still let me go over the page proofs and even make a couple of picky wording changes at the last minute. And in the final seconds I even reworked the last line.

Winburn: The graphics editors and copy editors didn't blow their cool. They love this craft, too. A strong writer-editor partnership can extend far beyond just writers and editors to the entire newsroom team.

Revising—Over and Over Again

ANNE HULL

Only editors know the awful truth: how bad even the best narrative stories look in the beginning. Successful rewriting requires a fierce sense of competition with yourself, not anyone else. You must be dogged in reaching for your personal best. When you begin a story's first draft, you must ask yourself hard questions.

Am I getting to the heart of my subject matter? When we begin redrafting—and, unfortunately, sometimes right through to the printed version—we're at the story's fringes. Finding the story's center is crucial; we usually write our way there. It takes many drafts, and there are no shortcuts.

Most newspaper prose uses language that distances readers and kills intimacy. The stories are so obviously *observed* that the reader can't get close to the main character, much less see things from her point of view. Try to think of your character's point of view. How does the world look to that person? Answering questions like this happens organically through reporting, hanging out with people, and learning the tone of their voices, their dialects, and their reactions to specific things.

There are three ways to get to the heart of the story: reporting, thinking, and rewriting.

Reporting

If you haven't done enough reporting, the story will look like a giant comb-over. Every reader will know you're trying to cover bald spots in your reporting. Try to write absolutely everything down while reporting. Note-taking is dredging the lake; you can sort it all out later.

My notes also include whatever upsets, frightens, or maddens me. These notes become benchmarks as I write. They reinvigorate me, returning me to that moment in time and allowing me to render it on paper.

Every line of your story—every single one—must have a fact in it. If it doesn't, it serves no purpose. A fact can be an observed moment, something overheard, or a detail from a think tank report. Before a story runs, fact-check every line. Look at each sentence separately and ask yourself: *How do I know that?* Double-check every source in your notes.

Thinking

Thinking is the most underused skill in the newsroom. Narrative journalists must do more than tell gripping stories; they must tell stories with larger messages. As I report a story, I constantly wonder, *What is this story about?* As I begin to write a draft, my answer to that question sometimes changes.

One test of how well I've answered that question is whether I can write a nutgraf. I used to consider nutgrafs unnecessary intrusions that restricted my writing. Now I understand how essential they are. The key is writing the nutgraf in the language of the story so that it blends in with its surroundings. No matter what you are writing, you must be able to explain its importance to the reader. The nutgraf throws down a gauntlet, saying to the reader: *I am going to show you something about this world I've visited. Let's go there together.*

Rewriting

Love the subject, not your rendering of it. When a good editor or another reader gives you feedback, listen hard to everything she or he says. This isn't a time to protect your ego; it's an opportunity to re-explore your story and force yourself to delve even deeper. Rewriting almost always requires more reporting. The first draft shows you the holes in your notebook or your characterization or the historical context.

Every writer needs a good reader. Some need one more than others. A few journalists work well alone, turning in drafts that are nearly completed but needing an editor to help them take it that last 5 percent. I'm not like that. I can only get to 30 percent before I need someone to work through the story with me. When I start a draft, it's as if I'm in a dark room fumbling for the light switch. If my editor makes very few marks on one of my drafts, I know that I have not yet found the switch.

If you put yourself in a challenging environment and force yourself to stretch, you *will* improve. That means you must always be shifting your location slightly so that you are always around people who are better than you.

Set aside your ego while you revise a story draft so you can concentrate on the work that must be done. Sometimes I'll keep a line that my editor strikes from a draft. I don't plan to include it but use it as a guidepost, to remind me of my goal. It won't end up in the story, but it informs what does go in.

Once you have a full draft, look at it with a brutal eye, asking yourself: *How can I make this better? How can I sandblast off all the extra writing?* Sitting down with a hard copy of the story and going over it with a pen is the fun part—you've finished the hardest work. The sandblasting elevates the piece from 70 percent finished to 90 percent finished. Writers often don't leave enough time for this step. Even if you only have a few minutes, do it. Change that cliché. Eliminate those extra words. Cut as close to the bone as possible.

Every word is important; examine the meaning of each one. If you

aren't absolutely sure, look it up. Avoid phrases that sound too familiar. Sometimes when writing an early draft you have to go ahead and
use the wrong word, just to keep putting one word in front of another. Later, search for just the right word.

Revision requires patience, a quality many journalists lack, and a
long attention span, also rare. Some reporters get bored and don't
want to take the final steps. They aren't lazy, but they're ready to start
the next story. Some journalists consider redrafting a form of punish-
ment, but I consider it a luxury—the chance to make the story better.

Transforming One Hundred Notebooks into Thirty-five Thousand Words

SONIA NAZARIO

My *Los Angeles Times* series "Enrique's Journey" narrated the experience of a fourteen-year-old boy, Enrique, one of thousands of Central American children who travel alone from their home countries
to the United States. These children are often following mothers
who left them behind and came to the United States to work. The series re-created Enrique's life from age five, when his mother left him,
until he found her eleven years later in North Carolina.

"Enrique's Journey" highlighted a huge social issue: illegal immigration. It also told a personal story with a universal theme: a boy setting out to travel through a hostile world in search of his mother. I
spent two years reporting and writing the story. After it was published
in the *Los Angeles Times*, I expanded it into a book, published by Random House and optioned by HBO for a miniseries.

When I began my reporting, I knew that it would be impossible to
follow one child all the way through Mexico to the United States, so I
looked for one who had already completed most of the journey. I
found Enrique once he had reached the United States–Mexico border. I followed him for two weeks while he was in Mexico—trying to
survive and find a way to cross the border into the United States.
Then I rejoined him in North Carolina. After that, I retraced his steps
from Honduras through Guatemala and Mexico. I interviewed many
people he had encountered along the way as well as other migrants
who had made the journey. Enrique's journey lasted 122 days and cov-

ered twelve thousand miles because the Mexican authorities caught him several times and returned him to the Guatemalan border.

The published series included about one-tenth of the material I had gathered. I believe in gathering far more material than I can use, but in this case I gathered too much. I spent three months retracing Enrique's steps, and three months before that doing related interviews and research for the series. When I finally got back to my desk, I had 110 notebooks, hundreds of hours of taped interviews, and typed notes from more than one hundred phone interviews. I was overcome with a feeling of paralysis; I didn't want to face the mountain of material.

My editor, Rick Meyer, insisted that I transcribe all my notes and tapes. I balked at first, but it was the right thing to do. It took me six full weeks. Using a Microsoft Word application, I created a ledger that allowed me to divide all my material by topic, theme, and sub-theme. After I had typed all my notes, I sorted them by topic. I printed the material and collected it in a binder. Transcribing the material gave me a general sense of what I had. It also made it easier to keep track of all the sources I would later need for the endnotes.

Next, I did what my editor calls "garbaging it down"—compressing the notes into a very rough first draft. As I worked my way toward that first draft, I tried to disengage the left side of my brain. I didn't want to dwell on the enormity of the overall project. My only goal was to get it down on paper. I put a sign above my computer that read, "It's the chronology, stupid!" The chronology of Enrique's journey provided the story structure, breaking naturally into six parts. Chapter 1 began the day Enrique's mother stepped off her mother's porch, leaving her five-year-old son behind. It ended the day Enrique decided to step off that same porch and find her. In the final chapter, Enrique crossed the Rio Grande into the United States and traveled to his mother in North Carolina.

It took six months to complete the first draft. I handed over the entire thing, 95,000 words, to Rick Meyer—an unusual strategy, but it worked. He had wanted me to get everything down on paper, thinking it would be the fastest way to move forward. He did a pencil edit of the entire draft, removing huge sections. I spent two months reworking the piece based on his edits, reducing it to 35,000 words and several sidebar stories totaling 11,000 words. The series would go through ten more drafts. Those ten drafts, along with preparing the layout, photography, design, and endnotes, took a year. The series appeared in October 2002.

Between the first and second drafts I had two goals: reducing the length and focusing relentlessly on the story's central purpose—getting readers to understand, empathize with, and invest in the main character. To make Enrique's story as gripping as possible, I ruthlessly cut out other characters. Even Enrique's mother became a secondary character. Several characters cut from the main narrative, whose stories were important to the overall topic of child migration, were included in sidebars.

I deleted the beginning or end of several chapters, although that meant leaving out major parts of the story's chronology. I learned that it's okay to skip ahead, to go from A to C and skip B. I cut some of the things that happened to Enrique to shorten the narrative and to avoid repetition. For example, he was robbed several times, but I described only one of those incidents. Rather than explain in my own voice why something happened, I included a series of short quotes, one after another, without attribution, of people explaining it themselves.

Once the draft was down to a manageable size, I turned to shaping the story. I repeated phrases to link disparate elements of a chapter. At the narrative high point of Chapter 4, local residents appeared and threw food to the migrants passing by on top of the trains. Some of the migrants hadn't eaten in days. In that chapter I included several nice things that happened to Enrique during that part of the journey, linking them by repeating the phrase "It is a gift." I minimized the bad things that happened in that time frame, in keeping with that chapter's theme.

I also repeated details that would become important later in the story. Someone steals one of Enrique's shoes. He finds another, ending up with two left shoes. I included that detail, though minor. After he crossed the Rio Grande, I noted that he put his two left shoes back on. Those details set up the moment later in the story when he speaks to his mother on the phone. She wonders whether it's really him since she hasn't often spoken with him on the phone. She asks, "What do you have on?" He tells her, "Two left shoes," and she knows it's really Enrique.

Although I wrote the story chronologically, at several points I grouped related material to keep the story moving. For example, in Chapter 4, Enrique passes by a statue of Jesus Christ. At that point I digress to include other religious references: how travelers carried Bibles, how prayer strengthened them, and how Enrique thought about religion.

After I had a solid story structure, I tightened the narrative. The final version that appeared in the newspaper included a 25,000-word main story, five sidebars totaling 9,000 words, and 7,000 words of endnotes. Even sentence-level edits became much tighter. For example, a second-draft passage read:

He hangs out at an encampment near the river. In time, he makes it his home. The camps are a haven for migrants, coyotes, junkies and criminals, but it is safer than anywhere else in Nuevo Laredo, a city of more than half a million people and swarming with *migra* and every kind of police. If he is nabbed in town for loitering, say, the authorities will jail him for two or three days and then might deport him to Guatemala. Worse than stuck, he would be at the beginning.

The final draft read:

The encampment he has joined is a haven for migrants, coyotes, junkies and criminals, but it is safer for him than anywhere else in Nuevo Laredo, a city of half a million and swarming with immigration agents, or *la migra*, and all kinds of police who might catch him and deport him.

I varied paragraph length to move the narrative along. One-line paragraphs added suspense or anger, or signaled the reader to pay close attention to a single sentence. I added detail to slow the pace, and removed it to speed things up. A first-draft scene of Enrique riding with a trucker in northern Mexico, nearing the United States, read like this:

The first checkpoint is a few miles north of Matehuala in Los Pocitos. "Checkpoint in 100 Meters" the sign warns, shortly after Enrique begins the journey. His truck idles in a line waiting to get through. When Enrique's truck gets to the officers, they ask what he's carrying, and they want to see his papers. They peer through the big windshield at Enrique, but they never ask about the boy. They assume, the driver tells Enrique later, that he is his assistant. That's what the trucker plans to say if they ask. A few feet further the army stops every vehicle to search for drugs and firearms. A couple of fresh-faced crew cut young soldiers wave them through.

This is the published version:

A sign at Los Pocitos says, "Checkpoint in 100 Meters." The truck idles in line. Then it inches forward. Judicial police officers ask the driver what he is carrying. They want his papers. They peer at Enrique.

The driver is ready: My assistant.
But the officers do not ask.

I also used sentence fragments. In the first draft, Enrique's
mother talks to the smugglers about the fee for bringing Enrique to
her: "Now a female smuggler is on the phone. The woman says, 'We
have your son in Texas, but twelve hundred is not enough.' Now the
woman explains that they want seventeen hundred." The final draft
read, "The woman says, 'We have your son in Texas, but twelve hundred is not enough. Seventeen hundred.'"

Trimming fat writing is difficult on the eleventh draft. I tried to
take a fresh look at each sentence and ask myself: *Is this really necessary? How much is lost by cutting it? How much would be gained by speeding
up the narrative? If I keep it, how can I make it better, shorter?* I questioned
every single word.

How to Come Up Short

TOM HALLMAN

I don't have a master's degree from Columbia, I never did an intern-
ship at the *Washington Post*, and I was fired from my first job as a copy
editor in New York: I'm an extremely average reporter. Extremely average reporters can win Pulitzers if they learn how to tell stories.

The actual words in my stories aren't that beautiful. I love reporting, but I really dislike writing. Before you can tell a story, you have to
learn how to *see* a story. There is no single secret to good storytelling,
but there is one idea that guides me: *Feelings are more important than
rules.* A story is a living thing. It doesn't come from an incident or the
right combination of words and imagery or the perfect structure.
Once the story moves you, the writer, you arrange the events, words,
imagery, and structure of the piece to *make the reader feel something.*

Writers are insecure. Every time we draft a story that includes emotion, we're crawling out on a limb. Our insecurities tell us to crawl back
to safety, but doing so eliminates the story's heart and soul—what
makes the story work. Emotion lives in nearly everyone, though it's
sometimes asleep. The writer must awaken it. We can do this in our
stories—even the ones that begin as the most mundane assignments.

While I was working the Saturday shift, I was assigned to cover the

Lewis & Clark College graduation. The press release focused on a professor receiving a special award; no one but his mother would be interested in that story. I called the school, asked a few questions, and learned there was an older student graduating: Juan Morales, who worked at the college as a custodian.

I called Juan. He started to talk immediately, but I told him, "Listen, I don't want to talk to you now. How about I come to your house Saturday? We can talk then, and I'll go to graduation with you." I reported and wrote the story in three hours. This passage appeared near the beginning of the story:

"This is where I study," says Juan Morales as he leads the way to the kitchen, which has cracked countertops and a sagging floor. Next to the microwave is a stack of World Books published in the 1960s. He bought the set at a used bookstore. When he eats, Morales randomly selects a volume and reads. He does not care what he reads. Any subject will do.

"I wasted too many years," he says. "Too many years dreaming, wandering, not doing anything."

He shakes his head.

"Let me show you something," he says.

He walks into the living room and points to a dirty wall that needs paint. Earlier this morning, he pounded a nail into the wall.

"That," he says, "is where the diploma will hang."

Emotion guides the story's structure. I wasn't looking for a complication, point of insight, or resolution, but for the emotional center. While reporting that story, I wrote down everything I saw and heard at Juan's house, and also everything I felt. That led me to the realization that the story was Juan Morales's journey, not the graduation ceremony.

Juan Morales, 38, the youngest child of a poor family, would receive his bachelor of arts degree in history.

"I wanted my mother there to watch," he says. "In March, she went to the U.S. Embassy for a visa. My family and I all chipped in for an airline ticket for her. Tonight, I plan on taking her to dinner.

"The money?" he asks.

He smiles and rolls up his right shirt-sleeve. He points to a dark spot on his skin.

"I am very familiar with the plasma clinic," he says. "I got $25 yesterday. We will use the money for dinner."

Graduate school a possibility.

He closes the door to his home in Fairview and walks to the car he bought for $100. To start it, he must connect two wires under the dashboard. He lets it idle for a while.

The story ends like this:

As he pulls into the campus, a Latino security guard spots Morales and gives him a thumbs up. He stops Morales, shakes his hand and then pounds on the roof of his car. The guard can't stop smiling. Morales parks his Datsun 210 next to a Volvo and joins the hundreds of young graduates making their way to the student center.

"I know every single office on this campus," he says. "I cleaned every one of them."

In the student center, he goes to the restroom to wash his hands. He looks at himself in the mirror, in his cap and gown.

"I cleaned this bathroom," he says. "Me, Juan Morales."

He adjusts his cap and joins the other graduates. He receives his material and learns that he will be student No. 247 out of 404 to receive a degree this Sunday. He clutches his number close to his chest and walks away, quickly swallowed up by a roiling sea of black.

I followed Juan Morales from his house to Lewis & Clark College in my car. As I drove, I wrote the story in my head. I had to finish the article by noon. I knew that going to the graduation ceremony itself would ruin the story. I wanted Juan to disappear into the sea of black gowns. The story ends before the graduation ceremony even begins. The details, like the Datsun 210 parking next to the Volvo, communicate the story's theme. Facts are neutral; they have no meaning. The writer must impose the meaning after discovering it.

If you want to write slightly more challenging narratives, don't wait for an assignment. You don't have to tell your editor immediately about every story idea. I was chatting with a woman at the gym, and she mentioned that her child was in dancing school—the same school I had attended when I was twelve. I saw a story, but I didn't tell my editor right away. I needed time to figure out why I was interested in a dancing school for twelve-year-olds.

I spent an evening at the school, looking around and thinking about what moved me. This is what I found:

Life gets confusing when a boy turns 12. Perhaps not all of life but certainly the part involving girls. When he's younger, girls are no big deal. Then he hits seventh grade and then—bam—they change or he does. At 12, a boy can find that just thinking about girls makes his hands sweat.

Though it wasn't any sort of traditional news story, it did have a nutgraf: "The truth is, dancing school is not really about dancing. It's about boys and girls discovering the mystery of difference. It is about children standing on the threshold of change. It is about being 12." I included this from my conversation with the instructor and his wife:

Walker hears the music in his head and springs from his seat. "This is the right way to do the cha-cha," he says. "Do you see that one-two-three rhythm, smooth. It's supposed to be smooth. Well, when the kids do it, they think it's fun to stamp their feet."

His wife looks pained. "That's not dancing," she says.

Walker still dances and smiles. "No, honey," he says. "That's adolescence."

I didn't write about how the instructor taught the kids to dance but how he deals with the fact that they are twelve-year-olds. I spent five hours with one of his students before he went to his dance lesson, but I wrote only about him getting ready to leave the house:

He carpools to dancing school with his best friend, Tommy, and Abby, a girl he's known since fourth grade. "You know, Abby, she looks different in a dress," he says. "I've never seen her look like that." He peers around the corner to make sure his brother isn't eavesdropping. "You know, Tommy and I don't goof off as much around her when she's dressed up like that."

He checks his hair once more, then walks to the kitchen to wait for his ride. The kid in him polishes off a handful of Oreo cookies, a glass of milk and a ribbon of spicy beef jerky. The man in him pats his coat pocket to make sure he has a Certs.

Often these slice-of-life stories don't have natural endings, so the narrator drops in for a bit, imposing an ending on the story:

Decades later you barely remember the box step, but you hold the door for your wife, teach your children please and thank you, and are somehow mindful of the value of good manners. What you carry with you still is the seventh grade.

Many reporters laugh at stories like these. Who would want to cover dancing school or a college graduation? Readers might forget 90 percent of what they read in the newspaper each day, but they will remember stories like these.

Newsrooms are not always supportive places. There is a lot of jealousy, which plays into our insecurities. You might really stretch and try to write a good story, but nobody will tell you, "Good job." You just have to trust yourself—and develop a thick skin.

You don't have to work at *The New Yorker* to write stories that move people; you can be at the smallest newspaper. The key is believing in yourself.

Narrative in Four Boxes

JACQUI BANASZYNSKI

The term *narrative*, as used in newspapers, doesn't only mean ten-part serials that take two years to report and write. It also means a single paragraph within a standard news story. I divide narrative writing into four general categories.

Nano-Narratives

I adopted the term *nano-narrative* from writing coach Mary Ann Hogan to refer to a bit of storytelling within a standard news report. You can transform an animated debate at a town council meeting into a narrative moment or slip in a paragraph-long profile of one of the councilors. Plane crashes, fires, and other disasters can be portrayed narratively through a single scene in a longer news article. These small scenes and characterizations bring the news to life for readers.

News-Driven Narratives

News events are, by definition, stories with beginnings, middles, and ends. Reporters can transform a true story into a narrative. This is the best way to get narrative stories on the front page. When an event occurs, whether it's Mother's Day or a plane crash, both writers and editors should stop and ask whether it should be covered using narrative techniques.

Lt. Col. Michael Anderson, one of the astronauts killed when the space shuttle Columbia crashed, was from Spokane, Washington. The only Black astronaut on the shuttle, he came from a nearly all-white city. We wrote a standard profile of him for the next day's *Seattle Times*. We asked ourselves: *How did Anderson, probably one of the few Black students in his school, grow up to become an astronaut?* This led to a further question: *What does it take to become an astronaut?* A week after the shuttle crash, we ran a follow-up story, "The Making of an Astronaut," a deeper profile of Anderson and his profession.

Narratives Revealing News Trends

Stories about real characters are among the best ways to help people understand larger social issues and trends. Narrative stories can answer boring-but-important questions, such as: How is money allocated for the school budget?

To figure out when narrative can best reveal a news trend, use the ladder of abstraction (see page 70). Ask yourself two questions: *Does this specific story also have universal meaning? Is the story also timely?* If you get two yeses, you might use the moment to tell a story that teaches readers about this issue.

Every news event opens a window of opportunity, a period during which you can cover it. How long that window stays open depends on the importance of the story in society *and* what your media outlet does with the story. Editors must consider that window while deciding when to use narrative.

True Narratives

Nonfiction stories that have universal meaning comprise this fourth level of narrative. Tom Hallman's series in the *Oregonian*, "The Boy Behind the Mask" (2001 Pulitzer Prize winner for Feature Writing), is an example. The story had nothing to do with any news trend; it was a timeless story about acceptance.

These stories encompass both ends of the ladder of abstraction: a specific example of a universal idea. They are the rarest stories to find and the hardest to write.

The same news story, topic, or trend might merit several articles. At the *Seattle Times*, we often do what we call a "one-two-three punch." We write the main news article as breaking news and then run the obvious follow-up story. Later, we return with a deeper story on the same topic. The earlier stories prepare our readers, tempt them into absorbing a long, intricate piece. The earlier pieces create buzz, and then the big story answers a question that the previous stories have brought to readers' minds.

Serial Narratives

TOM FRENCH

The three most beautiful words in the English language are not "I love you" but "To be continued." I've always savored the feeling of wanting to know *what happens next*. It's odd that I grew up loving stories so much because my father is a story saboteur. He picks up a book, flips to the last page, and reads it. If he likes it, then he reads the first page. If he likes that, too, he reads what's in between. I've had long, tortured discussions with him. "Please, I'm begging you, Dad," I say. "The author wrote it in that order for a reason. You are depriving yourself of the experience, and you are hurting that poor author, wherever he or she may be." He answers, "I'm sorry, son. I've just got to get to the bottom line."

Meanwhile, I've built my career on writing serialized narratives that appear in the newspaper one chapter at a time. Maybe my whole professional life has been an elaborate attempt to force my father to read a story from beginning to end.

Serialized narratives exert a wonderful pull on us; the power comes from that enforced waiting. We long for completion of the cycle. Serialized stories surround us: the Bible, *The Iliad*, soap operas, and many comic strips. Newspaper serials were popular in the early twentieth century and then fell out of favor. In the mid-1980s, they became popular again.

Before you try writing a serial narrative, study the stories all around you. Many newspaper reporters go home from the newsroom carrying only reports related to their regular beats. That is a terrible mistake; the best writers I know read for pleasure. Pay attention to your guilty pleasures. Analyze the pacing of a soap opera—watch especially closely on Mondays and Fridays. Pick up a comic book. Read the Harry Potter books. J. K. Rowling knows how to hold a reader by her side, an essential skill in serial writing.

Serials must be immensely, intensely, inescapably readable. Unlike other newspaper articles, serials are judged almost entirely by the number of people who read them. One way to attract readers is to create an irresistible central character, one the reader truly cares about. If readers don't care what happens to the character, they won't keep reading. Reward readers for staying with you. Give them great moments, memorable snatches of dialogue, and surprise turns in the plot.

While preparing to write, map all the events on a time line. Even if I don't plan to write a story chronologically, I still have to understand the chronology before I can write it at all. This is even more important in stories with more than one primary character. The characters intersect: One may open a door in one part of your narrative, just as another closes a door someplace else. You can't make these connections work without a clear time line.

Once you gain command of the chronology, you must find a frame for the story so the reader can understand it. You can't just write about football. You can follow H. G. Bissinger's example in *Friday Night Lights*. He picked one small town, one high school, and one football season. The more complex the story, the simpler the frame must be. The more macroscopic the theme, the more microscopic the frame you should choose.

Think cinematically. Transform the story's important events into scenes. For readers to lose themselves inside your story, you must choose scene details and dialogue very carefully. Your characters must talk to one another, not only to you. And they shouldn't just *talk* to one another but scream, whisper, curse, and flirt. People care about the facts that appear in the newspaper because of the river of emotion that runs beneath them. Emotion is essential.

Don't rush to the bottom line. In 2000, Anne Hull, Sue Carlton, and I wrote a serial narrative about a murder trial in real time. The narrative was the *St. Petersburg Times*'s primary coverage of that important local trial. On the next to last day, the jury deliberated all day. The defendant, a fifteen-year-old girl accused of killing her mother, sat in a holding cell. By regular news standards only one thing happened all day: The jury sent out a note around 5:00 P.M. asking to go home for the night. Our editors learned this and said, "Today's story will be really short, right?" *Wrong*.

The waiting held great power. We wrote about what the families of the victim and defendant said to each other, what the lawyers did, and—most important—what the defendant did as she waited in her cold, stinking cell with nothing to read but the graffiti on the walls.

Her lawyers went in every hour or so just to check on her. We asked them to write down some of the graffiti. The defendant, the lawyers, and the families were all waiting. We made the readers wait, too.

The story's ending must bring a payoff. If the story can't end on a hopeful note, it must at least offer the reader new understanding. After readers have stuck with the serial for several days, an utterly bleak ending is too little payoff for their investment. This can limit the sorts of stories that are likely to make successful serial narratives.

Every story contains an *engine*: the unanswered question that keeps the reader going. The engine is always a simple question, some version of *What happens next?* Think carefully about the stories around you and ask yourself: *What's the engine?* It is *not* the story's topic or its theme; it is the raw power that makes the story *go*. The engine of the movie *Jaws* is: Who ends up as a shark snack? You can choose any road, destination, or focus for your story, but the engine is intrinsic to it. The story already contained its engine when you chose to follow it. Your job as the writer is to identify and understand the engine so you can harness it.

I wrote the series "South of Heaven" about a year in the life of several high school students. The engine was simple: Would this character drop out? Would that character make it to graduation without cracking up? The engines were embedded in the characters' lives.

For another series I followed a group of children through the two years they spent in preschool. The mother of one of the children died of leukemia halfway through the two-year period. The story's engine became how the teachers helped the little girl grieve and begin healing as she continued what she needed to learn. I realized that the purpose of preschool is not to prepare children for kindergarten but to prepare them for *life*.

The serial narrative's power comes from the very fact that it unfolds gradually. In that sense, serials resemble life. Most important events don't begin, unfold, and end in one day. They take time. When a story takes time, it enters our lives in a way that is different from something that can be consumed in one sitting. If the reader can't get to the ending immediately, if the story lingers beyond the cycle of a single day and night, something powerful happens. We go to sleep at night with the characters and their problems in our brains, still unfolding, unresolved. They seep inside our consciousness and enter our dreams. When we wake up the next morning, they are still living inside us.

Care and Feeding of Editors and Writers

JACQUI BANASZYNSKI

I became an editor about ten years ago. Before that I spent nearly twenty years as an insecure, overachieving, sometimes even bratty reporter. It never occurred to me that the mission to "challenge authority" stopped at the newsroom door, so challenge I did.

Early in my career I wrapped myself in Christmas lights to protest the ban on newsroom Christmas trees and stood on a desk, blinking. Longtime friends swear I called one of my first assigning editors a "persnickety little sh**." (We have since become good friends.) During the 1970s' battles for women's rights, I presented a managing editor with a personal flowchart for every woman in the newsroom so he would never again have to ask whether any of us were "on the rag" if we happened to be in a testy mood. And then there was the time I marched into the executive editor's office, threw the morning paper on his desk, and jabbed at the front page. The top devoted five columns to a hockey tournament win and one column to a crucial decision about RU486, the "morning-after" pill. "Who's the dumb SOB who okayed this page?" I railed. His calm reply: "Well, that dumb SOB would be me."

Clearly, I'm an expert on how *not* to work with editors.

But after years of trial and error (mostly their trial, my error), I've also learned a bit about how to work *with* them. Good editors are godsends. They are backstoppers and butt savers and problem solvers. Every day an editor negotiates countless logistical minefields that reporters seldom worry about: how to balance finite resources between breaking news and enterprise reporting; what to do when the Saturday police reporter calls in sick; how to secure good images for a not-very-visual story assignment. And then there's managing a flock of prickly writer personalities—every one of them different and in some way demanding.

It took me too long to figure all that out. Still, thanks to those who put up with me, I did. I had spent years blaming some editor for holding me back, for not knowing I was afraid of failing, for not having perfectly tuned ears. But about fifteen years into my career, after I inherited a new editor, I walked into his office and handed him a document. "This is my owner's manual," I said. "I call it 'The Care and Feeding of a Banaszynski.'" It was my guide to how best to manage me, based on a bit of reporting on, well, *me*. It was made up of two simple lists: *Do* and *Don't*. If the editor followed the Do list, I would be loyal, productive, and his best advocate in the newsroom. (Example: Tell me once a week you're glad I work here and make me believe it.) But follow the Don't list, and I'd have to hunt him down in the dead of a Minnesota winter night with a snowplow and block his garage door. Or, worse, I wouldn't do my best work. (Top of that list: Don't gasp at the length of my story until after you've read it.)

Then I asked him to write his own manual for me. It took him a long time to finish, perhaps because writers so rarely ask their editors such questions as *What do you need from* me? *What are* you *up against? How can* I *best manage* you?

Without planning it, we were creating a contract—one that we returned to whenever things got snarly. When I became an editor myself, I tried to do the same with the writers I worked with: *Here's my operating manual. What's yours?*

Caring for Editors

Writers: Think of your primary editor as your first reader. As the reporter you are the story's expert, the translator between the specialists and the readership. Your editor can help you translate better, asking the questions that readers will ask. Use your editor as a sounding board. Take her out for a beer and tell her what you have learned through your reporting. Her instinctive response will tell you what's worth writing about and what isn't.

Think of your newsroom as a beat and your editor as your most important source. Talk to him, listen to him, be patient with him, meet him on his terms, and nurture the relationship.

Caring for Writers

Editors: There is no such thing as too much or overly constructive feedback for a writer. Most editors are very good at telling writers what's wrong with their copy. Too few help them come up with ideas for improving it.

Think of each reporter you work with in terms of one-year investments. Match the complexity of the assignment to the writer's skills. Raise the bar a little at a time. Each year choose three skills you want the writer to focus on, or that she wants to develop. Support story assignments that will strengthen those skills.

Give the writer "edit memos" on story drafts whenever you can. Cite three things the writer did especially well and three things you want him to tackle in a rewrite. Be specific: "Your sourcing is deep and transparent. I really trust your reporting." "Try to avoid intransitive verbs; they slow down the narrative."

Each month do a "Magic Marker exercise" with each of your writers. Take five of the writer's stories and choose one of her writing habits: overuse of adverbs, poor attribution, excessive dependent clauses. Using a highlighter, underline examples in all five stories. Review them with the writer, encouraging her to focus on that one writing issue in her next story. (Don't forget to highlight the positive habits, too.)

The editor-writer relationship is like any other primary relationship; it can be as difficult and messy as a marriage. I believe in a "seven-of-ten" rule: Of the ten things you most want from a boss, life partner, job, or house, you will get seven if you are smart and lucky, and work at it. Don't lament the missing three, because here's the deal: You can change your job or your partner or your house to get those other three things, but overall you still won't have more than seven.

No editor can be everything to a writer. Some editors are puzzle masters, good at figuring how to arrange the pieces of a story and identify the holes. Others are excellent wordsmiths or good handholders, or they maneuver well through newsroom politics. Few, if any, are naturals at everything the job demands.

That's where the care-and-feeding manual comes in. Writers need to determine which seven things they really need from their primary editor and which they can do without—or safely get from someone else. And editors need to let go of territory. Give what you can to best help your writers, including permission for them to get help from others who *can* meet their particular needs.

PART VIII

NARRATIVE
IN THE NEWS
ORGANIZATION

Introduction

MARK KRAMER AND WENDY CALL

Are the reporters at your local newspaper friendly? Probably, but do they sound personable in print? Here is an example from our hometown newspaper: "Four people were killed in two vehicle rollovers caused by speeding, including three children who were crammed in the cargo area of an overcrowded sport utility vehicle that flipped on Interstate 495 in Westford, police said yesterday."

Friends don't speak that way to one another. Even strangers sharing information in the crowd standing near the accident scene don't. The reporter who wrote that passage is probably an articulate, thoughtful person, appropriately saddened by those deaths, who was given only a few minutes to write a news brief. The resulting piece sounds official but not companionable. Newspaper reporters are generally trained to write with a one-size-fits-all efficiency of voice on the premise that "news voice" goes along with dispassion and so-called objectivity.

The acceptable range of tone in newspaper writing is not broad, but there *is* a range. The standard voice of the newspaper can be made friendly and real. A voice that is authoritative *and* companionable is good for circulation. That voice also enables deeper discussion of complicated ideas and events.

When there were thirty newspapers in Boston—at least one for each ethnicity, neighborhood, education level, and faith—they enjoyed automatic intimacy. Each writer knew precisely who would read his words. Now that our city has two daily newspapers (one more than many cities have), the journalist must work harder and more consciously to develop relationships with her diverse readers.

Some small-town newspapers maintain their intimacy. The writing might not always be elegant, but it's good company. The reporters know their readers' concerns with specifics: what's happening at the school construction site, progress on the search for a new road-crew manager, and who attended Mary and George Gleason's fifty-seventh anniversary party at Rose's Tea Room.

Many narrative reporters have worked hard at humanizing the newspaper's bureaucratic default voice. The change in tone allows writers to go where they couldn't before. Why should an individual reporter take the risk? At the 2002 Nieman Conference Jan Winburn, who has edited several Pulitzer Prize–winning stories, explained:

> Per capita, Baltimore is the most violent city in America. Every day in our newspaper we record murder and mayhem. On our editorial page we run a chalk drawing of a body with a number in it. You wouldn't know from those chalk drawings the story of a boy who was turning his life around but got caught up with his old friends. There are stories behind the numbers. Narrative writing tells those stories. Many important human stories never make our news pages. We don't write enough about the wildernesses that individuals and communities enter and emerge from—if not whole, at least courageously. When we can write intimately about those stories, we give our readers a more complete picture of their world.

In this section of *Telling True Stories*, three editors, five writers, and one photographer give tips for creating a whole world within the confines of the newspaper.

Beginning in Narrative
WALT HARRINGTON

Yes, we are fish wrap. We are on the bottom of the birdcage. We are only as good as our next story. Yet, as journalists, we are also the "rememberers" for our tribe, as the journalist Pete Hamill puts it. Newspaper and magazine journalists play a cultural role. We are real-time anthropologists, keeping a daily record of our culture. Historians go back to the newspapers from one hundred years ago; they study the advertisements, obituaries, and photographs to understand the past.

As rememberers, we do a very good job of recording many things: yesterday's weather, Michael Jordan's amazing 69-point game against Cleveland, insurgency in Peru, Monica Lewinsky under the desk, celebrities getting married, celebrities getting divorced, the dollar going up and down, the death of an old man in Omaha, the birth of a baby in Taos. It is an honor to have this place in our culture. Our audience, our fellow members of the tribe, allows us this luxury. They are often grateful for our work and reward us for it.

Still, there are other things we don't remember very well. We don't, for instance, record or remember very well the feeling that a child has when she receives her first communion, the feeling that a farmer has when he latches the barn door for the last time on his bankrupt farm, the feeling that a schoolteacher has when a bad student becomes a good student, the feeling that a father has when he buries his firstborn son.

What I call *intimate journalism*—in-depth, sophisticated, serious journalism—records the acts of ordinary people and their everyday lives, something all too rare in our profession. These stories record the behaviors, motives, feelings, faiths, attitudes, grievances, hopes, fears, accomplishments, and aspirations of people as they seek meaning and purpose in their own lives. They help people understand their places in the world.

Intimate journalism has a simple goal: to understand other people's worlds from the inside out and to portray people as they understand themselves. I once did a story about a family whose teenage boy had committed suicide two years earlier. I tried to explain to the family the sort of story I wanted to do, how deep the questioning would be. The father listened and listened, and then finally said, "So, you want to know what I think when I say my prayers in a quiet room." *Yes.* The question that drives intimate journalism is, in its simplest form: *How do people live, and what do they value?*

When I started as a journalist, I would cover an event, return to the newsroom, and write the article. The next day I would read my piece in the newspaper and realize there was little relationship between what I had experienced and what I had just read. That bothered me. What was missing? I put myself on a program of reading what I had missed before: fine journalism, travel literature, and great realistic fiction.

My interest in intimate journalism grew from my graduate school background in sociology. That training led me to think of feature stories not as little throwaway brighteners for the newspaper but as case studies. There is a subversive quality to that outlook, and I kept it to myself. Imagine if my city editor at the *Washington Post* had asked me, "Okay, Harrington, what kind of journalism do you want to do?" And I had said, "Well, I want to evoke the feeling of a lived experience." He would have thought me some kind of nut. My ambition for many years was a private one; the work had to speak for itself.

Becoming a storytelling journalist doesn't happen in one fell swoop. John McPhee has a famous collection of stories called *Pieces of the Frame*. The title encapsulates how aspiring intimate journalists should think about their work. Cut one piece of the frame, sand it, finish it, master it, and move on to the next piece. Eventually, you will learn to create an entire frame. Start simple.

Take advantage of stories that let you work on small pieces of the frame. Don't start with massively conceptual stories that require mastery of many skills. Don't destine yourself for failure. Master the frame one piece at a time. Over time, they will join together in a seamless whole. Mike Sager, who used to write for the *Washington Post* and now writes for *Esquire*, once said to me, "There is no reason why character, action and theme have to all come together at the end of a story, but in twenty years I have never done a story where it didn't happen."

How can you get there? Learn to crave criticism. Develop a persona that makes other people willing to criticize you. It's a double challenge: You must learn how to take criticism and use it, but you must also learn when to resist criticism. You don't want to lose touch with the voice and spirit that you bring to the story in the first place.

A Brief History of Narrative in Newspaper

JACK HART

Narrative journalism is hardly new; examples of it date to the earliest days of English-language journalism. Even the inverted pyramid, which we think of as a relatively modern development, has roots reaching back further than the first printed newspapers. Consider this report from the *Fuggerzeitungen*, the handwritten newsletters passed from city to city by the members of a large commercial family active throughout Central Europe in the sixteenth century: "Walpura Hausmannin, evil and wretched woman, now imprisoned and in chains has, under solicitous questioning, as well as torture, confessed her witchcraft and made the following admissions."

It is a classic inverted-pyramid lede, written in 1587, with the same who-what-where-when-and-why emphasis that we expect from a modern traffic accident or burglary report. On the other hand, note this story by Ned Ward from a 1699 issue of the *London Spy*: "Thus we prattled away our time, 'till we came in sight of a noble pile of a building. . . . I conceived it to be my Lord Mayor's palace. . . . [My] companion smiled at my innocent conjecture, and informed me that this was Bedlam, a hospital for mad folk."

And so continues the tale, a neat little explanatory narrative in the spirit of John McPhee. Ward and his perhaps apocryphal companion stroll through London's insane asylum. They note this and that as they go, giving readers a firsthand look at Bedlam, an institution with a name that has become a synonym for confusion and chaos.

Louis Snyder and Richard Morris's wonderful anthology, *A Treasury of Great Reporting*, the source of the examples used here, documents the continuing presence of both reports and narratives as the twin pillars of modern journalism.

The dominance of the realistic novel in the nineteenth century created a bridge between literature and journalism, and the era's narrative masters routinely crossed it. Walt Whitman, Mark Twain, and Stephen Crane all wrote for newspapers. Charles Dickens submitted "Traveling Letters" to the *London Daily News*, which in 1846 published a Dickens story with this enticing narrative lede: "On Friday, as he was dining with the other prisoners, they came and told him he was to be beheaded the next morning, and took him away."

Richard Harding Davis, a newspaper journalist largely forgotten in the twentieth century but celebrated in the nineteenth, was the son of an accomplished short-story writer. Polished, mass-market narrative technique powered not only his fiction but also the wartime dispatches that made him famous. World War I, his last great campaign, gave him the material for his most frequently quoted narrative lede:

> The entrance of the German army into Brussels has lost the human quality. It was lost as soon as the three soldiers who led the army bicycled into the Boulevard du Regent and asked the way to

the Gare du Nord. When they passed, the human note passed with them.

What came after them, and 24 hours later is still coming, is not men marching, but a force of nature.

That sort of literary crossover continued into the first half of the twentieth century. Ernest Hemingway, Damon Runyon, John Steinbeck, and others used the techniques of realism—still the most popular form of fiction—in both their fiction and their newspaper writing.

Ben Hecht—whose play *The Front Page* (written with Charles MacArthur) crystallized the stereotype of the 1920s newshound—began one of his best-known newspaper stories in a style indistinguishable from the era's short fiction: "Carl Wanderer, freshly shaved and his brown suit neatly pressed, stood looking over the back porch of his home at 4732 North Campbell Avenue. His wife, who was murdered last night by a holdup man in the doorway downstairs, lay in their bedroom."

The narrative tradition continued through World War II. Newspaper luminaries such as Jack Lait and Ernie Pyle exploited the form to near universal acclaim, but already a rift had appeared between the more abstract, just-the-facts-ma'am style of report writing and more literary, narrative-style storytelling. The fault line appeared as early as 1896, when Richard Harding Davis recognized it in his short story, "The Red Cross Girl."

The story, which takes place in a newsroom, concerns a reporter dispatched to cover the opening of a convalescent center. He fails to produce the expected report on the ceremonies with prominent mention of the philanthropists who had paid for the center. Instead, he hands in a more literary account focusing on a Red Cross volunteer.

The copy editor protests: "It's an editorial, an essay, a spring poem." It was most assuredly not a newspaper story. The managing editor nonetheless decides to run the piece, causing a protest that echoes in twenty-first-century newsrooms. "But," sputters the copy editor, "it's not news."

As is so often the case, the copy editor's view ultimately prevails. By the mid-1950s, bureaucratization, uniformity, and the it's-not-news ethic had driven most narrative storytelling out of North American newspapers. It survived in only a few corners of U.S. culture, most notably in *The New Yorker,* where James Thurber, Brendan Gill, Lillian Ross, Joseph Mitchell, and John Hersey guarded the flickering flame.

It burned long enough to eventually set afire a new generation of nonfiction writers: Tom Wolfe, Joan Didion, Norman Mailer, Hunter Thompson, and others. Ultimately, it would return to newspapers, where it had been such a lively presence more than 250 years earlier.

Nurturing Narrative in the Newsroom

JACK HART

Most newsrooms lack a storytelling lexicon. We call *everything* a story whether or not it contains any true story elements. However, a specific language of story is well understood in Hollywood. We need to bring some of that understanding to news editors' desks. The *Oregonian* publishes a monthly in-house newsletter called *Second Takes,* in which we review our own writing. In its early years much of the publication was devoted to teaching our newsroom staff the language of story.

It's a language that newspapers once spoke. The Dark Ages of newspaper journalism came in the mid-twentieth century with the rise of the corporate newspaper; all those creative individuals were banished from the newsroom. We can revive this creative force; definitions for a newsroom storyteller's lexicon are part of a beginning (see "A Storyteller's Lexicon" on page 235).

If your news organization's top management isn't narrative-friendly, find a safe haven further down. All it takes is one determined writer and a sympathetic editor who controls a little space in the newspaper. I began working on narrative writing at the *Oregonian* while I was editor of our Sunday magazine. After you publish a short narrative story, collect all the positive responses you receive; file the e-mails and save the voice mail messages. They will help show that readers appreciate narrative writing. For the top brass at your newspaper that means that narrative sells newspapers.

Regardless of how nicely it reads or how well it sells, narrative must be, above all, accurate. Here are some organizational ways to ensure that it is.

Early Editor Involvement

Make sure that editor-reporter conversations happen before, during, and after the reporting process. Part of the reporter's job is to make sure the editor understands what's happening. Talking with the editor about the story can help it develop shape and meaning. The editor's job is to ask questions that help the reporter identify themes and determine what additional reporting is needed. Editors may want to visit important settings or meet key sources to avoid adding inaccuracies to the reporter's material during the editing process.

Information Management

Carefully organize all the notes, background material, and other documentation gathered while doing long-form narrative reporting. Consider tape-recording and transcribing interviews to overcome the accuracy problems caused by stale notes and overwhelming quantities of material.

Feedback Loops

Once the story begins to emerge from the material, review key scenes and technical descriptions with key sources. Check not only for factual accuracy but for nuances that reveal the ways characters view their worlds. As issues arise during editing, call sources again and clarify matters. Double-check technical terms. Ask about titles, sequencing, and anything else in question.

Cooperation with Other Departments

Involve copy editors early, making sure they understand the story's theme and underlying structure. Involve them in the goals for engaging readers with the story's emotional impact. Discuss the tone, sequencing, and dramatic qualities of the story with designers, too. Make sure the design works well with the copy and photographs. Give photographers and photo editors early story outlines so they can plan their shoots accordingly. Make sure that writers, photographers, editors, and photo editors all see and approve cutlines, and that those elements don't give away a surprise story ending.

Collaborative Polishing

The editor and reporter should sit side by side during the final stage of the editing process, with the editor reading the copy aloud and the reporter approving and improving changes.

Prosecution-Style Editing

Editors should constantly ask, *How do we know this?* They should weigh the evidence and seek more where needed every step of the way.

Clear Review Process

Print separate copies for editors, writers, photographers, and senior editors. Collect all questions and corrections on a master version. Do the final round of editing side by side to deal with everything
raised by all these readers.

Narrative must be accurate, and it must not be forced. Once we
have an idea for a narrative story, we look at the ingredients and ask:
*Is there a protagonist? Is there a complication? Is there a sequence of events
that leads to some kind of dramatic tension? Is that tension resolved?* When
the answer is no, we don't force it. It is better to publish no narrative
writing than bad examples of it.

A Storyteller's Lexicon

JACK HART

Action Lines and Dramatic Tension

Anecdote: A staple of magazine nonfiction; a short account that
has its own action line. It usually contributes more to exposition and
characterization than to advancing the main action line.

Flashback: An interruption in the narrative chronology to describe a
scene that took place earlier in time. The second scene in a story that
began *in media res* (see below) is almost always a flashback.

Flash-forward: A scene that jumps ahead in the narrative chronology. It is much less frequent than a flashback, in part because of the
tense problems it causes.

Foreshadowing: Hinting at something significant that lies ahead in
the text.

Full Circle Ending: The most satisfying story ending, it gives the
sense that the story has come back to where it began. The structure of
the first and last paragraphs can provide this sense of satisfaction.

Full Dialogue: Speech that unfolds in the real time of the story between two or more of the characters.

Half Dialogue: The words of one participant interspersed with narrative.

In Media Res: Beginning a story in the middle of the action rather than at the beginning of the chronology. The term refers to the point at which the story's outcome hangs in the balance.

Internal Monologue: The narrator tells the reader in third person what the character is thinking at a particular point in the action. Internal monologue made conventional journalists uncomfortable when the New Journalists introduced it in the 1960s. Now it's a staple for successful narrative nonfiction writers.

Kicker Quote: A punchy quotation that ends a paragraph, creating a sense of finality and clearing the way for what follows in the narrative. The rhythm of these quotes is important, and the best ones end with a monosyllable.

Ominous Object: An item that a writer lingers on to give it greater importance. Chekhov's shotgun (see below) is a classic example.

Participative Dialogue: Discussion in which the storyteller participates.

Sentence Forms: Transitive verbs advance the action line by depicting movement. Linking verbs, such as forms of "to be," slow action down because they merely define.

Shotgun Rule: Anton Chekhov wrote that if a play opens with a shotgun hanging above a mantel, the gun must be fired before the end of the third act. In other words, every detail must do some work: help develop character, provide background information, or—most important— advance the action line.

Speculative Action: Filling out an action line with an intelligent guess about what might have happened, being careful to note the speculation to the reader.

Vignette: An anecdote without a punch line.

Scene Setting

Collective Details: Elements that characterize a group of people or objects rather than individuals.

Establishing Shots: Wide-angle views of a scene used to give a general sense of the setting before the writer focuses on a specific location.

Figurative Language: Similes, metaphors, allusions, or personifications that help set scenes by translating unfamiliar aspects of a scene into the familiar.

Texture: Clashing elements that help characterize a scene.

Thematic Details: Elements that develop central story themes. For example, in his famed profile of a *New York Times* obituary writer, Gay Talese noted that on his train ride to work he passed billboards advertising funeral parlors.

Characterization

Anecdotes and Vignettes: Snippets of action in a dramatic narrative that elucidate character.

Climax: The point at which the story's complication is resolved.

Complication: The development that disturbs the status quo, forcing the protagonist to react and thereby setting the story in motion. It can be physical or psychological and usually produces some sort of conflict.

Denouement: Falling action or the wrapping up of loose ends after the story climax.

Dialect: Dialogue that reveals distinct patterns of speech. Good dialect is difficult to do well. It is often just suggested, using the character's speech patterns only occasionally in the story.

Direct Characterization: Abstract observations about a character's personality or appearance.

Exposition: Devices used to inform readers of necessary background information. It is most effective when blended into the action line. It typically shows up in subordinate clauses, modifiers, appositives, and other incidental text elements.

False Climax: A technique in which the complication reasserts itself after the writer has led the readers to believe that it has been resolved. It is used to increase dramatic tension.

Indirect Characterization: The selection of external details that reveal character by showing rather than telling.

Physical Description: Details of appearance that suggest character traits or help bring the image of the character to life in the reader's mind.

Plot Point #1: When the protagonist first encounters the complication, which is usually at the end of the opening section.

Plot Point #2: When the protagonist's insight or change resolves the complication of the story.

Protagonist: The character driving the story line, who is not necessarily the story's hero or heroine.

Rising Action: The part of the story in which the protagonist becomes increasingly engaged with the complication. The protagonist often struggles with the complication and fails, raising the level of dramatic tension and setting up the climax.

Status Indicators: Details that reveal a character's place in the social order.

Point of View and Tone

Angle of Approach: The entry point the writer uses for the story.

Atmospheric Detail: A feature specifically selected to create mood.

Choice of Person: The perspective from which the story is told: first, second, or third person.

Level of Diction: The degree of formality of a story's language. Unlike the writer's *voice*, which is relatively constant, the diction may shift, depending on the subject and the writer's goal.

Psychological Distance: The separation the narrator maintains from the protagonist. *Close psychological distance* puts the reader inside the character's head. *Middle distance* steps back a bit, describing what happens to the protagonist as a close observer. *Remote distance* describes only what a stranger could see at some remove.

Stance: Where the writer places the tripod that holds the mental camera used for viewing the action. Typical journalistic distance is like a hanging balloon, in which the writer seems to be observing the action from a spot somewhere about twenty feet over the characters' heads.

Story Framing: The value sets and objectives that the writer brings to the story.

Voice: The overall personality of the writer as perceived through the text.

Structure

Character Sequencing: The order and timing used by the writer to introduce key characters. It creates story structure because it influences the type and placement of scenes as well as the direction of narrative.

Parallel Structure: Creating similarities in structural forms as a way to make larger points.

Scenic Structure: A story constructed scene by scene, each one unfolding in a specific place and time. A typical three-thousand-word story might contain three to five scenes.

Topical Structure: Ordering the story by subject matter rather than by story line.

Typographic Indicators: Devices that break the text into structural elements. The star-line break is the traditional indicator of a major break between scenes or topics.

Unifying Devices: Repetition of key details throughout the structure as a way of holding the story together.

Narrative as a Daily Habit

LANE DEGREGORY

Colleagues tell me, "All the people you write about are kind of weird, Lane," but I think of my subjects as ordinary people. I became a journalist to write about *all* kinds of people.

I usually write one or two short pieces each week. The longest story I've ever written took ten months to report and write; I continued publishing daily stories the whole time.

Most of my stories run in the features section; I'm the one in the newsroom who has to write the obligatory Christmas and Mother's Day stories. I even had to write a Christmas feature about people having their photos taken with their pets. Here are thirteen ways to find great story ideas so you can avoid writing about doggie Santa pictures.

Tip #1: Talk to strangers.

Be a nosy neighbor. Sit by the old woman on the swing. Walk the docks. Chat with people everywhere you go. I once chatted with the gravedigger while I waited for the family to arrive at a funeral I was covering. "This is a boring funeral," he told me. "We have one tomorrow where the man is being buried in a coffeepot." That man's sons and daughters decided to do that because he constantly asked, "Who's got my coffee?" I returned to the cemetery the next day and wrote a one-day story about it.

Tip #2: Play hooky.

Many of my stories come to me when I'm supposed to be at the office. The second week I lived in Florida, while driving to work, I saw a big sign that read FLORIDA FUR. I just *had* to know who would run a furrier in *Florida.* I went to the warehouse and interviewed an old man who had come from New York and set up a humidity-controlled warehouse where northerners could store their furs.

Tip #3: Read the walls.

I read everything everywhere I go—free drugstore papers, bulletin boards at the Laundromat, and especially the classifieds. One day an ad in the paper read, "To the girl with a face like a flower. Our eyes met for just a few seconds as you left Kathy's Deli last Wednesday around noon. I was the tall guy standing by one of the small tables in front of the deli. If you see this note, call me."

I called him and wrote a story about his efforts to find that woman. He never found her, but my article won him about forty other dates.

Tip #4: Eat lunch alone.

Sometimes I'll sit in a restaurant or on a park bench with a book propped in front of me just to listen to nearby conversations. After I hear something interesting, I'll say, "Excuse me, but I overheard you. . . . Can I talk to you about that?" People are usually receptive.

Tip #5: Get a life.

Watch out for interesting stories that you find in your own day-to-day life. A friend of mine teaches motorcycle riding at a Harley-Davidson dealership. He told me about a woman in her fifties struggling to ride a huge $130,000 Harley. Her husband had committed suicide a week after he bought the motorcycle, saddling her with the payments. She was trying to decide whether to sell the motorcycle or embrace the chance to experience something new.

Tip #6: Ignore important people.

Most of the time I find it boring to write about important people; others have already written it all. I was assigned the Miss Florida Pageant, the worst assignment. I was supposed to focus on the local contestant, Miss St. Petersburg, trying for the third time to become Miss Florida. I ended up writing about her wardrobe consultant, a gay diner waiter who was savoring his moment in the limelight.

Sometimes important people ignore me, and then I'll gladly write about them. Darryl Strawberry had been in the news a lot in Florida.

I wondered why his wife, Charise, continued to stand by him. She refused to talk to me, but the story had been scheduled so I couldn't back out. What could I do? I read everything I could find about her and then followed her around for three days, through one of her husband's court cases. I even borrowed a friend's pickup truck so I looked like a contractor and drove into the gated community where she lived. I wrote about how she reacted to things happening around her even though I couldn't interview her.

Tip #7: Celebrate losers.

Too much is written about people whose dreams come true. People facing failure or setbacks are far more fascinating. The tension is built into the story: *Where do they go from here? How have the crises changed their lives?*

I wrote about a man who tried to start an ecological farm and intentional community in central Florida. He had bought a big piece of land and put ads in an alternative newspaper looking for community members. The only people who replied were drunks, drug addicts, and fugitives from the law. His wife, who was supporting the venture financially, gave him just one more month to get the community going. My story followed him through that month as he faced the question: *What do I do when my lifelong dream doesn't work out?*

Tip # 8: Wonder "Who would ever _____?"

Ask yourself questions like: Who empties the septic tanks of Porta-Potties? Who cleans up under the bleachers after a Bucs game at Raymond James Stadium? I wrote an article about a public health department nurse known as "Momma V"—that's *V* for *vasectomy*. She had received a grant and made Pinellas County, Florida, the nation's top county for vasectomies done in a year.

Tip #9: Hang out at bars.

Everyone tells stories in bars. Even if you don't drink, you can sit there with a Diet Coke and listen to things you would never hear in the newsroom, at the city council meeting, or even out on the sidewalk.

Tip #10: Give everyone your phone number.

I usually wear my reporter tag. People stop me and say, "Oh, you work for the paper." I always say, "Yes, I do. Do you have any stories?" I hand out my card everywhere: the vet, the subway, the gas station. People do call, sometimes years later, with story tips. My e-mail and phone number now appear at the bottom of all my stories. That also generates a huge number of tips, some of them good ones.

Tip #11: Work holidays.

Somehow I became the person expected to do the holiday stories in my bureau. I turned it into a personal challenge: What would I do *this* Valentine's Day? I started thinking about holidays several months in advance, since I knew the stories would be dumped in my lap.

For the Fourth of July I wrote a story answering the question: How can there be so many fireworks stands when fireworks are illegal in Florida? It turns out that the buyers just had to sign a statement saying, "I'm only going to use the fireworks for blasting around fish hatcheries to get rid of annoying birds."

Tip #12: Grab the stories nobody else wants.

Those assignments that make colleagues roll their eyes can turn into truly interesting stories. We received a press release announcing, "Clubhouse for mentally ill opens." I was the only reporter who would take the story. A group of mentally ill people who attended the same day-treatment program started the place. Their program kicked them out between 4:00 and 7:00 in the afternoon so the staff could clean and prepare dinner. They didn't have anywhere to go, and some had been arrested for loitering. I followed them as they prepared for their grand opening and wrote about their excitement and the deep meaning the clubhouse held for them.

Tip #13: Look for the bruise on the apple.

I spent several weeks reporting on a group of orphaned Russian children who had come to Tampa. Each child had been assigned to a family for a few weeks in the hope that the family would adopt the child. I followed one couple as they readied a boy's room and bought clothes and a Scooby-Doo toothbrush for him. They even went to watch their niece and nephew being bathed to learn how to do it. The couple was in their fifties and really wanted children. In the end, they didn't get their little boy because of paperwork problems.

I had to make a decision: Should I write about the forty families who adopted children or this one couple who didn't? I wrote about that couple and their heartbreak because the bruise held my interest more than the shine on the rest of the apple.

When we open our eyes and ears, stop being snobs, realize we haven't heard it all before, and allow ourselves to witness other

worlds with honest wonder, stories emerge. Sometimes, like the blue-
bird of happiness, the best ones appear in our own backyards.

Building a Narrative Team
MARIA CARRILLO

Writers wanted. You'd rather be out and about, turning up stories in unlikely places, than sitting in the office. You're insatiably
curious. You notice the details that make readers see, laugh, cry,
think. And, of course, you write like a dream.

Boy, do we have a job for you.

Here's the deal: We want to bring together a storytelling team
of three or four reporters from among the paper's strongest writers, to go in search of great stories.

That was the job posting that appeared in the newsroom of the
Virginian-Pilot, a 200,000-circulation paper in Norfolk, Virginia. We
wanted ideas. We wanted talent. We wanted people who weren't going to sit around the office, who were experienced but not drained.
We wanted everything.

That's how our narrative team was born. The decision to create it followed closed-door debates among senior editors about the merits of the
idea and whether the newspaper could afford it. Looking back, the decision seems remarkable—made in the midst of downsizing at a newspaper that had a spotty commitment to feature writing through most of
the 1990s. Twice in the seven years before our team's formation, the *Pilot* had created features staffs—one called the Flex Team, another Real
Life. They shared an approach: Both were to write for every section of the
paper, to bring a writerly voice to news, business, and sports stories as
well as traditional features. They also shared a fate: Neither lasted long.

Those earlier teams were axed for some reasons unique to the *Pilot*
and for others familiar to many news organizations: eroding political support from newsroom leaders, misapprehension by leaders as
to the time and labor required for effective storytelling, and Stone
Age notions of how a successful news article should read.

After that, a "features just happen" philosophy took over. A veteran on my narrative team, who had lived through the earlier team

initiatives, joked that the *Pilot* started to read like "something that was good for you." Features became mere spin-offs of the regular news beats. The paper had lost its attention to craft. Our editor, Kay Tucker Addis, believed that a group devoted to good writing would not only bring great stories to our readers but would also set an example for the rest of the staff. She wanted to create a home for veteran writers, those who didn't wish to become editors but didn't want to keep covering city council meetings, either.

I arrived at the *Pilot* during these conversations. After two months I was given the job of choosing and leading the team. Sixteen people applied to be team members, including a business reporter, a metro editor, a military beat reporter, someone from the North Carolina news bureau, and a sportswriter. They turned in résumés, clips, and cover letters. I was new to the paper, so I sat down with each candidate, trying to get to know them and discern who the storytellers were. We narrowed the pool to seven and eventually chose four. Seven years later we still have a four-person team.

I hadn't just considered the applicants' clips but also their ideas. Could they see stories? Narrative writers tend to see possibilities that other writers don't—the story behind the story or the one a bit off to the side. I chose people who *wanted* constructive criticism and who could share it with the others.

I added one more criterion: I gave each of them a color. I wanted diversity of personality. My most intense and opinionated writer, definitely a red. I also chose a blue (thoughtful, curious), a lavender (creative, fearless), and a pink (energetic and emotional). The pink left the paper, and we picked a yellow (eager, empathetic). It has proved a powerful blend of characters, interests, and talents.

At first, narrative team appointments had limited duration. After two years people could reapply and receive three-year terms. Now they can stay on as long as they want. We have invested in them; we want to keep them around.

Our team is a little laboratory of narrative thinkers constantly hunting for stories. We meet weekly to discuss stories we've produced and study good examples from elsewhere. We have become much better at sensing what will and won't work.

Team members make suggestions to our beat writers and try to be gracious and collaborative with the rest of the staff. The team has set an example for other writers and has greatly improved the paper.

Resentment lingers, of course. Members of this kind of special team are bound to be labeled prima donnas, and they *do* get time and space that most of our reporters aren't afforded. Last year, to encourage even more narrative work from other members of the staff, we began a "story sabbatical." Two or three times a year we offer beat reporters a month to pursue one story with my guidance, as a fifth member of my team. The sabbatical has encouraged some ambitious ideas and given those reporters a real taste of what it takes to pull together a narrative story.

Beyond the sabbatical, if other reporters have great ideas, we encourage them to take the initiative and invest the front-end work. Then we help them pursue the project. I work with a lot of other reporters and with their editors who come to me with ideas. I may poke holes in those ideas, but only to strengthen them. We work together all the way through the story process.

My team's stories generally appear on page A1 or in the features section, sometimes on the local section front page, and occasionally in the sports pages. We tell stories that few others at the paper are interested in writing or have the time to do. We react to the news, and we revisit it later. We try to give readers the unexpected—in topic and treatment.

At first our goal was to be in the paper a lot, with both short and long pieces. We tested ourselves to make sure we could tell a quick story, use more dialogue, and improve our field reporting.

We cover breaking news, too. When Hurricane Isabel hit, a narrative team member was the lead writer who put together the storm story because we wanted somebody who could tell it well.

I attend the newspaper's budget meetings, and I try to cultivate the culture of narrative across the newsroom. I challenge old and tired approaches. Occasionally, an item in the budget even inspires an idea for the narrative team.

I hold regular sessions that are open to all reporters and editors. We zero in on a specific topic—story endings, for example—and discuss it for an hour over lunch. Sometimes I lead the discussion; other times I recruit someone else to get us started. I help produce an in-house newsletter. At one session a military reporter and a business reporter, both of whom have been at the paper for decades, showed up to hear about storytelling on deadline. I thought, "*Now* I can retire!"

Two Visions, One Series:
A Writer and an Editor
Talk About What They Do

JACQUI BANASZYNSKI AND TOMAS ALEX TIZON

Tomas Alex Tizon: On September 12, 2001, the day after the World Trade Center disaster, a photographer and I hit the road in a rented truck. We spent three weeks traveling from Seattle to New York City and wrote fourteen stories for the *Seattle Times*. The series, called "Crossing America," consisted of reported personal narratives and photographs.

On September 11, I worked on the main news story that ran the next day. That afternoon a couple of editors asked me, "How would you like to go to New York City?" An hour later I received a call from my own editor, Jacqui Banaszynski.

Jacqui Banaszynski: I was in Columbia, Missouri, where I teach part of each week. With the nation's flights grounded, I was stuck in a university bubble, unable to get to the newsroom or home to my family. One of the *Seattle Times*'s political reporters had come up with the basic idea: Go out and discover the "New" America. As we discussed this nontraditional project, it quickly became clear that it wasn't a question of *what* to write or *how* to report it but, rather, *who* should do it. There was one person in the newsroom who was a natural for the assignment. The original reporter, bless his heart, agreed with our decision. So I called Alex.

Tizon: My response was "You want me to do *what*?"

Banaszynski: Alex has a history of not reacting warmly to editors' ideas. Usually when I approached Alex with a story idea, he would take a few days to shape the assignment and then agree to it. But this time he had to be on the road the following morning. We rented a truck for him (no small feat on September 11 with every airport in the country shut down) without his knowing about it since he hadn't yet agreed to do the story.

Tizon: The next day, Wednesday, as Alan Berner and I drove across the Cascade Mountains, I finally called Jacqui and said, "Okay, we'll do it." But Alan and I had no idea *what* to do. Should we should stop and spend a week in one place and write a long story? Or stop in two places? Or write a story every day from a different town? We felt terrified. Alan said, "I'm going as far as the Washington state border, then I'm heading home." That's exactly what he did.

Meanwhile, we had to have our first story to Jacqui by Friday. Our first stop was Ellensberg, a town in central Washington. We brainstormed, making a list of places we could go: a bowling alley, church, shopping mall, City Hall. We decided on a school. We talked with the principal and listened to the students recite the pledge of allegiance. The beginning of that first piece set the tone for the series:

> Seattle to Ellensberg. Beware of visions that come in the middle of a headache, especially when the headache is part of a bigger ache that you can't put your finger on.
>
> It hit first in the stomach as I watched video coverage of the World Trade Center collapsing like a mountain caving in on itself. It pierced the heart as I saw pictures of men and women leaping from the tops of what at one time were the tallest buildings on earth. By the end of Tuesday, September 11, 2001, my head was so crowded with impossible images that it hurt.
>
> A voice said, "Go east." So I am, not entirely sure why.
>
> The journey feels right even in its vagueness. I'm a pacer. When I need to process something, I get up and walk. This will be my form of walking, only I'll do it in a rented Ford Expedition and cover 3,000 miles. Many of you are in the same mental and emotional space I am and I invite you to come with me in spirit across the country. Like true Seattleites we can process this thing together.

I invited the whole city of Seattle to come with me. But what if they didn't?

Banaszynski: Even as Alex and Alan made their list of places to go, editors in the newsroom made their own lists. One editor had a map in his office full of pins. While I dealt with the editors' various opinions, I worked with the graphics department and news desk to develop a logo and headline, and figure out where in the paper to place the series.

Some of the news desk editors protested: "The biggest news story in the history of America is happening, and you want to put some personal piece that you can't describe *on the front page?*"

Yes. That time required journalism that tapped into emotion. I trusted that the photographer and reporter would do that even if none of us knew *how* they would do it.

Tizon: I knew nothing about Jacqui's newsroom debates.

Banaszynski: My conversations with Alex weren't about *where* or *what* but about *tone*. We talked about the series' architecture, about its soul. The idea was *go find America*. I believed the series had to be written personally, yet I had to ensure that the stories were journalism so they would make sense to the other editors and to our readers.

Tizon: Writing in first person wasn't difficult for me. I like the sense that there is a *person* behind the words, an orienting consciousness, even if the word "I" isn't included.

Banaszynski: Younger reporters who want to write first-person journalism or journalism with a strong point of view should keep in mind that Alex spent twenty years learning the tools of the trade before he wrote pieces like this series.

Tizon: After the first piece ran, I received seventy e-mail messages from readers. The personal tone resonated with people's feelings.

Banaszynski: Readers wrote us notes like "I wish I could go with you. I can't, but here are the directions to my aunt's house in North Dakota. I'd like to call ahead and have her make a cherry pie." Those messages helped convince the rest of the newsroom that the series deserved to be on the front page.

As Alex mentioned, the photographer left at the Washington-Idaho border, because of the cost as well as the pressure of other assignments. The photos disappeared after the first two stories. Once I managed to fly from Columbia, Missouri, back to Seattle, I lobbied the photo editor and other top editors each day. I showed them Alex's stories with no photos and said, "Gosh, isn't it too bad our readers can't see this person?" Later, I argued that Alex was such a good writer that readers could practically *see* the people he wrote about even without photos. That's when the photographer rejoined Alex. At that point, readers began responding in even greater numbers.

While Alex traveled without a photographer, it was much harder to get the story on the front page. Conversely, once I carved out front-page space, I had to make sure a story came in to fill it. Several times I called Alex in the evening to tell him I needed a story by eight in the morning. He wrote on his laptop while Alan drove. A few times the managing editor had to step in to ensure that the story remained on the front page.

"Crossing America" became something of a turning point for

the *Seattle Times*. Since then we have published several personal, emotional, intimate stories. Their genesis can be traced back to Alex and Alan's work.

Tizon: Although Jacqui fought to have a photographer with me, I wanted to work alone. Generally, I prefer reporting alone; having someone with me can feel cumbersome. I lost that fight. Still, after I picked Alan up at the Denver airport, I knew that it meant the project had won over the newsroom. The photo department had been the most skeptical about it.

Banaszynski: In the nearly twenty years I worked as a writer, I always wanted to have a photographer with me. Good photographers—and the large majority of them are good—see the world in a way I can't. They offer a knowing pair of eyes uninterrupted by the notebook.

Tizon: Jacqui and I also disagreed about the pace. I wanted to write less often; Jacqui wanted more stories. We finally settled on a story every two to three days. That was manageable, though it meant working sixteen hours each day.

We spent most mornings traveling. Alan did most of the driving while I read background information from the *Seattle Times* researcher as well as anything we could find on the way. Once we arrived someplace, we stopped at a supermarket for coffee and all the local publications we could find. Then we spent the afternoon reporting. I usually slept on it one night, then got up really early and spent one to four hours writing. We would hit the road again and the cycle started over.

Banaszynski: I insisted they go to Oklahoma City. Alex resisted. The story he ended up writing included this:

> On the afternoon we were there Bonnie Martinez, dressed in a formal white gown and tiara, came to honor her father on her quinceñera, a Latino ceremony marking a woman's 15th birthday.
>
> Her father, the Reverend Gilbert Martinez, was on the first floor helping a friend fill out Social Security forms when the bomb found its mark. It was supposed to be a quick errand. Bonnie was in the third grade at the time.
>
> Her teacher mistook the explosion for an earthquake and told her students to crouch under their desks.
>
> It would be hours later, after school, when Bonnie arrived home to weeping relatives that she found out. "I miss everything about him," she says plainly. She had learned to summarize six years of grieving into a single idea.

Those four paragraphs form the series' heart. No matter how massive the event, the grieving is individual. Alan, the photographer, found Bonnie Martinez.

Tizon: I hadn't wanted to go to Oklahoma City because that story could so easily lapse into cliché. I started that story by presenting my argument for not going there: "We had not planned to come here. What was there left to say?" It's okay to approach sentimentality in your writing as long as you don't actually get there. Emotion is built into the situation—no need to talk about it.

Banaszynski: I did very little line editing on the "Crossing America" stories. Most of my editing involved variations on the question: "How do you know that?" Even in first-person stories like these, I don't care how Alex feels, I care about how he translates the experience to the reader.

Tizon: The series' narrative arc began with our departure from Seattle amidst anguish and nervousness, and ended with our arrival in New York. It wasn't until we got to Wyoming that we developed a rhythm. That is when the master narrative—the journey—became clearer to us. Each day's story was a mininarrative within the larger story arc. I often began the pieces with our arrival in a town and ended with our departure. The characters we met, their feelings and thoughts, became the stories' central tension.

As the series continued, we received suggestions from readers— some of which we took. One reader wrote to us, "You should go to Louisville, Kentucky. It's interesting because it's partly southern, partly northern." We went there, planning to write about the boxing gym where Muhammad Ali had started or his ties with Islam. We learned that most of the city's boxing gyms had closed down, victims of gentrification. We couldn't find anyone who actually knew Muhammad Ali. We found a minister who said that he would show us the site where Ali's gym used to be. On the way, we passed an old, broken-down house with a huge American flag draped over it. Two old women in overalls, flannel shirts, and straw hats sat in rocking chairs out front. We spent that afternoon with them; they became our story.

More than half the time we ended up with completely different stories from what we had planned when we rolled into town.

Banaszynski: Alex started saying, "I think we should just veer off before we get to New York." I began to panic, thinking, *How do I talk him into going to New York?* After they did a story about the crash site in Pennsylvania, Alex started to feel more connected to the actual event. I told him he had to go to New York, but if he didn't find a story, we could deal with that when the time came.

Tizon: The New York story ended up being one of the better ones in the series.

Banaszynski: Anyone who does this sort of writing must be a very good reporter. Theme becomes evident through the reporting. Each piece in the series begins with a strong foreshadowing of the theme, making these personal narratives more acceptable to newsroom traditionalists.

The third piece in the series began "What do little old ladies do in times of war? While driving through the eastern foothills of the Bitterroot Mountains one late afternoon, as the nation neared a new and terrible one week mark, I met two and asked them."

That phrase, *as the nation neared a new and terrible one week mark*, functioned as the nutgraf, a tether that kept the story from wandering off through the clouds.

Tizon: The series was so successful that we repeated the process in 2002, traveling across the country again to arrive in New York for the first anniversary. The second series was better written; we had the time to plan it properly. Still, it didn't have the emotional impact that the 2001 series did. The first one worked because it was done at the right time. It offered a personal voice when readers most needed that.

Team Storytelling
LOUISE KIERNAN

I worked on a team of sixty-four reporters and photographers to put together a series called "Gateway to Gridlock" for the *Chicago Tribune*. The team included graphics reporters, artists, and myriad editors. Like many projects, this one began with one person's experiences: Our editor, Ann Marie Lipinski, had a terrible time trying to fly home to Chicago from Florida with her young daughter. She decided the *Tribune* should take a look at problems with the air travel industry.

I wrote the lead article in the four-part series and was one of the reporters for the piece. We planned the story as a day in the life of the air travel system. The day we chose was picked arbitrarily after extensive negotiations with the FAA and major airlines. By sheer luck—good or bad, depending on your perspective—two massive thunderstorms collided over Chicago's O'Hare airport that afternoon. Thousands of people were stranded in the airport overnight, and air travel was disrupted throughout the country. With *Tribune* reporters and photographers stationed all over the United States—at airports, on planes, in FAA control towers, and at the headquarters of major airlines—we had one day to get the story right.

Editors began planning the series in July 2000, and I became involved in the project in August. Our reporting day was a Monday in September. The story ran the third weekend in November. We had nine weeks between the reporting day and publication—a lightning flash in the world of long projects.

On team stories one important tactic is to report *before* you report. Make sure that all who are working on the project know what to look for when they go out. Two of the reporters on our team covered the airlines on their regular beats, and they laid out some of the larger themes and issues we should look for as we reported. One focus, for example, was to find out whether airlines gave misleading information to their passengers. The more you can prepare your team, the better reporting they can do.

Whenever possible, the lead writer on a team project should also work as a reporter. I couldn't have written "Gateway to Gridlock" if I hadn't been in O'Hare airport that day myself, seeing the wadded-up hamburger wrappers and smelling the stale beer breath of the people stranded there. The writer's involvement also builds a sense of teamwork. Reporters who spend sixteen hours walking around an airport terminal need to know that the writer isn't back in the office sipping a cappuccino.

No matter the size of the team, each reporter should have a specific assignment. You can't unleash people and just tell them to "go get some good quotes." For the "Gateway" project we gave each team member clear directions: Stay with the baggage handlers or patrol Terminal 2 or shadow the airport administrator. We wanted people to understand that if they persisted with their assignment and took careful notes, good material would eventually emerge.

At the same time we needed flexibility. A reporter who had been scheduled to fly to Denver that morning found himself stuck, like everyone else, at O'Hare. But he and a photographer came across a woman who was stranded with her baby, her toddler, and no diapers. The reporter and photographer followed her for the next day, all the way to her mother's home in Buffalo, New York. She became a main character in the story.

One of our largest challenges was helping roving reporters understand that we weren't doing a news round-up. The goal wasn't ten quotes from ten different people but quality and depth. For many of the reporters this was their first narrative project or their first project of any kind. Convincing them that it was okay to talk to just one person, as long as it was the *right* person, took some persuasion.

We created a mechanism so that everyone could stay in close communication before, during, and after the reporting day. People spoke constantly by cell phone. One of my responsibilities at O'Hare airport was to coordinate a short meeting every few hours. The meeting wasn't mandatory; reporters could skip it if they were in the middle of something interesting. We just wanted people to have a way to touch base if they got stuck or needed direction.

Communication was vital; it made a much better story. For example, a reporter at the American Airlines operations center in Texas called the city desk in Chicago to report that one plane had been sitting on an O'Hare runway for almost five hours. A reporter went to the gate and caught the only passenger allowed off the plane—to take his dog to the bathroom. Because of our communications system, we were in the right place at the right time.

After the reporting day, the reporters gave me their notes. First, I read through all the material and highlighted everything that seemed interesting. Next, I constructed a rough chronology of the day. I tried to fit all the stories together, assembling the pieces of a large puzzle. In several places, one person's notes linked with something another person saw elsewhere. Someone heard an exchange between a pilot and the control tower, for example, that turned out to be from a flight whose passengers we had interviewed.

When I mentioned to the team that we would be lucky if 10 to 15 percent of the material we gathered found its way into the final story, people laughed. But that ended up being a fairly accurate estimate. Pages of interviews and description were sometimes reduced to a single strong image, such as a person's foot swinging over the head of someone sleeping on the floor below him.

I went back to reporters to get more information, where possible, on pieces that we were likely to use. On team projects it is important for individual reporters to do as much of their own follow-up reporting as possible. As a practical matter, it would have been impossible for me to do all the follow-up for "Gateway to Gridlock." More important, allowing reporters to remain responsible for their own work reduces the possibility of errors creeping into the story.

Throughout the writing process I kept in close contact with the reporters, checking to ensure that I had interpreted their notes correctly. Before we published the story, I sent all the reporters the portions of the final draft that included their material to make sure it was accurate.

With such a large team, convincing people that their particular contribution mattered was a challenge. Not all gave their best efforts but most did. And not everyone's work made the final cut. We recognized the team members who contributed the most in a box that ran with the story.

After the series won the Pulitzer Prize for Explanatory Reporting, our editor, Ann Marie, put the prize money toward the cost of having replicas of the award made for every member of the team. That certainly helped people feel that their hard work was appreciated.

Photographer as Narrative Storyteller

MOLLY BINGHAM

Text and photographs can be a powerful pair: Each presents discrete information that the reader/viewer could not get from either one alone. Too frequently, though, editors select photographs that are merely illustrations of the text rather than allowing each image to speak its thousand words—as the saying goes. Any photographer creating multiple images on the same subject is a narrative journalist, telling a story. Most publications could do a better job deploying narrative photojournalism to tell complicated, in-depth stories.

It often seems there is a huge brick wall between text and photo editors. Publications gain by bringing photographers into the editorial process: considering story ideas, shaping reporting angles, and deciding on tactics for in-depth narratives. By bringing photographers in on discussions for story ideas, photographers will become full-fledged team members in story development. Photographers tend to be treated as second-class citizens in the journalistic process. Not every photographer is a genius, but neither is every writer. Unlike most editors and many writers, photographers must leave the building and venture out into the rough world every day.

It is difficult, if not impossible, for photographers to pitch stories directly to magazines and newspapers. Story editors might like a photographer's story idea and hire a writer to do it, but photo editors won't like being told which photographer to hire for that story. A freelance photographer can end up losing the story completely. This gap between the text and photo sides of a publication represents a missed opportunity. Photographers see things differently—and see different things—than writers do.

Editors frequently tell photographers that there is a much more limited budget than there was a few years ago. Stories must now be shot "quick and dirty" in one or two days. Some magazines used to give photographers a week to provide the visuals for a story. Reducing the photo budget means less space for visual story presentation, which adds deeper meaning. In this restricted work environment, what is lost?

The sophistication of visual storytelling is lost. Good photojournalism takes time. The power of imagery is widely recognized in advertising. However, creating that critical image that "just says it all" takes much more time in the real world of photojournalism than in the advertising studio. Photographers must encourage subjects to open up and allow events to unfold in front of them. This process can't be rushed. Writers can reconstruct crucial scenes they missed, but photographers can't.

The creative tension between images and text is also lost. The two need not run on the same track, though they should run roughly parallel. Readers often gain the most when photographs address issues not directly treated in the text. Stories that run with just one image reduce the photography to mere illustration, repeating information already transmitted by the text. This is a disservice to readers.

Editors should give photographers time to explore a story, to figure out the visual elements, find the right character to follow, gain that person's trust, and allow that person to lose self-consciousness about being photographed. Photographers need time with the subject when they are doing whatever it is they do, engaged with the story's subject matter—not when they are being interviewed about it. Interviews between writer and subject present the worst possible environment for taking quality photos: The subject sits in a dark corner, her mouth open, making faces and rolling her eyes.

Some images speak for themselves while others need long captions. I always file photographs with much more text than any publication would use. Some images are more metaphorical in their meaning or are revealing only after the viewer learns a fact or two. These sorts of images need explanation. But this raises a problem: The same mentality that prevents photographers from pitching stories leaves our explanatory prose at the mercy of both writers and editors. Our photographs sometimes run with stories that misrepresent our own reporting, particularly if the photographer is freelance. This is even more likely to happen if our images are bought as "stock" from our agencies, not assigned by the publication. On some stories we might be able to collaborate with freelance writers, but if the editor doesn't like the text, our photos are killed, too, regardless of their merit.

In the best cases, writers and photographers collaborate on stories. Like marriages, photographer-writer relationships can be glorious, merely workable, or downright failures. Successful collaboration requires mutual respect and clear, fluid communication. Writers and photographers need not be connected at the hip, but they must exchange the information they accumulate each day or week. People behave differently in front of photographers and in interviews. They might make an offhand comment to the photographer or confide in her, providing a key sentence in the story.

Photographers often see a story's wider context as they build a collection of images around the central subject. At the same time, the information gleaned by the writer through interviews, research, and observation can help the photographer understand precisely how the visual story meshes with the text story. Photographer and writer both seek truth but do so in different ways.

All stories benefit from a genuinely collaborative relationship between text and pictures, one that integrates photographers into the story development process and fosters communication in the field. Fine photographic work—especially visual storytelling that relies on the nuance of character and situation—takes just as much time as fine writing.

Subversive Storytellers: Starting a Narrative Group

BOB BATZ JR.

My newspaper, the *Pittsburgh Post-Gazette*, isn't a narrative journalism incubator like the *Oregonian* in Portland or the *Sun* in Baltimore. Many news organizations in the country still aren't particularly supportive of narrative writing. Those of us working for such publications can still improve our writing and even slip some stories into our newspapers.

Although I had been a features writer for fourteen years before I attended my first narrative writers' conference, that experience fundamentally changed my work. I returned to Pittsburgh and worked with our writing coach, Peter Leo, to keep the spirit of the Nieman conference going, and fight the storyteller revolution from the ground up.

Our newspaper already had an in-house training program. I had attended "Post-Gazette University" talks for years. All that talk hadn't done much to help the *Post-Gazette* blossom into the next *Oregonian*. Peter Leo challenged me to form a narrative writing group. I wanted to start with a small number of fellow travelers, people I knew were interested in narrative reporting. We purposely invited photographers and writers from several departments, but no editors. I asked a photographer to co-lead the group, in part because photography was important to our storytelling vision.

At our first meeting we didn't even turn on the conference room lights. We wanted to avoid attention. We called ourselves "the Subversive Storytellers." We could discuss the writing we aspired to without worrying about an editor saying, "That's a great idea, Bob, and we'll need it in three days." Our first few meetings had only six participants and one agenda item: *How can we stop complaining about how bad things are in newspaper journalism and actually* do *something about it?*

Peter Leo proposed an in-house newsletter, a sort of underground newspaper within our newspaper. In the first issue of *Extra!* our top story announced the Subversive Storytellers. We hinted at our wish that editors not attend; we wanted all reporters to feel comfortable. Later, we loosened up, and several editors now attend. We had a great turnout for that first public meeting; there was more interest in storytelling than I had realized.

After meeting for several months, I worried that the Storytellers, as we became known, was becoming another group that talked a lot but did little. Then an editor threw us our first project. In early 2001, a new baseball stadium opened in Pittsburgh. For five years the *Post-Gazette* had written about the new stadium: from the passage of the tax bill, through the construction, and all the way to seeding the grass. By opening day there was nothing left to write. It became the story that nobody wanted. One day in the snack bar, the local news editor, Tom Birdsong, said to me, "Hey, Batz, opening day is coming up this weekend. Why don't you and that group of yours cover it?"

It wasn't a friendly invitation but a challenge. Perhaps stupidly, I said yes. I convened our group and presented the idea. "If we believe in narrative, here's our chance," I said. Everyone agreed. Opening Day was only a week away. We had never worked on a story together, much less a big story. We sat down and carefully planned our coverage. We decided on an inning-by-inning structure, beginning with the first pitch.

We didn't just decide how to coordinate our reporting, we outlined the basics of narrative coverage. We gave examples: "We don't want to talk to the dad who brought his son to the game and get a quote like 'It was really important for me to bring Jimmy to this historic event.' We want someone to be there when Jimmy says, 'Dad?' and then hurls up his nachos because he ate too many." This might sound elementary, but for our group at that time it wasn't. We talked to the copy editors and graphic artists and designers, so no one would be surprised by the story we created.

On Opening Day seven reporters and four photographers headed to the ballpark. I played the role of informal team leader. They all had a deer-in-the-headlights look in their eyes. *Could we pull it off? Would we find material from every inning? Would we know what to look for?* In the end we had a surplus of good material.

Back in the newsroom, the collaboration was beautiful: a sportswriter sat at a terminal with a hard news reporter, something that hardly ever happens. An arts writer and a young intern worked together. The story started on page A1 with a lede about the first pitch and a offbeat photograph of it: a spectator's feet propped up at the edge of the field, the pitcher tiny in the background. That photograph captured both the action of the ball and the spirit of Opening Day fans.

We completed a two-page narrative in just a few hours. The story was far from perfect, but it *was* a story—an experiential narrative in words and images. We had a group clip, which gave us credibility in the newsroom. Perhaps some of our colleagues hadn't wanted us to succeed, but after that story came out, they must have thought, "I'm not sure what that group is, but they do more than just talk about writing."

Our colleagues at both the *Post-Gazette* and other newspapers responded positively. "Makes you realize," one wrote to us, "how much atmosphere you miss at a ballgame when you buy a ticket and sit in one seat." Feedback from readers confirmed that we had given them compelling scenes and images they don't usually see in the newspaper. People were surprised; most were pleased. One self-described "longtime subscriber" wrote to the photographer who took the page 1 photograph, Steve Mellon, complaining, "36,984 people attended the home opener and for some strange reason, you chose . . . a shot of some jerk's big, fat, ugly, smelly feet!"

We deconstructed the story at our next group meeting. The group moved on to several other story projects. For Labor Day—a day we knew the paper would be happy to have a feature—we threw around some rather crazy ideas and then settled on a series of profiles of people and special tools of their trades. After getting a thumbs-up from some editors, we wrote about a well-known grill cook who had used the same spatula for a decade, and a woman who had become one of the first African-American members of the local floor coverers union. Her vinyl tile cutter had been a gift from someone who had really wanted her to succeed—and she had. The published story began on page 1. It wasn't a perfect narrative, but it had the important elements: ground-level reporting, good writing, strong collaboration between the photography staff and the writers, a real human element, and deeper meaning.

Sustaining a group like this is challenging. The people you most want to participate—the most talented journalists—are the busiest in the newsroom. The *Post-Gazette* lost several young reporters, and our group lost energy. Even without joint projects, a narrative group can be a powerful resource. We read articles and books together and discuss them. Reporters and photographers bring their projects, and we figure out how to improve them. In some ways our group stands in for relationships that people wish they had with their editors. At the same time, we feel free to say things we wouldn't say at an editors' meeting. We share unformed ideas because there is no danger of being laughed at or getting assigned the story too soon.

PART IX

BUILDING
A CAREER IN
MAGAZINES
AND BOOKS

Introduction

MARK KRAMER AND WENDY CALL

In the world of magazines and books, the most widely published writers aren't necessarily the best, but are the most persistent. Unless you are on an assigned project, a finished manuscript rarely means a completed project. Writing the story is hard enough, but before, during, and after the writing it is usually your job to sell it, too.

This involves time as well as personal, professional, and financial risk. Here is what Adrian Nicole LeBlanc, author of the book *Random Family*, says of freelancing:

> You really are gambling. Even if you win the jackpot, you don't make much money. It might be a losing game, but that's what you're choosing to do. The benefit is the time to do something you really care about. The sacrifice is that you must prove to everyone—your sources, your editors and your readers—that your story is worth *their* time. You must believe in yourself and in your project, because you have a lot of big people to convince. Once you do that successfully a few times, the ball will start to roll.

In this final section of *Telling True Stories*, one agent, two editors, and five writers explain how to get that ball rolling.

Making It as a Freelancer

JIM COLLINS

Freelancing as a narrative writer hasn't ever been an easy way to earn a living, and recent changes in the magazine industry have made it even tougher. The 1960s and 1970s were the golden era for narrative journalism in magazines like *Esquire, Rolling Stone,* and *The New Yorker.* Since then, ever fewer big magazines publish long narratives. *Rolling Stone* held on for a long time, but it has shifted to much shorter, celebrity-driven articles.

Magazines that depend on subscriptions can no longer compete with those relying on advertising income. Most thriving magazines are not general-interest publications such as *Harper's* and *The Atlantic Monthly* but vertical magazines—each with a narrow and clearly defined focus, providing information for niche audiences. *Outside* and *Field and Stream* succeed because they provide specific readerships for advertisers. Vertical magazines provide most of the opportunities for freelance writers. We all aspire to see our byline in the *Atlantic,* but that's not where most writers break into the magazine world. Some vertical magazines, such as *Condé Nast Traveler* and *National Geographic Adventure,* publish good narrative writing.

While getting started as a freelancer, you must spend as much time pitching stories (and accepting rejection) as you do writing them. I know only one writer who has made his entire living on freelance income from the beginning. As soon as he finished school, he began working as a full-time freelancer. His first year he sold fifty-eight pieces and earned $30,000. His big client was *Concrete Today,* an industry newsletter. He took on all the work he could find—the good stuff and the cheap stuff. One piece for *Glamour* earned him $5,400, but he also wrote newsletters for his wife's PTA for small change. *Glamour* was his big break. He soon wrote for that magazine regularly, and the *Glamour* editor passed him on to *Mademoiselle.* Now he makes much more money writing many fewer pieces. He has earned it.

More commonly, people move slowly into freelance writing from positions as staff writers or editors. They moonlight to get freelance careers moving, jumping in full-time when their freelance income hits $25,000 or $30,000 a year. Most freelancers have a few publications or contracts that yield most of their income. I write a monthly column for the US Airways magazine, earning $1,800 per column. It puts nearly $22,000 a year into the family budget. I know that I can also write two or three long features—three thousand or four thousand words each—every year. With this income and a slice of a book advance, my annual income comes to around $50,000.

Magazine rates vary greatly. Some alumni magazines pay a dollar per word for features. That is also what *Boston* magazine—a glossy regional magazine—pays its writers. Airline magazines also typically pay a dollar a word for features but might offer only half that for departmental pieces. A dollar a word might be something to aspire to, but that figure hasn't increased in a long time; it's the same rate I aspired to fifteen years ago. The best magazines pay two dollars per word or more—sometimes quite a bit more—but generally only to well-established, first-rate writers.

In-flight magazines are a great market for narrative writers. My US Airways editor has just one rule: Don't write about death, injury, bad weather, or anything that might remind readers they are on an airplane. These magazines might take chances on interesting offbeat subjects of interest to business-class passengers. You could write a short narrative about Tiddly Winks as a multimillion-dollar industry because it's a top-selling game in Asia.

When looking for potential outlets, don't judge a magazine by its cover. Peruse any magazine that looks vaguely interesting. How long are the features? Are author bylines in the table of contents? What are the writers' credentials? Do the editors seem to allow individual voices in the writing? Do the articles show depth, creativity, complexity?

Once you have a list of potential magazines to query, *refine* your story idea to fit each one. Begin reporting your story before you pitch it. You don't need a magazine assignment to start reporting. *We* know the title "freelance writer" could mean a stay-at-home dad having a midlife crisis, but the rest of the world doesn't. Approach potential subjects saying, "I'm gathering material for an article that I think could be really interesting." Most people are excited to talk about their lives, work, and predicaments. Project amiability and confidence. Answer their questions honestly, but don't start by apologizing, "I don't have an assignment, but . . ."

You must do some research before you can pitch a story idea successfully. You need to say who the characters will be, include at least one good scene you might use, and describe the likely story arc—the

dramatic elements that suggest movement in the story, a clear beginning and end. You might have to invest lots of weekend and evening
time at first, working on spec. You don't know whether it will pay off,
but it's the only way.

After that legwork, sit down and think hard about how to *frame*
your query. You have to sell not only your story idea but also the
meaning below the story line—why this story should resonate for this
particular magazine. In pitching a story to a regional magazine, for
instance, explain how the story's subtext reveals a subtle change in
the region's historical character.

First, *read* the magazine. If you absolutely can't get a copy where you
live, call the magazine and ask for a sample. Study the publication's departments. Short narrative pieces can satisfy the needs of most magazine departments, including food, travel, and fashion. Editors tend to
focus on features, but they must also fill the department slots in every
single issue. Improve your odds by pitching stories that fill those slots.

Invest your time carefully. Making your work do double duty is the
only way to make a living as a freelancer. For example, my monthly column for US Airways is called "How It Works." While writing my book
about the Cape Cod Baseball League, I wanted to use some of the material in the column. Early on, I wrote about the physics of wood bats
versus aluminum bats. Just as the book came out, eighteen months
later, I published an article about the changing demographics of major league baseball and the annual baseball draft.

Make sure your query shows that you have mastered the basics of
narrative craft. Use telling details that animate a character. Make sure
those details show *why* the subject is worthy of a central place in your
story. Think about the dramatic potential in the feature or longer departmental piece you propose. A successful feature will have conflict
or tension that will be resolved in the course of the narrative.

Enclose only one or two clips of your previous work with your
query letter; editors are too overworked to read more than that. Send
clips only if they strengthen your pitch. Clips should showcase the
kind of article you propose. Don't send a personal essay—even a
good one—when proposing a narrative nonfiction feature that requires reporting. An essay won't tell the editor about your reporting
skills and how you put facts together. Clips should prove your ability
to think through a story, to write clearly, to make smooth transitions,
and to elevate a story to include meaning. Clips are solid evidence
that you are a professional; bad or irrelevant clips are worse than
none at all.

When I was editor of *Yankee* magazine, we received fifty to seventy-five proposals—query letters or manuscripts—each week. More than half were inappropriate to the magazine. Most of the others offered only topic summaries and gave no sense of why we should select them. We so rarely received detailed narrative proposals showing evidence of reporting, even interns recognized those rare queries, knowing to put them on the "editor-to-read" pile. I winnowed that pile, looking for evidence of the writer's voice. I looked for passion, a sense that the writer truly wanted to tell a particular story.

Newcomers are likely to run into trouble sending multiple submissions. Editors want to believe the writer is thinking only about their magazine. Each query must be crafted to a particular magazine. If you have an idea that will fit more than one, tailor each query and send proposals sequentially. Each magazine should receive a unique pitch. Send the query to your top-choice publication, noting, "I think there might be other magazines interested in this; it's a timely topic. Could you get back to me within a month?" If you don't hear back, move on to the next magazine. Above all, don't let rejections bother you or slow down your submissions.

Here are some strategies that can increase your odds when you approach a magazine editor for the first time.

Think of a story idea that only you can write.

Take account of your life experience and expertise as well as your personal and professional networks. Think about the region where you live, your neighborhood, where you grew up, what you do on weekends. Those esoteric areas of your life will lead to story ideas that you are especially qualified to write about. If you have unique access, the editor can't get the story without taking you, too.

Follow up.

If the editor turns down your query saying, "We have a similar piece in the pipeline," make a note to yourself to follow up. If the subject hasn't appeared in the magazine six months later, send the editor a friendly e-mail, with your original query attached, asking what happened. Might he still be interested in your query?

Think small.

Newspaper reporters write about more weighty subjects as they build their careers. If they move into magazine work, they often believe they must find still weightier topics. That is not how magazine editors think. They are simply interested in stories that tell readers how the world works, how people see the world and make their way through it. Magazines illuminate daily life. Wonderful narrative is often built around small but revealing events.

Think about anniversary hooks.

Seasonal hooks and event anniversaries are good opportunities for magazine articles. Monthly magazines have more flexibility than newspapers do for annual subjects. The alewife run on Cape Cod happens for just two weeks each spring, but an article about it can appear in the April or May issue. Keep in mind that some magazines have long time lines. At *Yankee* our standard deadlines fell five months prior to publication, and it wasn't uncommon to ask for pieces a full year or more ahead of time. Fortunately, we could pay the writer on acceptance of the manuscript—as do most good magazines.

All but the most successful freelancers probably need to write for a variety of magazines and accept a mix of assignments, not just serious narrative journalism. My goal has been to increase the narrative part of the mix over time. If you are devoted to the craft, an increasing amount of your work will be challenging and rewarding, both personally and financially.

Not Stopping: Time Management for Writers

STEWART O'NAN

Joseph Conrad, a prolific writer, said there are only two difficult things about writing: starting and not stopping. That's absolutely true. Sooner or later almost every writer takes on a large independent project. To succeed, you must find the time or make the time or even steal the time. Precisely because the project is independent, no one else will help you with it, or pressure you to complete it. To have any chance of finishing, you have to make your own rules—rules to *not stop*.

When I was just beginning to write, while still working full-time as an engineer, I often lost interest in my short stories and novels halfway through and abandoned them. As a writer you should finish things whether or not you like them. Even after you have fallen out of love with your project, you can go back and improve it. Abandoning projects can become a bad habit; avoid it altogether.

I learned from David Bradley, a great fiction writer, that all first drafts are crap. Sometimes that's hard to realize about your first draft. You have been inching forward, writing very carefully, putting well-crafted sentences and marvelous images on the page, creating the right mood. It's still going to be a crappy first draft, but that's okay. You can fix it later.

I studied novelist John Gardner's personal papers and looked at early drafts of marvelous novels like *Grendel*. They were terrible. Like most good writers, he couldn't write, but he had the energy and determination to *rewrite*. He wrote each novel over and over until it became the vivid, continuous dream that I loved to read. How can we emulate that? How can we keep the work rolling even while working for somebody else?

The first rule: Make yourself accountable to yourself. Some writers write themselves contracts: *I will deliver my book by xxx date.* One writer I know, Chip Scanlan, actually signs these contracts and pins them to his office wall.

Second rule: Keep the manuscript with you at all times. I always carry the pages that I'm working on. Whenever I have a few moments, I can move it forward. Even if you just take the very last sentence you wrote on an index card, you can take five seconds to look at it and ponder what to write next. I used to go to my engineering job each day and say, "I'm going to write one sentence today."

An actors' trick is to keep their scripts with them at all times so they are always delving more deeply into the character. Do that with your manuscript so you can move more deeply into the material. Somehow, keeping the work physically close to me helped me stay connected to it even when I was immersed in my job, my family, my two-hour daily commute.

Third rule: Take your lunch hour. Take your sick time. Sit in the bathroom and think about your writing. Take *all* the time you are entitled to at your job.

Fourth rule: Always have a notebook and pen with you.

Fifth rule: Carry your characters with you. I often put on the mask of my main character and try to slip into that person's point of view. I'll go through my day trying to imagine how what I see would strike that person. If my main character is a woman waiting twenty-five years for her husband to get out of prison, I'll walk into a hotel lobby and think about everyone there enjoying their freedom.

Sixth rule: Never let the project sit for too long. If you go for several weeks without working on it, you'll never finish it. Now that I'm writing full-time, I aim for one page each day. When I had another job, a paragraph was a good day. I can't write more than five hours a day no matter how many hours I have available. I spend my best hours writing and then use the rest of my work time revising, doing research, or fact-checking.

Seventh rule: Write, don't talk. Try not to talk too much about a project that you are just beginning. Sometimes you can talk the mystery out of a project and lose your passion for it.

Eighth rule: Ask people what they know. If you need information or sources for your project, ask everyone you encounter about it.

Ninth rule: Isolate yourself. Spend your lunch hours where no one can find you. Stay at your desk after everyone else has gone home, or show up before anyone else arrives. Use that time for your own project.

Tenth rule: Budget your time carefully. If you're self-employed, give your best hours of the day to your big project and your less-alert hours to the stuff that just pays the bills. Figure out your peak hours and try to arrange your schedule so that you can give those to the work you care about the most.

Eleventh rule: Give your best effort and your best turns of phrase to your own project. Do a good job for your employer, but do a better job for yourself.

Twelfth rule: Never force yourself to begin from a dead stop. The way to do this, of course, is never stop. Keep the project in mind. Each time you leave the writing, give yourself a note or a prompt to get you started the next day.

Thirteenth rule: Get it on paper. All the research and reporting in the world are meaningless without the words coming one after another on the computer screen or on the page.

Fourteenth rule: Take extreme measures. I actually used to tie myself to my chair with a piece of yarn to force myself to face the cursor. When revising, I find that I keep as much from the days that felt awful as from the days when the writing seemed to flow easily.

Just sit there for as much time as you have. Put maximum pressure on yourself to get into the chair. Once you're there, ease off the pressure a bit. Robert Frost said it best: "The art of writing is the art of applying the seat of the pants to the seat of the chair." It's a lot easier if you're tied to the chair.

Fifteenth rule: Write down your dreams. I've woken up in the middle of the night and had entire short stories announce themselves.

Sixteenth rule: Find the time and the space. Your writing desk must welcome you. Use lighting, music, a warm blanket, or noise-canceling headphones to make your desk a comfortable place to spend time each day.

Seventeenth rule: Enjoy yourself. You can't be sure that the book you're working on will make it. You must enjoy the time you spend writing it. Everything that happens after that manuscript leaves your desk is not real. Everything that happens at your desk *is* real. If your book wins the National Book Award and makes millions of dollars, wonderful. If it's a complete flop and goes out of print within six months, wonderful. Either way, the book is no better or worse by one word.

Lessons from the Jury Box

JACK HART

As usual, the feature writing jurors for the 2002 Pulitzer Prizes were the last to leave their meeting room at the Columbia Graduate School of Journalism. On the final afternoon, after we had picked the three finalists, we sat around the table, exhausted. The also-rans were stacked in a huge pile under the table. All the finalists were narrative pieces, as were about half of all the entries.

Jim Warren, a *Chicago Tribune* editor, posed a question to the rest of us: "What did we learn about feature writing as a result of having gone through this process?" Here is the list of tips that we produced:

1. Have a point.
2. Be skeptical of victim stories.
3. Have a narrative structure. Read a screenwriting book.
4. Strive for clear organization.
5. Have a dramatic engine.
6. Don't be conventional.
7. Think about your story's selling point. How will the story benefit readers?
8. Don't create false heroes.
9. Don't be afraid to show complexity or ambiguity.

Working with an Agent

MELISSA FAY GREENE

After you have spent some time publishing newspaper and magazine articles, a 2,000-word article may start to strike you as absurd. Pretty soon 10,000 words may not seem like enough to capture the whole story you want to tell. You begin lusting after more and more words. Why not 20,000? Or 100,000? It might be time to think about a book.

How do you get a book idea off your desk and into the hands of an acquisitions editor at a publishing house? You will need help to find your way through the half-insane, labyrinthine, political, erudite, hip, market-driven, celebrity-obsessed New York publishing world. You will need a literary agent. Think of literary agents as realtors, and yourself as a home owner with a house to sell. The first thing to do is spruce up the place. Sweep the basement, clean out closets, wax the floors. You'll want the realtor to think (a) this is a gem, (b) this would be a fun sale, (c) we'll get top dollar for this, and possibly even (d) I already have a buyer in mind.

Your submission to a literary agent must sparkle. The first sentence should read like a dream and flow into the second sentence. The paragraph at the bottom of your first page had better be a page-turner. Good agents are extremely busy, with manuscripts piling up on their desk, telephones ringing, and assistants running back and forth between FedEx and the photocopier. Agents lunch with editors every day between eleven and two at little restaurants featuring olive bread and radicchio. They never actually read published books, but they always lug around unpublished manuscripts and book proposals to read on subways, in taxis, and while waiting for editors to show up at the little restaurants.

My agent receives ten to twenty manuscript submissions per day. Your submission must squeeze through a very tiny window and catch an agent's attention. There are four ways to climb in that window.

One: Publish pieces in the newspapers or periodicals that literary agents read. My agent, for example, subscribes to at least a dozen major newspapers, scanning them for good writers. If you publish something truly noteworthy, an agent might call. This is the easiest—and least likely—way to find an agent.

Two: Have a successful agented author refer you to his or her agent. If this is an option for you, it's a terrific approach.

Three: Look up agents in the *Literary Marketplace* or a similar publishing guide. This is the most difficult route to take; your proposal will join that pile of ten to twenty daily submissions. Generally, agents end up representing fewer than one of every hundred of the unsolicited submissions they receive. But it *does* happen.

Four: Find an agent through a book he or she has represented. This is the advice my agent gives to serious authors. Go into a big bookstore and find the shelf where your book belongs. Look for the books that are as close as possible to yours and read the acknowledgments, find the agent's name, and take home the books. Read them and then write each agent a personal letter about that book—and your own.

Agents look for two things: a person's ability to write and ability to see the larger picture. Does the author know the lay of the land outside the specific focus of this book? Does the author really grasp where this book is heading? What is the book's premise? Beyond the excellent prose, what drives the book? Returning to the real estate analogy, literary agents don't have time for fixer-uppers. They want something marketable.

It's not easy, but writers and agents do find each other. Once you and your agent have found each other, you've reached the next step: preparing your book proposal. Even if you have developed a full book proposal during your search for an agent, it will need substantial revision before editors see it. Each of my book proposals took me six to ten months to complete and ran over one hundred pages. It is torture, but my agent insists on it because he wants the writer to think through the entire project. It is protection—for writer, agent, and publisher—against books that the author can't bring to fruition.

The proposal for my first book, *Praying for Sheetrock*, laid out the book's whole story. It included the table of contents and six sample chapters. The logical question is: How can a journalist or nonfiction writer complete six chapters before finishing half the research? The answer: A proposal is not nonfiction. I think of my book proposals as great works of fiction about the greatest nonfiction books ever to be written. Of course you don't know what the finished book will look like before you've done all the research. Just keep in mind that you will rewrite—probably many times—the chapters included in your book proposal. Publishers know you have not written your book or finished the research. They just need an educated guess, the feel of a project.

For example, the *Praying for Sheetrock* proposal included no white people. I had spent ten years as a visitor, a legal aid worker, and friend in the African-American community of McIntosh County, Georgia. I didn't even know any white people there when I wrote the book proposal. In the actual book, about half of the events and characters came from the white community. That means my proposal probably missed the mark by 50 percent.

By the time I decided to write *The Temple Bombing*, my second book, *Praying for Sheetrock* had become a big success. I thought, "The publisher loves me, I'm happy with my agent and my editor, so I'm all set. I'll just tell them what my next book will be about. But my agent said, "Go write a book proposal." I was shocked. "I bet when James Michener has a new book idea, he just writes 'Poland' on a cocktail napkin and sends it in," I sputtered. "And they send him eight million dollars." My agent replied, "You're right. That is what James Michener does. Now go get started on your proposal."

What Makes a Good Book?

HELENE ATWAN

Think about the best nonfiction books you have read that began as newspaper or magazine articles. What made them such good books? Why was the subject worthy of 100,000 words? That is the first question to ask yourself when considering a book idea: *Does this topic have life as a book?*

Sometimes a subject is so complex that it demands many more words than can be crammed into an article. Jeff Toobin's book *A Vast Conspiracy*, about the Clinton impeachment, ran more than four hundred pages—probably 150,000 words. Laurie Garrett's *The Coming Plague* had about 300,000 words in it, most of them creepy. These subjects demanded book-length treatment.

Other books contain stories that transcend the moment of publication. *Hiroshima* by John Hersey, *Silent Spring* by Rachel Carson, and *All the President's Men* by Carl Bernstein and Bob Woodward were all timely but also took on subjects of lasting value and importance. All are still in print. Even for books that don't reach this lofty standard, topics must command as much interest three years from now as they do today. Once you have a story idea that requires 100,000 words, you must have the writing skill and style to bring it to fruition. After all, the author must keep the reader engaged for a long time.

After publishing several magazine or newspaper articles about a subject, the writer's perspective on it might take an analytical or speculative or more personal turn. That happened with Adam Pertman's *Adoption Nation* and Tom Wolfe's *The Right Stuff.* After he had reported on adoption for the *Boston Globe*, Pertman's personal experiences with adoption made for a rich book. In *The Right Stuff*, what began as a story about a particular group of astronauts and how they got into the space program became a book about the notion of masculinity. In expanding a piece of narrative journalism into a book, the author can—and must—editorialize, including his thoughts about the reporting and research or her analysis of the meaning and impact of the events.

No matter how many articles you have written on your book's subject, you likely will do more reporting before you write your book. One of the first books I edited at Beacon Press was commissioned from Philip Winslow, a journalist who had been reporting on land mines. He had spent eighteen months reporting in Africa before we began the book, but he had to return because the book required a different type of reporting. He had to go find the character who would become the book's centerpiece. He spent four months at a refugee camp in Angola, focusing on a woman who had been injured by a land mine. He needed that single character to get behind the mind-numbing statistics. He wanted readers to know the character as well as the broader story about the problem of land mines.

For book-length narrative to be successful, it must have strong narrative drive as well as characters that develop and a story that progresses. It is much more difficult to interest publishers in a collection of short pieces because they are hard to sell. Many *New Yorker* authors do collections, but *The New Yorker* is exceptional. It establishes writers like no other magazine or newspaper can.

Big commercial publishers count on a few of their books selling in huge numbers to make up for many more than don't sell well at all. Smaller, independent houses look for solid books—though they might sell only modestly—in a very tough marketplace. Many books from Beacon Press are adopted for university courses and stay in print for twenty or thirty years.

Most nonfiction books used to sell in the range of twenty thousand to thirty thousand copies. Now, very few sell in that range. While a small press like Beacon is still thrilled when a book sells thirty thousand, that won't even turn on the lights at Random House. Commercial publishers seek books that have the potential to sell far beyond that number. They must focus on marketing the books most likely to succeed rather than carefully editing and thoughtfully marketing all the books they publish. The economics of the industry make it impossible to give much attention to meticulously editing manuscripts.

Most books published don't end up selling hundreds of thousands of copies, of course. To deal with this fact, big publishers often cut their losses—even after the contract has been signed and the author has delivered the manuscript. If they have decided that a book is unlikely to sell well, they print a small number of copies and barely promote it. As a result, books that might have sold twenty thousand or thirty thousand a decade ago will sell just five or six thousand copies today.

A first-time author might get an advance of just $5,000 or $7,500. If the publisher thinks the book will be the next *A Civil Action*, the author might get $150,000 or even $200,000. When trying to sell your book, don't think just about the advance. Look for a publisher you really believe in, who will stand behind you. It is much harder to sell a second book than a first one. For many first-time authors it is better to choose a publisher with a smaller list so that you don't get lost. Your first book may make or break your career as a writer. No matter how big your advance, if your house abandons your first book, you might find it hard to sell another.

From Book Idea to Book Contract

JIM COLLINS

Here was my book idea: a narrative account of the Cape Cod League, where the country's very best college baseball players spend the summer. I had played college baseball, so I knew the mystique of the league. Even twenty years after letting go of the dream of playing major league baseball, I still wondered what it took to play at that level. What was it like for a twenty-year-old all-star, suddenly surrounded by the other twenty-year-old all-stars, to learn for the first time where he really stood? How I sold the idea—though it is just one example—might offer a glimpse into the mysterious workings of the book publishing world.

Developing a proposal for this idea was my first real experience selling myself in the book marketplace, even though I had worked for decades as a magazine editor and writer. I didn't think I could fake my way through several sample chapters since I hadn't yet done the research. Instead, I wrote a speculative book proposal. The proposal said briefly: "Here's the league and its history. These are the stakes. This is how a typical season unfolds." I put my best writing and my heart into many drafts.

At that time I had recently left my position as editor of *Yankee* magazine, which is well-known in New England. I was primarily a regional writer; I had never written for the *New York Times Magazine* or the *Atlantic*. I knew people who had, though, and I asked them to recommend agents. I submitted the same proposal to five agents.

The proposal was only thirty-eight pages long. My marketing analysis amounted to one sentence: "I see this as a book about baseball in the same way that *In These Girls, Hope Is a Muscle* was a book about basketball and *Friday Night Lights* was a book about football." That sentence told them I was familiar with sportswriting, I knew the difference between sportswriting and sports literature, and I aspired to the latter.

Four of the five agents I contacted wanted to represent the book. One agent said she didn't know baseball well enough to represent it. She ran into another agent at a cocktail party and mentioned the proposal. She thought he would be perfect for it. It turned out that he was one of the other four. I had just made my first mistake: sending simultaneous submissions. I should have indicated to each agent that it wasn't an exclusive submission.

Still, it turned out well. I met with three of the agents, interviewed them (as they interviewed me), and chose the one who seemed like the best fit. He represented authors who had written successful books about Cape Cod, and he had a terrific reputation with New England booksellers.

I signed with my agent, and then he said, "I love your proposal. Now, go and do the research so you can do a real proposal for publishers." He thought we would garner more interest in the book and more money after I did one season's worth of research.

My wife and I took financial risks to make this happen. I cashed in my life insurance policy to pay ten weeks of summer rent on Cape Cod. We hoped the book advance would allow us to pay back the policy. More important, we also hoped the book would give me access to a new level of magazine editors, boosting my career.

The proposal my agent and I sent to publishers was also short, just forty pages. It included two of my clips, both sportswriting, and two newspaper profiles about me. I didn't write a sample chapter but included a table of contents, the story line for each chapter, the narrative arc of the whole book, and detailed descriptions of the setting, the league's history, the teams, and the book's main characters.

My agent sent the proposal to twenty-two editors. Within a week fourteen had contacted him, interested in buying the book. Though I was amazed, my agent wished the number were higher. His reaction surprised me. "Wait until they start talking to their sales departments," he told me. One by one the publishers fell out of the running. Those fourteen publishers shrank to six as the acquisitions editors talked to the marketing staffs. Several editors made offers, and I ended up signing with Perseus for a $75,000 advance. I was very pleased with that figure.

According to the Web site Publisher's Lunch, I got a "nice deal." Above that is "good deal," "significant deal," and then "major deal." I was on the lowest rung, according to Publisher's Lunch, but I was on the ladder, and that made me happy. Some good writers I know have received advances of just $10,000 or $12,000.

My editor, Amanda Cook, said the voice of my book proposal is what grabbed her attention. She isn't a baseball fan, but she knew she wanted to read the book. She receives five to ten proposals a week and buys about ten books each year. After I turned in my manuscript, I asked Amanda how she knew which books would make that one-in-fifty cut. "It's like pornography," she replied. "You know it when you see it."

Your Book and the Marketplace

GERI THOMA

There is one thing every nonfiction writer should try to keep in mind: *Book publishers, agents, and editors all love you.* We may love you too much or in the wrong way, but we *do* love you, because you have jobs that pay your rent, because you are used to rejection, and because you understand deadlines.

Short story writers are the hardest writers for agents to represent because they are reaching for the smallest market. Academics are the easiest because they have tenure and they come to trade publishing having made it through the painful slog of writing books from their dissertations. Journalists fall somewhere in between these two groups. Sometimes they don't know quite what they are signing up for when they decide to write a book. It is impossible to calculate just how hard it will be to complete a book if you have an enormous number of competing obligations—especially if one of those obligations is regular journalistic reporting.

After completing their first book, many nonfiction writers describe themselves as having gone through a very particular form of hell. In the midst of it they have ceased talking with their friends, family members, and, most of all, their spouses. For far too long they have done nothing but eat, breathe, and sleep their book. They emerge utterly exhausted by the effort and find it hard to imagine ever doing it again—especially with a full-time job. Still, many *do* write more books.

Before you decide to write a book, you must have a powerful sense that no matter what the cost of time and energy, you have a story that must be told at book length. Journalists feel the pain of that longer length more than other writers do. My academic clients worry about writing too long, while my journalist clients call and ask, "How many words does the contract say I have to write?" Only journalists always know exactly how many words they have written toward that 100,000-word goal.

Eighteen-month book contracts are common. When a trade publisher signs a book, it is slotted to a publishing period in terms of profit. For more business-oriented publishers, such as HarperCollins and Simon & Schuster, a paid-out advance is a debit that had better turn into a credit once the book is published. These days, editors are under fierce pressure to cancel books that aren't delivered soon after the deadline in the contract. Sometimes an author can extend a contract, but a publisher faced with a delay might cancel the book instead. Traditional publishers, such as Knopf and Norton, tend to be more flexible about deadlines. They want the author more than the particular book.

Trade publishers seem to be more open to giving long contracts to academic writers. They understand that writing a history of the civil rights movement could take a while. An academic might say, "I have two sabbaticals in the next five years, so I can deliver the manuscript in five and a half years." Trade publishers push journalists to complete books more quickly.

By the time their books are published, many writers feel so worn out by the process, they find themselves thinking, "It can't possibly be my job to sell the book, too." Unfortunately, if it is not your job, it may not be anybody else's job, either. As the book's publication date draws near, you must be creative, forceful, and energetic to ensure your book's success.

Because you are in the business of research, you can be an invaluable aid to the overworked, underpaid, and underappreciated cadres of people in the promotion and publicity departments of publishing houses. The first, essential requirement is to be unfailingly kind to those young folk who may hold the fate of your book partially in their hands. As one client of mine did, you can come up with lists of names and addresses of newspaper columnists who might write about your book and journalists who have written on similar subjects and might offer a book blurb.

The writers I most enjoy working with want to be engaged in the publishing process but understand that they can't control it. They are willing to do whatever they can to help sell their book. Sales success of a book is an extraordinary and often heartbreaking roll of the dice. It often comes down to who reviews the book and whether the publicist assigned to the book is sharp enough.

Six years ago if I asked young editors what sorts of books they wanted, their answers would usually include "spirituality." Book upon book came out as cozy little paperbacks: *Twelve Zen Rules for This* and *Seven Zen Rules for That*. Most of these books failed. Editors rarely say they want to buy books about spirituality anymore. Three years ago that same bright group of young editors began to say they wanted "narrative journalism." Still, successful writers sell themselves on the strength of their writing, not the strength of a fad.

Most book buyers who read serious nonfiction cruise new book aisles for *authors*, not for topics. A reader buying *King Leopold's Ghost* generally isn't thinking, "I really want to read a book about King Leopold." She's thinking, "Adam Hochschild is a really interesting writer. I'll bet he wrote a good book about the Congo."

All agents are looking for literary writers whose work is powerful enough that readers will never forget the experience of reading their work—and will want to know about whatever subject they turn to next.

Crossing Over:
From Advocacy to Narrative

SAMANTHA POWER

In writing my book, *A Problem from Hell: America and the Age of Genocide,* I had to cross over from activism and human rights advocacy to history and investigative reporting. I shifted into the sort of objectivity— which is not to say neutrality—required to write a book. I also had to leave the walls of academia and enter the real world.

I wrote the book because of a trio of questions that burned in my mind: *Why does the United States do so little about genocide? Why haven't we noticed how little we do? Why are we able to still say "never again" as if the genocides of the 1990s didn't happen?*

I spent six years reporting for *A Problem from Hell.* I interviewed hundreds of victims, bystanders, and perpetrators of the atrocities in countries where genocide had happened: Turkey, Germany, Cambodia, Bosnia, Rwanda. Still, the book's emphasis was on America and Americans: journalists, governmental leaders, and decision makers in nongovernmental organizations. After I finished reporting, I faced three key challenges.

How could I avoid anachronism when everyone already knew how all the cases turned out? We know that six million Jews were killed in the Holocaust and that 800,000 were murdered in Rwanda. How could I create suspense for my readers as I tried to get them to care about the human stakes of these massive crises?

How could I write about moral stakes without sounding like a moralist? I was so moved by the gravity of the events, how could I pull back and get out of the way of the story?

How could I write a book about things that didn't *happen?* My book was about nondecisions or decisions *not* to decide—sins of omission rather than commission. This is a common problem when writing about social justice issues. Many individuals within bureaucracies don't consider themselves responsible for injustice. They consider themselves inheritors of structures that have led to great suffering. How could I capture both the limits of my characters' agency and also the agency that they exhibit by tamely deferring to "rules of the game" that they made no effort to contest?

The first challenge, avoiding anachronism, was excruciating. I was trying to trace—in the cases of the Armenian genocide, the Holocaust, Pol Pot's rule, and the Rwandan genocide—when U.S. officials learned what was happening. When did they actually receive intelligence on the atrocities occurring? When did that intelligence become knowledge? When did that knowledge become the sort of gut-wrenching, knee-buckling knowledge that might have made a person shudder or cry? How and why did a particular individual move along that continuum of knowledge? We all know how these stories turned out but not how they developed.

In reporting the book, it was very difficult to convince U.S. officials to go back over their experiences and offer their perspectives on them. Unsurprisingly, because so few individuals took a stand within the U.S. government, they were largely reluctant to review their actions as events unfolded.

The Freedom of Information Act proved invaluable to me. A former government official might say, "I didn't know about the 800,000 deaths until we went in after the genocide and the graves were excavated." I could prove otherwise after finding that person's signature on a document showing that he or she knew about the massacres long before the excavations. And I was able to find a few people within the U.S. government who *were* interested in excavating their memories with me. They went back to their diaries, notebooks, and e-mails. I tried to match press accounts of events to the personal memorabilia and recollections of these officials. To avoid anachronism, I tracked down real-time documentation of people's attitudes and agendas.

The second challenge I faced was writing about moral themes without seeming moralistic. I started the book because I had been a journalist in Bosnia during the war. I had felt immensely frustrated by the carnage I witnessed on the ground while watching NATO airplanes flying overhead, monitoring the killing but doing nothing to stop it. I covered the fall of Srebrenica in 1995. Eight thousand Muslim men and boys were systematically executed while television cameras rolled. I wanted to know why. *Why had we learned so little in the fifty years between the Holocaust and the Srebrenica massacre?*

My book's first draft was not something that anyone would want to read. I was angry. After I finished the first draft, I set it aside and distanced myself from it. When I returned to it, I approached the book as if I were the editor of a manuscript about a topic that interested me. I've always considered myself a better editor than writer.

Handing the story over to my characters was key. A writer should develop a strong voice, but not one that rises to such a pitch that it distracts readers. Instead of arguing with me because my voice was so loud, I needed to make sure readers would pick their fights with U.S. officials such as George Schultz, Warren Christopher, and Franklin D. Roosevelt.

Inhabiting the gray areas of morality was essential. Very few of the people who commit evil acts, even perpetrators of genocide, think of themselves as doing bad things. They tell themselves potent moral stories. Portrayals that don't give voice to the stories the perpetrators tell themselves—however hypocritical or outlandish those stories seem—reduce our capacity to recognize people who perform in similar ways in the future.

I told my story about bystanding genocide through *upstanders*, people who tried to stop the genocides. One of the book's main characters is Raphael Lemkin, a Polish Jew who lost forty-nine family members in the Holocaust. In the 1930s, he told European lawyers that crimes like the Holocaust were bound to happen, not just to Jews but also to Armenians and Mongols and Huguenots. In 1944, he invented the word *genocide*. In addition to all his good deeds, he was an unbearable jerk and a colossal plagiarist. Just as evil is more gray than black, goodness is less than lily-white. This was an important lesson for me to learn and try to convey in the book.

There were some villains in the Clinton administration during the Rwanda genocide who had very simple attitudes: *Getting involved is not in our national interest. African citizens don't vote in this country, and we have an election coming up.* Anthony Lake, Clinton's National Security Advisor, was not one of those people. His story was much more complicated and much more compelling to readers. Of all the people I interviewed, Lake was the most accessible. He opened himself up and puzzled over what had happened. In the end, my book exposed him the most, and I was grateful that he allowed that.

The third challenge I faced was depicting nonevents and nondecisions. When it came to responding to genocide, U.S. officials frequently made decisions not to decide. It was very difficult to get officials to remember their actions, because they had done so little in the face of these horrors. The National Security Archive, a nongovernmental organization in Washington, D.C., succeeded in getting government documents declassified soon after the Rwanda genocide. Because the U.S. government hadn't done anything, the declassifiers were quite generous. Their reasoning seemed to be that the United States had nothing to hide because it didn't do anything in Rwanda. The documents helped me trace U.S. attitudes at the time of the genocides—the book's narrative drive. But to make a book dramatic, action is usually required. Here I was fortunate to learn about individuals who pushed, unsuccessfully, for more to be done. Their confrontations with those who did not want to act provided considerable dramatic tension. I built suspense by meticulously conveying the indeterminacy of a moment—an indeterminacy that disappears only with hindsight.

Writing a book is, as George Orwell said, like contracting a disease. I've come to the conclusion that I should write a book only when I cannot live with its absence, when I have a question burning in my mind that must be answered. When one is embarking on a book project, the most important decision is how to frame the question. Had I known how torturous the process would be or how long it would take to complete, I probably would not have started. Writing serious nonfiction requires becoming quite antisocial for a time. Enduring that degree of antisocial behavior requires stubbornness and an almost desperate desire to satiate one's curiosity. Don't ever write a book merely for the sake of having done it; there is plenty of other essential writing to be done.

A Passion for Writing

SUSAN ORLEAN

Any successful writer must have a passion for writing. Being a writer *and* caring about passion is a paradox of sorts because writers are, by definition, outsiders. While working on my book *Saturday Night*, I asked myself, "Why on earth did I pick this job? I hate being an outsider. I hate being not included." I was writing a book about the American passion for spending one night of the week doing something special. I discovered that most people want to spend Saturday night with people they care about. I discovered this by spending five years' worth of Saturday nights with people I'd never met before.

Many writers have heightened senses of disconnectedness, making us especially suited to this work. While I was reporting *The Orchid Thief*, I envied the people I wrote about. They were all deeply connected to something they really cared about. The orchid poachers' desire to find the rarest orchids answered questions about their lives: how to spend their time and money, who their friends would be, where they would travel.

Spending time with the orchid poachers made me realize that I do have one real passion: for my work and the idea that it matters. Narrative nonfiction has a bit of a self-esteem problem. How can we justify writing long, time-consuming pieces about small stories? I think it's easy to justify: We are a species that communicates, that wants to know about the rest of our species. As writers we go out and learn about the world, and then come back and tell others. Any story can be worth telling if the author is passionate about it.

Occasional discomfort, both physical and emotional, is one of the burdens of being a narrative writer. This isn't a desk job. As much as I might resist getting out there, it's the only thing that works. Every time I push myself out the door, I try to remember that there will be a payoff. Often when I'm out reporting, my deepest desire is to go home. By forcing myself to stay out there, I usually discover something on which the whole story turns.

I once wrote a profile of Jean Jennings, editor of *Automobile* magazine. Toward the end of my reporting she decided to drive to Louisiana with her gynecologist to go duck hunting. I thought, "Well, that sounds like a mess." As much as I wanted to go home, a voice in the back of my mind nagged at me: *I really should go duck hunting.* Here's what happened:

> Jean Jennings and Doctor Ledfoot drive very, very fast. Doctor Ledfoot has another name, under which she practices gynecology in Ann Arbor, Michigan, presumably at approved speeds. Jean Jennings is one of Doctor Ledfoot's patients; she is also the editor-in-chief of *Automobile* and is always on the move. One recent morning, Jean and the Doctor were heading down to Louisiana so they could shoot some ducks. They were in a silver 2001 Chevrolet Suburban loaded with three boxes of ammunition; three shotguns; Jean's two Chesapeake Bay retrievers, Ronald and Sandra Lou; camouflage shirts, jackets, pants, shoes, umbrellas, me, and a six-pack of Diet Coke. Their plan was to leave Ann Arbor by 5:30 in the morning and drive straight through—fill-ups and bathroom visits only, except for a rolling

stop in Nashville to drop me at the airport—ending up in a duck blind near New Orleans by the next dawn. To manage this, they were going to have to average about 85 miles per hour. The two of them had never traveled together before. Jean, who is used to being the fastest driver wherever she goes, hadn't been sure what to expect from her gynecologist, but fortunately, Dr. Ledfoot did not disappoint.

"This vehicle corners pretty good at 90, Jeannie," the Doctor said, wrenching the Suburban to the right.

"It sure as hell does." Jean said, "even now that it's raining pretty goddam hard."

"Hey, Jeannie," the Doctor said, "The goddam Robo DUK better be there when we get to Louisiana." The Robo DUK is a hunting decoy that Jean had ordered the day before. Suddenly a yellow car streaked past us on the right. "Son of a bitch," the Doctor said. "That Mustang is hauling ass. Let's see if I can get him."

"He's gone, Doc," Jean said, leaning forward to check out the Mustang. "Whew. He's in the next county already. That dude's cookin' with gas."

"Shit," the Doctor said disconsolately. She pushed the Suburban up to 95 and closed in on a muddy truck lumbering along in the left lane. She braked sharply and then looked at Jean and rolled her eyes.

"Another member of the Anti-Destination League," Jean said.

Sometimes you're going to wish you had a desk job. Still, nothing is more thrilling than watching something unfold in front of you as you're reporting. At those moments you think, *I couldn't do anything else in the world.*

Here are a few questions to ask yourself as you embark on this journey.

Why did you want to be a writer? It seems simplistic, but it's a question worth asking yourself over and over. Did you become a writer because you like talking to people? Or because you like telling stories? What is it? Writing isn't the world's easiest profession, and it's certainly not the most lucrative. It works only when done with a high degree of commitment and authentic desire.

Do you love language? Language thrills me. Sometimes I will read a word that I haven't come across in a long time or that I don't know, and I can't wait to include the word in a story.

Are you deeply curious? Do you really wonder about the world around you? If you don't, this isn't the right profession for you.

Even more important: *Are you a bit of a control freak?* Being a control freak is a very valuable thing. You have readers in the backseat of your car, and you're taking them somewhere. You must be in control. As you're reporting, you must be humble, but when you return to your desk and start writing, you must take charge and say to your readers, "Sit down. I'm going to take you for a great ride."

Most important of all: *Do you find the world and the people in it a marvel?* Bring to your work the sense of excitement and discovery that kids have. We're all mature adults who have seen and done a lot. Still, when you go out to find a story, do it with a sense of delight. If you feel it, your readers will, too.

When I write about a ten-year-old boy, his wisdom about ten-year-old-hood is far greater than mine. Regardless of the subject's expertise, we can learn from it. We each have something we feel we have mastered. Remember this as you head out into the world. In different people this quality ranges from the genuinely wonderful to the mildly psychotic, but it's never silly. It's about being in love with something—and love is never silly.

SUGGESTED READING

Many of these books are noted in the text of the anthology. Others come recommended by one or more contributors. In the latter case, the person's name—or initials, for those who recommended more than one—appears at the end of the listing.

Basic Skills

Blumenthal, Joseph C. *English 3200 with Writing Applications: A Programmed Course in Grammar and Usage*, fourth ed. Belmont, CA: Thomson-Heinle, 1994.

Harrison Smith, Sarah. *The Fact Checker's Bible: A Guide to Getting It Right*, New York: Anchor Books, 2004.

O'Conner, Patricia T. *Woe is I*, expanded ed. New York: Riverhead Books, 2003. —Jacqui Banaszynski

Rowland, Robin. *The Creative Guide to Research: How to Find What You Need . . . Online or Offline*, Franklin Lakes, NJ: Career Press, 2000.

Strunk, William Jr., and E. B. White. *Elements of Style*, fourth ed. New York: Longman, 2000.

Swift, Kate and Casey Miller. *The Handbook of Nonsexist Writing*, second ed. Lincoln, NE: iUniverse, 2001.

Zinsser, William. *On Writing Well: The Classic Guide to Writing Nonfiction*, thirtieth anniversary ed. New York: HarperResource, 2006.

The Craft of Writing

Blundell, William E. *The Art and Craft of Feature Writing*, New York: Plume, 1988. —Jack Hart

Boynton, Robert. *The New New Journalism: Conversations with America's Best Nonfiction Writers on Their Craft*. New York: Vintage, 2005.

Burroway, Janet. *Imaginative Writing: The Elements of Craft.* New York: Longman, 2002. —JH

Cheney, Theodor. *Writing Creative Nonfiction,* Cincinnati, OH: Writer's Digest Books, 1987. —JH

Clark, Roy Peter, and Cole C. Campbell. *The Values and Craft of American Journalism: Essays from the Poynter Institute.* Gainesville: University Press of Florida, 2005.

Elbow, Peter. *Writing with Power: Techniques for Mastering the Writing Process.* New York: Oxford University Press, 1981.

Field, Syd. *The Screenwriter's Workbook.* New York: DTP Publishers, 1988. —Jon Franklin

Forche, Carolyn, and Philip Gerard, eds. *Writing Narrative Nonfiction.* New York: Writer's Digest Books, 2001.

Franklin, Jon. *Writing for Story: Craft Secrets of Dramatic Nonfiction by a Two-Time Pulitzer Prize Winner,* reprint ed. New York: Plume, 1994. —JH

Gardner, John. *The Art of Fiction: Notes on Craft for Young Writers,* reissue ed. New York: Vintage, 1991. —JH

Gerard, Philip. *Writing a Book That Makes a Difference.* Cincinnati, OH: Story Press Books, 2000.

Gornick, Vivian. *The Situation and the Story: The Art of Personal Narrative.* New York: Farrar, Straus and Giroux, 2002.

Hayakawa, S. I. *Language in Thought and Action,* 2nd ed. New York: Harcourt, Brace & World, 1964.

LeGuin, Ursula. *Steering the Craft: Exercises and Discussions on Story Writing for the Lone Navigator or the Mutinous Crew.* Portland, OR: Eighth Mountain Press, 1998. —JB

McKee, Robert. *Story: Substance, Structure, Style, and the Principles of Screenwriting.* London: Methuen Publishing Ltd., 1999.

Murray, Donald. *Writing for Your Readers: Notes on the Writers Craft from The Boston Globe.* Guilford, CT: Globe Pequot Press, 1992. —DeNeen L. Brown

Stewart, James B. *Follow the Story: How to Write Successful Nonfiction.* New York: Simon & Schuster, 1998. —JH

Vogler, Christopher. *The Writer's Journey: Mythic Structure for Storytellers and Screenwriters.* Studio City, CA: Michael Wiese Productions, 1999.

The Art of Writing

Atwood, Margaret. *Negotiating with the Dead: A Writer on Writing,* reprint ed. New York: Anchor Books, 2003. —DLB

Dillard, Annie. *The Writing Life.* Perennial, 1990. —JB

Goldberg, Natalie. *Writing Down the Bones: Freeing the Writer Within.* Boston: Shambala Books, 1986. —JB

King, Stephen. *On Writing.* New York: Scribner, 2002.—Loung Ung

Lamott, Anne. *Bird by Bird: Some Instructions on Writing and Life.* New York: Anchor Books, 1995. —JB

O'Neill, Dennis. *DC Comics Guide to Writing Comics.* New York: Watson-Guptill Publications, 2001. —Thomas French

Tan, Amy. *The Opposite of Fate: Memories of a Writing Life,* reprint ed. New York: Penguin Books, 2004. —LU

Anthologies of Narrative Nonfiction

American Society of Magazine Editors. *The Best American Magazine Writing* (annual). New York: HarperCollins.

Atwan, Robert, series ed. *Best American Essays* (annual). Boston: Houghton Mifflin. —Mark Kramer

Eggers, Dave, ed. *Best American Nonrequired Reading* (annual). Boston: Houghton Mifflin.

Harrington, Walt. *The Beholder's Eye: A Collection of America's Finest Personal Journalism.* New York: Grove Press, 2005.

Harrington, Walt. *Intimate Journalism: The Art and Craft of Reporting Everyday Life.* Thousand Oaks, CA: Sage Publications, 1997.

Howarth, William L. *The John McPhee Reader.* New York: Farrar, Straus and Giroux, 1985. —JB

Kerrane, Kevin and Ben Yagoda. *The Art of Fact: A Historical Anthology of Literary Journalism.* New York: Scribner 1997. —JH

Klement, Alice and Caroline Matalene, eds. *Telling Stories/Taking Risks: Journalism Writing at the Century's Edge.* Belmont, CA: Wadsworth Publishing, 1997. —JB

McPhee, John and Carol Rigolot, eds. *The Princeton Anthology of Writing.* Princeton, NJ: Princeton University Press, 2001.

Roorbach, Bill. *Contemporary Creative Nonfiction: The Art of Truth.* New York: Oxford University Press, 2001.

Root, Jr., Robert L., and Michael Steinberg. *The Fourth Genre: Contemporary Writers of/on Creative Nonfiction.* Boston: Allyn & Bacon, 1999.

Sims, Norman, and Mark Kramer. *Literary Journalism.* New York: Ballantine Books, 1995.

Sims, Patsy. *Literary Nonfiction: Learning by Example.* New York: Oxford University Press, 2001.

Snyder, Louis and Richard Morris. *A Treasury of Great Reporting*. New York: Simon & Schuster, 1950.

Wolfe, Tom, and Edward Warren Johnson. *The New Journalism*. New York: HarperCollins, 1973.

Critical Issues in Narrative Nonfiction

Adam, G. Stuart, and Roy Peter Clark. *Journalism: The Democratic Craft*. New York: Oxford University Press, 2005.

Black, Jay, Bob Steele, and Ralph Barney (The Poynter Institute). *Doing Ethics in Journalism: A Handbook in Case Studies*, third ed. New York: Allyn & Bacon, 1998. —JB

Christians, Clifford. *Good News: Social Ethics and the Press*. New York: Oxford University Press, 2001. —Walt Harrington

Hartsock, John. *A History of American Literary Journalism: The Emergence of a Modern Narrative Form*. Amherst, MA: University of Massachusetts Press, 2001.

Kovach, Bill, and Tom Rosenstiel. *The Elements of Journalism: What Newspeople Should Know and the Public Should Expect*, reprint ed. New York: Three Rivers Press, 2001. —WH

Malcolm, Janet. *The Journalist and the Murderer*, reprint ed. New York: Vintage, 1990. —MK

Patterson, Phil, and Lee C. Wilkins. *Media Ethics: Issues and Cases*, fourth ed. New York: McGraw Hill, 2001. —WH

Works of Narrative Nonfiction

Als, Hilton. *The Women*. New York: Noonday Press, 1998.

Bissinger, H. G. *Friday Night Lights: A Town, a Team, and a Dream*. Cambridge, MA: Da Capo Press, 2003.

Blais, Madeleine, and Geneve Oberholzer. *The Heart Is an Instrument*. Amherst, MA: University of Massachusetts Press, 1992.

Bowden, Charles. *Down by the River: Drugs, Money, Murder, and Family*. New York: Simon & Schuster, 2002.

Caro, Robert. *The Power Broker: Robert Moses and the Fall of New York*. New York: Random House, 1975. —WH

Carson, Rachel. *Silent Spring*, fortieth anniversary ed. Boston: Mariner Books, 2002. —Adrian Nicole LeBlanc

Collins, Jim. *The Last Best League*. Cambridge, MA: Da Capo Press, 2005.

Conover, Ted. *Newjack: Guarding Sing Sing*. New York: Vintage, 2001.

Dash, Leon. *Rosa Lee: A Mother and Her Family in Urban America.* New York: Plume, 1997.

Didion, Joan. *Where I Was From.* New York: Knopf, 2003.

Didion, Joan. *The White Album,* reissue ed. New York: Farrar, Straus and Giroux, 1990.

Fadiman, Anne. *The Spirit Catches You and You Fall Down: A Hmong Child, Her American Doctors and the Collision of Two Cultures.* New York: Farrar, Straus and Giroux, 1998.

Fonseca, Isabel. *Bury Me Standing: The Gypsies and Their Journey.* New York: Vintage, 1995.

Garrett, Laurie. *The Coming Plague: Newly Emerging Diseases in a World Out of Balance,* reprint ed. New York: Penguin Books, 1995. —Helene Atwan

Gawande, Atul. *Complications: A Surgeon's Notes on an Imperfect Science.* New York: Metropolitan Books, 2002.

Gourevitch, Philip. *We Wish to Inform You That Tomorrow We Will Be Killed with Our Families: Stories from Rwanda.* New York: Picador, 1999.

Greene, Melissa Fay. *Praying for Sheetrock,* reprint ed. New York: Ballantine Books, 1992.

Greene, Melissa Fay. *The Temple Bombing,* reprint ed. New York: Ballantine Books, 1997.

Guillermoprieto, Alma. *The Heart That Bleeds: Latin America Now.* New York: Vintage, 1995.

Halberstam, David. *Firehouse.* New York: Hyperion, 2002.

Halberstam, David. *The Teammates.* New York: Hyperion, 2003.

Halberstam, David and John S. McCain. *The Best and the Brightest,* reprint ed. New York: Modern Library, 2001. —WH

Hemingway, Ernest. *Death in the Afternoon,* reprint ed. New York: Scribner, 1996. —JF

Herr, Michael. *Dispatches,* reprint ed. New York: Vintage International, 1991. —HA

Hersey, John. *Hiroshima,* reprint ed. New York: Vintage, 1989. —DH

Hochschild, Adam. *Bury the Chains: Prophets and Rebels in the Fight to Free an Empire's Slaves.* Boston: Houghton Mifflin, 2005.

Hochschild, Adam. *King Leopold's Ghost: A Story of Greed, Terror, and Heroism in Colonial Africa.* Boston: Houghton Mifflin, 1999.

Iyer, Pico. *Sun After Dark: Flights into the Foreign.* New York: Knopf, 2004.

Kincaid, Jamaica. *Talk Stories.* New York: Farrar, Straus and Giroux, 2002.

Kramer, Mark. *Three Farms: Making Milk, Meat, and Money from the American Soil*, reprint ed. Cambridge, MA: Harvard University Press, 1987.

Langewiesche, William. *Cutting for Sign*, reprint ed. New York: Vintage, 1995. —Anne Hull

LeBlanc, Adrian Nicole. *Random Family: Love, Drugs, Trouble, and Coming of Age in the Bronx*. New York: Scribner, 2003.

Lemann, Nicholas. *The Big Test: The Secret History of the American Meritocracy*. New York: Farrar, Straus and Giroux, 2000.

Lewis, Michael. *Moneyball: The Art of Winning an Unfair Game*, reprint ed. New York: W. W. Norton, 2004.

Martínez, Rubén. *Crossing Over: A Mexican Family on the Migrant Trail*. New York: Picador, 2002.

McPhee, John. *Basin and Range*. New York: Farrar, Straus and Giroux, 1986.

McPhee, John. *Encounters with the Archdruid*, reissue ed. New York: Farrar, Straus and Giroux, 1977. —Adam Hochschild

Mehta, Suketu. *Maximum City: Bombay Lost and Found*. New York: Knopf, 2004.

Mitford, Jessica. *The American Way of Death Revisited*, reprint ed. New York: Vintage, 2000.

Momaday, N. Scott. *The Way to Rainy Mountain*. Albuquerque: University of New Mexico Press, 1976.

Nazario, Sonia. *Enrique's Journey: The Story of a Boy's Dangerous Odyssey to Reunite with His Mother*. New York: Random House, 2006.

Power, Samantha. *A Problem from Hell: America and the Age of Genocide*. New York: Perennial, 2003.

Rhodes, Richard. *Looking For America*. New York: Viking, 1980.

Ross, Lillian. *Portrait of Hemingway*. New York: Modern Library, 1999.

Sacco, Joe. *Palestine*. Seattle: Fantographics Books, 2002.

Siegel, Barry. *Actual Innocence*. New York: Ballantine Books, 2001.

Spence, Jonathan D. *The Question of Hu*. New York: Vintage, 1989.

Toobin, Jeffrey. *A Vast Conspiracy: The Real Story of the Sex Scandal That Nearly Brought Down a President*. New York: Touchstone, 2000. —HA

Urrea, Luis Alberto. *The Devil's Highway: A True Story*. New York: Little, Brown, 2004.

Wolfe, Tom. *The Right Stuff*, reprint ed. New York: Black Dog & Levanthal, 2005.

Works of Memoir and Personal Essay

Baldwin, James. *The Fire Next Time*, reissue ed. New York: Vintage, 1992.

Baldwin, James. *Notes of a Native Son*, reissue ed. Boston: Beacon Press, 1984.

Bergman, Ingmar. *The Magic Lantern: An Autobiography*. New York: Penguin Books, 1989. —AH

Brox, Jane. *Five Thousand Days Like This One: An American Family History*. Boston: Beacon Press, 2000. —Emily Hiestand

Colette, Roussant. *My Mother's House and Sido*. New York: Modern Library, 1995. —EH

Erlich, Gretel. *The Solace of Open Spaces*. New York: Penguin Books, 1986. —JB

Frankl, Viktor E. *A Man's Search for Meaning*, revised ed. New York: Pocket Books, 1997. —LU

Ginzburg, Eugenia. *Journey into the Whirlwind*. New York: Harvest, 2002. —AH

Harris, Eddy L. *Mississippi Solo: A River Quest*. New York: Harper & Row, 1988.

Lesy, Michael. *Wisconsin Death Trip*. Albuquerque: University of New Mexico Press, 2000. —WH

Levi, Primo. *The Reawakening*, reprint ed. New York: Touchstone, 1995.

Lopate, Phillip. *The Art of the Personal Essay: An Anthology from the Classical Era to the Present*. New York: Anchor Books, 1994.

Nabokov, Vladimir. *Speak, Memory*, reissue ed. New York: Vintage, 1989. —AH

Orwell, George. *Homage to Catalonia*. New York: Harvest, 1962. —AH

Quindlen, Anna. *Thinking Out Loud: On the Personal, the Political, the Public, and the Private*. New York: Ballantine Books, 1994. —Roy Peter Clark

Quintasket, Christine. *Mourning Dove: A Salishan Autobiography*. Lincoln: University of Nebraska Press, 1990.

Raines, Howell. *The One That Got Away: A Memoir*. New York: Scribner, 2006. —RPC

Ray, Janisse. *Ecology of a Cracker Childhood*. Minneapolis: Milkweed Editions, 2000. —EH

Rodriguez, Richard. *Brown: The Last Discovery of America*. New York: Penguin Books, 2003.

Talese, Gay. *A Writer's Life*. New York: Knopf, 2006.

Ung, Loung. *First They Killed My Father: A Daughter of Cambodia Remembers*. New York: Harper Perennial, 2001.

Ung, Loung. *Lucky Child: A Daughter of Cambodia Reunites with the Sister She Left Behind.* New York: Harper Perennial, 2005.

Wideman, John Edgar. *Brothers and Keepers.* New York: Vintage, 1995. —Debra Dickerson

Williams, Patricia. *Open House: Of Family, Friends, Food, Piano Lessons, and the Search for a Room of My Own.* New York: Farrar, Straus and Giroux, 2002.

"Good little magazines" to read for personal essays, recommended by Phillip Lopate: *American Scholar, Antioch Review, Boulevard, Creative Nonfiction, Fourth Genre, Hotel America, River Teeth, Salmagundi, Southwest Review, Three Penny Review, Yale Review*

Works of Fiction and Poetry

Agee, James. *A Death in the Family.* New York: Vintage International, 1998. —AH

Ashbury, John. *Self Portrait in a Convex Mirror.* New York: Penguin, 1990. —EH

Ephron, Nora. *Heartburn,* reissue ed. New York: Vintage, 1996.

García Márquez, Gabriel. *One Hundred Years of Solitude,* reprint ed. New York: Harper Perennial, 1998. —A. Hull

Giovanni, Nikki. *The Collected Poems: 1968-1998.* New York: William Morrow, 2003. —DLB

Hurston, Zora Neale. *Their Eyes Were Watching God,* reissue ed. New York: Harper Perennial, 1990. —LU

O'Brien, Tim. *The Things They Carried,* reprint ed. New York: Broadway, 1998. —JB

Orwell, George. *Down and Out in Paris and London.* New York: Harvest, 1972. —AH

Salter, James. *Light Years,* reissue ed. New York: Vintage International, 1995. —Stewart O'Nan

WEB SITES AND INTERNET RESOURCES

Maynard Institute: www.maynardije.org

Media Bistro: www.mediabistro.com

Nieman Narrative Digest: www.narrativedigest.org

Nieman Program on Narrative Journalism:
   www.nieman.harvard.edu/narrative

Poynter Institute: www.poynter.org

Transom: www.transom.org

WriterL: www.writerl.com

ABOUT THE EDITORS

Mark Kramer is director and writer-in-residence of the Nieman Program on Narrative Journalism at Harvard University. He was writer-in-residence and professor of journalism at Boston University from 1991 to 2001, and taught at Smith College for a decade before that. He has written for many newspapers and magazines. His books include *Three Farms, Invasive Procedures*, and *Travels with a Hungry Bear*. He coedited the anthology *Literary Journalism* as well as narrative journalism textbooks published in Danish and Japanese.

Wendy Call is a freelance writer and editor based in Seattle. She has been a Fellow of the Institute of Current World Affairs in southern Mexico, a Scholar at the Bread Loaf Writers' Conference, and writer-in-residence at Seattle's Richard Hugo House. Her narrative nonfiction has appeared in magazines and anthologies in six countries. Before turning to full-time writing and editing in 2000, she devoted a decade to working for grassroots, social justice organizations in Seattle and Boston.

ABOUT THE CONTRIBUTORS

Jay Allison, an independent broadcast journalist, has contributed to NPR's *All Things Considered*, PRI's *This American Life*, and other programs. He has received five Peabody Awards and an Edward R. Murrow Award, public radio's highest honor. He directs a public radio station for the Cape Cod region, where he lives.

Helene Atwan, born in Paris, began her publishing career at Random House in 1976. She has worked at Alfred A. Knopf, Viking Press, Farrar, Straus and Giroux, and Simon & Schuster. She was named director of Beacon Press, an independent nonprofit publisher, in 1995.

Jacqui Banaszynski holds the Knight Chair in Journalism at the University of Missouri, and teaches at the Poynter Institute. She has been an editor at newspapers in Seattle, Portland, and St. Paul. Her awards include the 1988 Pulitzer Prize for feature writing, and she has served as a Pulitzer juror.

Bob Batz Jr. has worked as a feature writer in Pittsburgh since 1986. He was part of the team that produced the *Pittsburgh Post-Gazette* special report "All Nine Alive! The story of the Quecreek Mine Rescue," which was published as a book.

Kelley Benham is a features writer for the *St. Petersburg Times*. She won the Ernie Pyle Award for human-interest writing in 2003 and the 2004 short feature-writing award from the American Association of Sunday and Feature Editors (AASFE). She is a former high school journalism teacher.

Molly Bingham, represented by World Picture News, has worked as a photographer since 1994. From 1998 to 2000 she was the official photographer for Vice President Al Gore. She has photographed stories in Central Africa, Iran, Iraq, Afghanistan, and the Gaza Strip, and was a 2005 Nieman Fellow.

Katherine Boo has been a staff writer at *The New Yorker* since 2003, and before that was a writer and editor for the *Washington Post* and *Washington Monthly*. She has received a Pulitzer Prize, National Magazine Award, and a MacArthur Fellowship. She lives in Washington, D.C.

Donna Britt has been a columnist for the *Washington Post* since 1992. She has received numerous awards, including top honors from the American Society of Newspaper Editors (ASNE) and the National Association of Black Journalists (NABJ). She lives in suburban Maryland with her husband, journalist Kevin Merida, and their three sons.

DeNeen L. Brown is a feature writer for the *Washington Post*. She has also been the newspaper's Canada bureau chief and a general assignment reporter, and has covered police, education, and government. She has won a 1999 ASNE Award as well as a Knight Fellowship and a *Post* Media Fellowship at Duke University.

Maria Carrillo is managing editor of the *Virginian-Pilot*. She previously directed most of the newspaper's projects, and oversaw a four-person narrative reporting team. Stories she edited have won awards from ASNE, NABJ, and AASFE, and three serials have been expanded and published as books.

Roy Peter Clark is vice president and senior scholar at the Poynter Institute, where he has taught writing since 1979. Before that he was the *St. Petersburg Times*'s writing coach. His most recent book is *Writing Tools: Fifty Essential Strategies for Every Writer.*

Jim Collins is author of *The Last Best League*, an *Attaché* contributing editor, and former editor of both the *Dartmouth Alumni Magazine* and *Yankee* magazine. During his tenure at *Yankee*, it received National Magazine Award nominations for general excellence and reporting. He lives in New Hampshire with his wife and two children.

Ted Conover's books include *Newjack*, a Pulitzer finalist and winner of the National Book Critics Circle (NBCC) Award for 2001; *Rolling Nowhere*; *Coyotes*; and *Whiteout*. He has been a Guggenheim Fellow and Visiting Fellow at Harvard University, and teaches at the Bread Loaf Writers' Conference and at New York University.

Lane DeGregory's writing has earned her awards from ASNE, NABJ, and AASFE, as well as the 2001 Outstanding Media Award from the National Alliance for the Mentally Ill. She is a features writer for the *St. Petersburg Times* and author of *The Insider's Guide to North Carolina's Outer Banks*.

Bruce DeSilva, worldwide writing coach for the Associated Press, has been a training consultant at forty newspapers and a frequent speaker at journalism conferences. Stories he edited have won ASNE, Ernie Pyle, Batten, Polk, and Livingston awards, and he helped edit a Pulitzer winner.

Debra Dickerson has been a senior editor at *U.S. News & World Report*, and a New America Foundation senior fellow. She is the author of *An American Story* and *The End of Blackness*. She is the daughter of Great Migration sharecroppers, and holds a doctorate of law from Harvard Law School.

Nora Ephron is a screenwriter, film director, author, and journalist. Her books include *Crazy Salad*, *Heartburn*, *Wallflower at the Orgy*, and *Scribble Scribble*. She received Academy Award nominations for Best Original Screenplay for *When Harry Met Sally*, *Silkwood*, and *Sleepless in Seattle*. She lives in New York.

Jon Franklin won the first Pulitzer Prizes awarded for feature writing (1979) and explanatory journalism (1985). He has directed both a university creative writing program and a journalism department, and currently teaches at the University of Maryland. His books include *Writing for Story*, *Molecules of the Mind*, and *Shocktrauma*.

Thomas French has been a staff writer at the *St. Petersburg Times* since 1981. His serial narrative "Angels and Demons" won a Pulitzer Prize for feature writing. His books include *A Cry in the Night* and *South of Heaven*, and he teaches in the MFA program at Goucher College.

Malcolm Gladwell has been a *New Yorker* staff writer since 1996. He has won the National Magazine Award for Profiles, and both his books, *The Tipping Point* and *Blink*, were *New York Times* number one best sellers. In 2005 he was named one of *Time* magazine's "100 Most Influential People."

Cynthia Gorney, a former *Washington Post* reporter, teaches journalism at the University of California, Berkeley. She is the author of *Articles of Faith: A Frontline History of the Abortion Wars* and a staff writer at *The New Yorker*. She has also written for *Harper's*, the *New York Times Magazine*, *Sports Illustrated*, and other magazines.

Melissa Fay Greene is the author of *Praying for Sheetrock*, *The Temple Bombing*, *Last Man Out*, and *There Is No Me Without You*, about Ethiopia's AIDS orphans. Winner of the Robert F. Kennedy Book Award and two-time finalist for the National Book Award, she lives in Atlanta with her husband and seven children.

Alma Guillermoprieto is a regular contributor to *The New Yorker* and the *New York Review of Books*, and author of *Samba* (finalist for the NBCC Award), *The Heart That Bleeds*, *Looking for History*, and *Dancing with Cuba*. Her awards include a MacArthur Fellowship and the Polk Award. She lives in Mexico City.

David Halberstam has written nineteen books, including *The Best and the Brightest*, *The Powers That Be*, *The Amateurs*, *The Children*, *Firehouse*, and *The Teammates*. He was a reporter for the *Nashville Tennessean* and the *New York Times*, and won a Pulitzer for his coverage of the Vietnam War.

Tom Hallman Jr. has written for the *Oregonian* since 1980, where he is currently senior feature writer. He won the 2001 Pulitzer Prize for feature writing for his series "The Mask." His other awards include the Ernie Pyle Award, two ASNE awards, and a Society of Professional Journalists award.

Walt Harrington was staff writer for the *Washington Post Magazine* for nearly fifteen years. His books include *Crossings*, *Intimate Journalism*, and *The Everlasting Stream*. He has won awards from NABJ and Sigma Delta Chi, as well as the Lowell Mellett Award. He is head of the University of Illinois' journalism department.

Jack Hart is managing editor and writing coach at the *Oregonian*. Stories he edited have won two Pulitzer Prizes as well as awards from the Overseas Press Club, ASNE, Scripps Howard, and Society of Professional Journalists. He is the author of *The Information Empire* and *A Writer's Coach*.

Emily Hiestand is a writer and photographer whose books include *The Very Rich Hours* and *Angela the Upside Down Girl*. Her writing has appeared in *The Atlantic Monthly*, *The Georgia Review*, and *The New Yorker*, and has won a National Magazine Award, Pushcart Prize, and Whiting Award. She lives in Massachusetts.

Adam Hochschild, a former newspaper reporter, cofounded *Mother Jones* magazine. His books include *Half the Way Home*, *Finding the Trapdoor*, *King Leopold's Ghost* (NBCC Award finalist), and *Bury the Chains* (National Book Award finalist). A Lannan Literary Award winner, he teaches writing at the University of California, Berkeley.

Anne Hull is a national reporter at the *Washington Post*. Before joining the *Post* in 2000, Hull was a reporter at the *St. Petersburg Times*. She has been a Pulitzer Prize finalist, won the ASNE Distinguished Writing Award, and was a 1995 Nieman Fellow.

S. Mitra Kalita is an award-winning business reporter at the *Washington Post* and past president of the South Asian Journalists Association. She is the author of *Suburban Sahibs: Three Immigrant Families and Their Passage from India to America*. She lives in Washington, D.C., with her husband and daughter.

Tracy Kidder is author of *My Detachment* (about his time as an Army officer in Vietnam), *Mountains Beyond Mountains*, *Home Town*, *Old Friends*, *Among Schoolchildren*, *House*, and *The Soul of a New Machine*. His awards include a Pulitzer Prize, National Book Award, and Robert F. Kennedy Award.

Louise Kiernan has been a reporter and editor for the *Chicago Tribune* since 1992. She wrote the lead article for a Pulitzer Prize—winning series in 2001, and was also a Pulitzer finalist in 2001. She has worked for the *Tribune*'s Sunday magazine, reported from abroad, and was a 2005 Nieman Fellow.

Adrian Nicole LeBlanc is the author of the best-selling *Random Family: Love, Drugs, Trouble, and Coming of Age in the Bronx*, an NBCC Award finalist. She has written for the *New York Times Magazine*, *The New Yorker*, *Esquire*, and the *Village Voice*. She teaches at the Columbia School of Journalism.

Nicholas Lemann joined *The New Yorker* as a staff writer in 1999. Before that he was national correspondent for *The Atlantic Monthly* and executive editor for the *Washington Monthly*. His books include best sellers *The Promised Land* and *The Big Test*. He is dean of the Columbia School of Journalism.

Jill Lepore's books include *The Name of War* (Bancroft Prize winner), *A Is for American*, and *New York Burning* (Anisfield-Wolf Award winner and a Pulitzer Prize finalist). Professor of history and chair of the History and Literature Program at Harvard University, she is also a contributor to *The New Yorker*.

Phillip Lopate is an essayist, novelist, and film critic. He is author of eight books, most recently *Waterfront* and *Totally, Tenderly, Tragically*; editor of the anthologies *The Art of the Personal Essay* and *Writing New York*; and series editor of *The Art of the Essay*. He lives in Brooklyn.

Victor Merina is a senior fellow at the University of Southern California's Annenberg Institute for Justice and Journalism. As a staff writer for the *Los Angeles Times*, he shared a 1993 Pulitzer Prize and was a 1997 Pulitzer finalist. He has taught journalism and essay writing across the country and internationally.

Sonia Nazario is a projects reporter for the *Los Angeles Times*. Her 2002 series "Enrique's Journey," now a Random House book, won more than a dozen national awards, including a Pulitzer Prize and the Robert F. Kennedy Grand Prize. She grew up in Kansas and Argentina, and lives in California.

Stanley Nelson is a 2002 MacArthur Fellow, Emmy winner, and executive producer of Firelight Media, a nonprofit documentary company dedicated to social justice. His documentaries include the award-winning *The Murder of Emmett Till* and *Sweet Honey in the Rock: Raise Your Voice*, which aired on PBS's American Masters Series.

Stewart O'Nan's novels include *A Prayer for the Dying, Everyday People, The Speed Queen, A World Away, The Names of the Dead,* and *Snow Angels.* His nonfiction books include *Faithful* (with Stephen King) and *A Circus Fire,* and his articles have appeared in *Outside, Oxford American,* and the *Boston Globe.*

Susan Orlean has been a *New Yorker* staff writer since 1992. Her books include *The Orchid Thief* (made into the film *Adaptation*), *My Kind of Place, The Bullfighter Checks Her Makeup, Saturday Night,* and *Red Sox and Blue Fish.* She has been a contributing editor at *Rolling Stone* and *Vogue.*

Lisa Pollak is a producer at the public radio program *This American Life.* Before that she was a features writer at the *Baltimore Sun* and the *News & Observer,* winning the Pulitzer Prize in feature writing in 1997 and the Ernie Pyle Award for Human Interest Writing in 1994.

Samantha Power's book *A Problem from Hell: America and the Age of Genocide* won the 2003 Pulitzer Prize and NBCC Award. From 1993 to 1996 she worked as a reporter in the Balkans. She is now a professor of human rights policy at the Kennedy School of Government, Harvard University.

Gay Talese is the author of nine books, including *A Writer's Life, The Gay Talese Reader, Fame and Obscurity,* and *The Kingdom and the Power,* about the history and internal workings of the *New York Times.* His magazine writing has appeared in *The New Yorker, Esquire,* and other publications.

Geri Thoma is a partner and literary agent at the Elaine Markson Agency in New York, where she has worked since 1980. The authors she represents include journalists writing about politics, race, education, culture, and food, as well as historians, biographers, sociologists, economists, and fiction writers.

Tomas Alex Tizon is a national correspondent for the *Los Angeles Times* and a former staff writer at the *Seattle Times,* where he shared the 1997 Pulitzer Prize for investigative reporting. He is a former Jefferson Fellow and holds degrees from Stanford and the University of Oregon.

Loung Ung is a survivor of the killing fields in Cambodia and the author of the best-selling books *First They Killed My Father* (which has been translated into twelve languages) and *Lucky Child*. She lectures widely and is national spokesperson for the Campaign for a Landmine Free World.

Isabel Wilkerson, the first African-American woman to win a Pulitzer Prize for journalism, has also won a Guggenheim Fellowship, a George S. Polk Award, and a Journalist of the Year award from the NABJ. She writes for the *New York Times* and is the author of *The Great Migration*.

Jan Winburn has been an editor at the *Philadelphia Inquirer, Hartford Courant*, and the *Baltimore Sun*, and is currently at the *Atlanta Journal-Constitution*. Stories she edited have won Pulitzer Prizes and an ASNE Award. She is the editor of the anthology *Shop Talk and War Stories: Journalists Examine Their Profession*.

Tom Wolfe is the author of more than a dozen books, including the nonfiction books *The Electric Kool-Aid Acid Test* and *The Right Stuff*, and the novels *The Bonfire of the Vanities* and *A Man in Full*. A native of Richmond, Virginia, he lives in New York City.

INDEX

Access
  contaminated, 26
  to subjects, 20, 25–26, 43–45, 59–60,
    166, 173–174, 176
Accountability, 91, 167–168, 170–172
Accuracy, importance of, 108, 132,
    174, 233–235
Action
  lines, 26, 141, 235–236
  rising, 142–143, 238
  speculative, 236
  unfolding, 20–22, 26
Activism, writing about, 133–134,
    202–205, 283
Adoption Nation (Pertman), 275
Advances, 276, 278, 279
"Against Joie de Vivre" (Lopate), 80
Agents, 76
  finding, 272–273, 277
  working with, 76, 272–274
"AIDS in the Heartland" series (Ba-
    naszynski), 66, 68
All the President's Men (Woodward and
    Bernstein), 274
Allison, Jay, 92–94
Allusion, 236
Ambiguity, 23, 81, 201
"American Man at Age Ten, The"
    (Orlean), 159
American Story, An (Dickerson), 107, 186
Anachronism, 88–89, 281, 282

Anecdote, 12, 117, 235, 237
"Angels and Demons" (French),
    189–191, 219–220
Angle of approach, 238
Anonymous sources, 167
Anthony, Ted, 118–119
Arlen, Michael, 75
*Art of Fiction, The: Notes on Craft for
    Young Writers* (Gardner), 103
Aspects of the Novel (Forster), 78
Associated Press, 48, 118
Atlantic Monthly, The, 52, 138, 264
Atmosphere
  detail and, 238
  importance of, 132
Attribution, 189–193
Atwan, Helene, 274–276
Atwood, Margaret, 103
Audience, 24, 56, 57, 101, 114,
    130–131, 192, 207
Authenticity, 174
Autobiography, 82–83, 150

Background information, 24, 25,
    27, 54
Baldwin, James, 79, 81
Baltimore Sun, 23, 24, 202, 256
Banaszynski, Jacqui, 3–6, 29, 66–69,
    216–218, 221–223, 246–251
Barringer, Dale, 185–186
Basin and Range (McPhee), 25

Bates, Steven, 170
Batz, Bob, Jr., 256–259
Beacon Press, 275, 276
Beginnings, 100–103, 143, 154
Behaviorism, 127
Benham, Kelley, 104–107
Berendt, John, 168
Berkes, Howard, 169
Berner, Alan, 246–250
Bernstein, Carl, 274
Best and the Brightest, The (Halberstam), 12
Big Test, The (Lemann), 114
Bingham, Molly, 254–256
Birdsong, Tom, 257
Bissinger, H. G., 16, 219
Black Hawk Down (Bowden), 191–192
Blumberg, Janice Rothschild, 88, 89
Boo, Katherine, 14–16, 89–92, 177–178
Book advances, 12, 276, 278, 279
Book contracts, 38, 276, 278, 279–280
Book-length topics, 274–276
Book proposals, 272–274, 277–278
Boston Globe, 275
Boston magazine, 265
Bowden, Mark, 151, 192
"Boy Behind the Mask, The" (Hallman), 217
Boyer, Glenn G., 165
Bradford, Jessica, 102–103
Bradley, David, 269
Bragg, Rick, 104
Britt, Donna, 83–85
Brodie, Laura, 203–205
Brown, DeNeen L., 81–83, 98, 100–103
Brown, Tina, 165
Bundy, Ted, 144–145
Bury the Chains: Prophets and Rebels in the Fight to Free an Empire's Slaves (Hochschild), 133–136

Call, Wendy, 19–20, 65–66, 97–98, 125–126, 163–164, 197–198, 227–228, 263
Camera angle, 136–137, 236, 238
Capote, Truman, 166
Carlton, Sue, 219
Carrillo, Maria, 243–245
Carson, Rachel, 274
Carter, Graydon, 11
Casert, Raf, 119–120
Cellini, Benvenuto, 150

Central America, 154–157
Character
    complication, 110
    composite, 166, 168
    definitions of, 126–127
    development of, 27, 129–132, 219
    first-person, 36, 78–81, 82–83, 93, 118
    historical figures, 86–87, 130–132
    motivations of, 73–74, 91, 127–128, 269–270
    sequencing, 238
    voice and, 159
Character profile (*see* Profile writing)
Characterization
    direct, 237
    indirect, 237
Cheese and the Worms, The: The Cosmos of a Sixteenth-Century Miller (Ginzburg), 88
Chekhov, Anton, 109, 143, 236
Chicago Boy (documentary), 130
Chicago Tribune, 15, 145, 251–254
Chronology, 109–111, 128, 139–140, 142, 168, 209, 210, 219, 253
Cinematic writing, 13, 98–100, 116, 132
Citizen Kane (film), 129
Clark, Roy Peter, 66, 70, 164–169, 189–192
Class, writing about, 14, 82–83, 151–153, 175–176
Climax
    false, 237
    of story, 144–145, 237
Clips, 266
Collective details, 236
Collins, Jim, 264–268, 276–278
Columbia School of Journalism, 7, 49
Column writing, 83–85
Coming Plague, The (Garrett), 274
Commentary, 66, 83–85
Complicated stories, 14, 145–148, 168, 219
Complication, of story, 237
Composite characters, 168
Condé Nast Traveler, 264
Confessions (Cellini), 150
Conflict, 79, 110, 143–144
Conover, Ted, 35–39
Conrad, Joseph, 268

Consent, securing, 176–177
Contaminated access, 26
Context, of story, 27, 49
Cook, Amanda, 278
Cradle-to-current profile, 68
Crane, Stephen, 153–154, 231
Crane, Townsend, 153
Creative nonfiction, 165
Crenson, Matt, 119
Cross-cultural reporting, 46–48
"Crossing America" series (Tizon),
    246–251
Curiosity, 7, 15, 287

Dahlberg, Tim, 139–140
Davis, Richard Harding, 231–232
Deadlines, 42
Defoe, Daniel, 150
DeFord, Frank, 11
DeGregory, Lane, 20–22, 239–243
Denouement, 237
Description, 88, 90, 237
    physical, 237
DeSilva, Bruce, 116–121, 139–140
Destination, of story, 28, 116, 121,
    137
Details
    atmospheric, 238
    collective, 236
    status, 129, 151, 238
    telling, 67–68, 117, 127, 128–129,
        139, 147, 157, 201
    thematic, 237
    use of, 128–129
Dialect, use of, 108, 237
Dialogue, 21, 29, 104–107, 112, 151,
    219, 237
    accuracy of, 21, 107–108
    full, 235
    half, 235
    importance of, 132–133
    participative, 236
    use of, 104–107
Dickens, Charles, 231
Dickerson, Debra, 107–109,
    184–187
Diction, level of, 238
Didion, Joan, 16, 79, 233
Direct characterization, 237
Discovery, sense of, 129, 130
Dixon, Phil, 102
Documentary film, 129–130
Documents

historical, 87, 133–134
    private, 133, 146, 282
    public, 133, 146, 282, 283
Dostoevsky, Fyodor, 79
Down and Out in Paris and London (Or-
    well), 150
Drafts
    revising, 53, 125, 206–208, 209–212,
        269, 282–283
    rough, 52–53, 97, 148–149, 204, 205,
        209, 269, 282
    writing, 28, 42, 51–54, 58–59, 60
Dramatic vs. summary narrative,
    111–112, 140

Editing process, 198, 209–211,
    222–223, 230, 233–235
Editor-writer relationships, 11, 53,
    101–102, 155, 158, 159, 169, 179,
    191, 197–198, 202–205, 209,
    221–223, 233–234, 246–251
Edwards, Elizabeth, 105
El Mozote massacre, 155
Eliot, George, 132
Emotion, in writing, 25, 111, 133,
    137, 151–154, 212–216, 219, 248,
    251
Emotional truth, 23
Empathy, 33, 172
End of History, The (Fukuyama), 150
Endings, 24
    effective, 117–121
    full circle, 235
    importance of, 116, 143
Endnotes, 164, 192–193
Enlightenment, 127
"Enrique's Journey" (Nazario), 164,
    178–182, 192, 208–212
Ephron, Nora, 98–100
Esquire magazine, 7, 230, 264
Ethics, 33, 163–193
    of accuracy, 164–169
    of attribution, 189–193
    code for journalists, 170–172
    dilemma of immersion journalism,
        182–183
    in personal writing, 184–187
    protection of subjects, 178–182
    responsibility to subjects, 172–176,
        177–178
    securing consent, 176–177
Exposition, 237
Eye contact, 47

Fact and fiction, line between, 164–169
Fact-checking, 62, 167, 192, 206, 234
Failure, writing about, 7–9, 241
Farewell to Arms, A (Hemingway), 111
Felt-life-level access, 26
Field and Stream magazine, 264
Fieldwork (*see* Reporting)
Filmmaking, 98–100
Finkel, David, 141–143
Firehouse (Halberstam), 11–12
First drafts (*see* Drafts, rough)
First They Killed My Father: A Daughter of Cambodia Remembers (Ung), 187
Fitzgerald, F. Scott, 7, 132
Flash-forward, 235
Flashback, 131, 235
Foreshadowing, 130, 149, 235, 251
Forster, E. M., 78
Frame, of story, 27, 238
Franklin, Jon, 29–30, 34–35, 109–111, 126–128, 197, 203
Freedom of Information Act, 146, 282
Freelancing, 76, 254–255, 263
  for magazines, 56–57, 59, 184–185, 264–268
  queries, 56–57, 59, 184–185, 264–268
  time management, 268–271
  working with agents, 272–274
French, Thomas, 140–145, 189–191, 218–221
Frey, Darcy, 16
Friday Night Lights (Bissinger), 219
"From Citizen to Activist: The Conversion of Laura Brodie" (Pollak), 202–205
Front Page, The (Hecht), 232
Frost, Robert, 270
Fukuyama, Francis, 150

García Márquez, Gabriel, 41, 156
Gardner, John, 103, 269
Garrett, Laurie, 274
"Gateway to Gridlock" series (*Chicago Tribune*), 251
Genocide, writing about, 281–284
Gill, Brendan, 232
Gill, Guy Roberto, 41
Ginzburg, Carlo, 88
"Give and Take on the Road to Somewhere" (Finkel), 141–142
Gladwell, Malcolm, 73–74

Glamour magazine, 264
"God and Country" (Ostling and Lieblich), 120–121
Goodbye, Columbus (Roth), 149
Gorney, Cynthia, 55–59
Grapes of Wrath, The (Steinbeck), 111
Great Gatsby, The (Fitzgerald), 7, 132
Greek myths, 72–73
Greene, Melissa Fay, 88–89, 272–274
Grendel (Gardner), 269
Guillermoprieto, Alma, 154–158
Guzy, Carol, 15

Halberstam, David, 10–13, 42
Hallman, Tom, Jr., 212–216, 217
Hamill, Pete, 228
Harper's magazine, 264
Harrington, Walt, 54, 97, 128–129, 148–149, 170–172, 228–230
Hart, Jack, 111–112, 230–239, 271
Harvard Law School, 184
Hayakawa, S. I., 70
Heart That Bleeds, The (Guillermoprieto), 156–157
Heartburn (Ephron), 100
Hecht, Ben, 232
Hegel, Georg Wilhelm, 152
Hemingway, Ernest, 111, 232
Hendrickson, Paul, 54
Hersey, John, 166, 232, 274
Hiestand, Emily, 198–202
Hill, Robert, 131
Hiroshima (Hersey), 166, 274
Historical writing, 66, 86–88
Hochschild, Adam, 16, 28–29, 74–78, 132–136, 280
Hogan, Mary Ann, 216
Homage to Catalonia (Orwell), 150
Homer, 74
Honesty, 23, 33, 36, 170 (*see also* Subjects)
House (Kidder), 52
Hull, Anne, 39–45, 90, 182–183, 198, 205–208, 219
Humor, 80, 113, 143, 159

Idea plot, 114, 115
Ideas, 10–13, 55–59 (*see also* Topics)
  weaving story and, 112–116
If No News, Send Rumors: Anecdotes of American Journalism (Bates), 170
Imagery, 147, 255

Immigrants
    writing about, 49–51, 108, 178–182, 208–212
    writing by, 187–189
"In Case We Die" (Sullivan and Casert), 119–120
In media res, 236
Indirect characterization, 237
Internal monologues, 168–169, 236
International topics, 3–4, 12, 76–78, 154–158, 187–189
Interviewing, 12, 48
    intercultural, 46–47
    profile writing and, 66–69
    psychological, 34–35, 127
    strategies for, 15, 30–33, 45–47, 61–62
Intimate journalism, 229–230
Inverted pyramid, 116–117, 201, 230, 231
Investigative reporting, 66, 89–92, 145–148

James, Henry, 26, 200
Johnson, Dirk, 23

Kalita, S. Mitra, 48–51
Kenner, Hugh, 169
Kidder, Tracy, 51–54, 176–177
Kiernan, Louise, 45, 145–148, 251–254
Killed assignments, 59, 61, 256
King Leopold's Ghost (Hochschild), 280
King of Hearts (Miller), 168
Kramer, Mark, 19–20, 24–28, 65–66, 97–98, 125–126, 136–139, 163–164, 197–198, 227–228, 263

Ladder of abstraction, 66, 70, 87–88, 217
Lait, John, 232
Langewiesche, William, 41
Language, 5, 238
    figurative, 236
    love of, 286–287
    specificity of, 43
    use of, 199
Language in Action (Hayakawa), 70
Lanpher, Katherine, 5
Latin American journalism, 154–157
LeBlanc, Adrian Nicole, 59–62, 263
Ledes, 143, 148, 156, 231
Lemann, Nicholas, 112–116, 192–193
Leo, Peter, 257

Lepore, Jill, 86–88
Levi, Primo, 75
Lewan, Todd, 139
Lewis, Michael, 151
Libel cases, 176
Lieblich, Julia, 120–121
Liebling, A. J., 16
Lippman, Laura, 23
Listening, 24, 30, 33, 62, 92
Listening posts, 46
Literary Marketplace, 273
Llosa, Mario Vargas, 156
London Spy, 231
Looking for the Light (Hendrickson), 54
Lopate, Philip, 78–81
Los Angeles Times, 13, 47, 164, 192, 208
Lucky Child: A Daughter of Cambodia Reunites with the Sister She Left Behind (Ung), 187–188

MacArthur, Charles, 232
MacLean, Paul, 111
Mademoiselle magazine, 264
Magazine freelancing, 56–58, 264–268
Maggie: A Girl of the Streets (Crane), 153
Mailer, Norman, 166, 233
"Manful Life of Nicholas, 10, The" (Wilkerson), 172–176
Marcus Garvey: Look for Me in the Whirlwind (documentary), 130–132
McPhee, John, 25, 169, 230, 231
Meaning, 22, 85, 109, 111, 129, 153
Media Ethics, 170
Memoir, 66, 78–81, 164, 165, 186–187, 189
Memory, reliability of, 34, 165
Merina, Victor, 46–48
Metaphor, 28, 236
Methods blocks, 191
Meyer, Rick, 209
Michener, James, 274
Middlemarch (Eliot), 132
Midnight in the Garden of Good and Evil (Berendt), 168
Miller, G. Wayne, 168
Mitchell, Joseph, 168, 232
Mitford, Jessica, 16
Monologues, internal, 168–169, 236
Montaigne, Michel de, 80
Moral themes, 281, 282
Morris, Edmund, 165
Morris, Richard, 231

Moss, Adam, 56–58
Music, 4, 5, 102, 111, 145
"Mysterious Killer" (Crenson and Ver-
    rengia), 119

Nano-narratives, 216
Narrative distance, 103–104
Narrator, 130, 215
    first-person, 78–83
Nation, The, 28
National Book Award, 149
National Geographic Adventure, 264
National Public Radio, 92
National Security Archive, 283–284
Nazario, Sonia, 164, 178–182, 192,
    208–212
Negotiating with the Dead: A Writer on
    Writing (Atwood), 103
Nelson, Stanley, 129–132
New Journalism, The (Wolfe), 101, 113
New Journalism movement, 151, 166
New Republic, The, 184
New York Post, 98–99
New York Times, 6–7, 8, 12, 13, 23, 30,
    48, 99, 155, 170, 172, 173, 237
New York Times Magazine, 38, 55–59, 60
New York Tribune, 153
New Yorker, The, 36, 37, 73, 232, 264,
    275
Newjack (Conover), 36–39
News-driven narratives, 216–217
Newsday, 50, 59
Newspapers
    future of, 154
    historical, 87, 133–134, 167, 229
    history of narrative in, 230–233
    local, 42–43
    voice of, 227–228
Newsrooms
    politics of, 216, 243, 244
    working in, 47–50, 216, 233–235
Newsweek magazine, 8
Nieman Conference on Narrative
    Journalism, 228, 257
Nieman Seminar for Narrative Editors,
    197
Note taking, 28–30, 38, 51–52, 60, 76,
    206
Notebooks, organizing, 52
"Notes of a Native Son" (Baldwin),
    79, 81
Nutgrafs, 71, 110, 115, 118, 148,
    206–207, 215, 251

Objectivity, 281
O'Brien, Tim, 4–5
Observation, importance of, 6, 40, 173
Odyssey (Homer), 74
Off the record, 171
O'Hara, John, 7
Ojito, Mirta, 48
Ominous object, 236
O'Nan, Stewart, 268–271
Orchid Thief, The (Orlean), 285
Oregonian, 233, 256, 257
Orion magazine, 198–199
Orlean, Susan, 158–159, 284–287
Orwell, George, 81, 150, 284
Ostling, Richard, 120–121
Outlines, 52, 148–149
Outside magazine, 264
Overnight angle, 99

Pace, 159, 201, 211, 219–221
Paragraph profile, 68, 69
Parallel structure, 238
Participant observation, 173
Participatory reporting, 35–39
Passage to Ararat (Arlen), 75
Patel, Harish, 49, 50
Pearlstine, Norman, 9
Person, choice of, 238
Personal essay, 66, 78–81, 199, 201
Personal space, 46
Personification, 236
Pertman, Adam, 275
Philadelphia Inquirer, 191–192
Photographer-writer relationships,
    246–250, 257
Photography, 54, 167–168, 249,
    254–256, 257
Physical description, 237
Pieces of the Frame (McPhee), 230
Piping, 165
Pittsburgh Post-Gazette, 256–259
Place
    sense of, 42, 43
    writing about, 46
Plot points, 109, 237
Point of insight, 110
Point of view, 53, 238
Pollak, Lisa, 202–205
Portnoy's Complaint (Roth), 149
Portrait of a Lady (James), 26
Power, Samantha, 281–284
Praying for Sheetrock (Greene), 273, 274
Presentism, 86

Privacy, 163
Private documents, 146
Problem from Hell, A: America and the Age of Genocide (Power), 281
Profile writing, 66–74, 285–286
Prosody, 200
Protagonist, 238
Psychological distance, 103–104, 238
Public documents, 146
Public radio, 92–94
Publick Occurrences, 167
Publishing
  book, 272–280
  magazine, 56–57, 264–268
Pulitzer Prize, 86
  jurors, 271
  nomination, 90
  winners, 189–191, 254
Pyle, Ernie, 232

Question of Hu, The (Spence), 88
Quindlen, Anna, 166
Quotations, 32, 135
  altering, 107–108
  inventing, 165
  kicker quote, 236
  recording, 29
  use of, 104–107, 112, 117
  use of informal English, 29, 108

Race, writing about, 48–51, 82–85, 175–176
Radio documentary, 66, 92–94
Raleigh *News & Observer*, 181
Random Family (LeBlanc), 59–60, 62, 263
Reawakening, The (Levi), 75
Reconstruction, 27, 132–135
Red Badge of Courage (Crane), 153
"Red Cross Girl, The" (Davis), 232
Remnick, David, 42
Reporting, 60–61, 275 (*see also* Ethics)
  immersion, 14–16, 24–27, 35–45, 60–61, 90, 170, 173–174, 182–183
  intercultural, 46–48
  from inside communities, 48–51
  international, 3–4, 12
  participatory, 35–39
  tape recording and, 28–30
Research, 27, 54, 91, 114, 133–135, 146–149
Revision, 205–208
Rhythm, 111, 159

Right Stuff, The (Wolfe), 113–114, 275
Riis, Jacob, 153
Risks of immersion reporting, 38, 178–182, 185
Robinson Crusoe (Defoe), 150
Rolling Stone, 59–60, 264
Rosenstiel, Tom, 165
Ross, Lillian, 232
Roth, Philip, 149, 150
Rothschild Blumberg, Janice, 88–89
'*Round Midnight* (film), 202
Rowling, J. K., 218
Runyon, Damon, 232

Sager, Mike, 230
St. Paul Pioneer Press, 4, 5
St. Petersburg Times, 13, 90, 143, 144, 189–191, 219
Saturday Evening Post, 109
Saturday Night (Orlean), 284
Scene
  development, 27
  reconstruction, 132–135, 137–138, 190–191
  setting, 27, 60, 136–139, 150, 236–237
  structure, 150, 239
Schwalbe, Will, 11
Scorsese, Martin, 100
Screenwriting, 98–100, 116, 201
Seattle Times, 68, 217, 246–248
Second Takes newsletter, 233
Sense of place, 42, 43
Sensory reporting, 27
Sentence forms, 236
September 11, 2001, 11–12, 50, 246, 247, 250, 251
Sequence
  character, 238
  of events, 26, 53
  in narrative, 140, 181
  principles of, 141–145
Serials, 209–210, 218–221, 247–251, 251–252
Shaw, Irwin, 7
"Shooting an Elephant" (Orwell), 150
Short narratives, 212–216, 216–217
Shotgun rule, 236
Signed releases, 176
Silent Spring (Carson), 274
Silkwood (film), 98–100
Simile, 236
Sims, Norman, 169

Smiling, 47
Smith, Gary, 23
Snyder, Louis, 231
Soul Food (film), 82
Soul of a New Machine, The (Kidder), 176
Source notes, 135, 164, 191, 192–193
Sources
  anonymous, 167
  inventing, 165
"South of Heaven" (French), 220
Spence, Jonathan, 88
Sportswriting, 8–9, 257–258, 277
Stance, journalistic, 238
Starbuck, George, 200
Statistics, use of, 91, 147
Status details, 129, 151, 238
Stavans, Ilan, 125
Steinbeck, John, 111, 232
Stewart, Ian, 118
Stewart, James B., 22
"Storm Gods and Heroes" (Lewan), 139
Story framing, 27, 238
Storytelling, importance of, 4–6, 156, 218, 233, 254, 256
Streep, Meryl, 99
Structure, 13, 97–100
  beginnings, 98, 100–103, 131
  endings, 116–121, 220
  experimentation with, 201
  parallel, 238
  scenic, 239
  story, 109–111, 213–214
  topical, 239
  voice and, 126
Style, 198–202
Subcultures, writing about, 74
Subjectivity, 166
Subjects, 6–8 (*see also* Ethics; Interviewing)
  background checks of, 41
  changing names of, 38
  developing trust, 32
  entering lives of, 15, 21, 27, 40–41, 44–45, 59–62
  finding, 203, 239–243
  profile writing and, 71–73
  protection of, 178–182
  relationships with, 30–33, 163–164
  responsibility to, 32, 172–176
  tape recording, 28–30

Suburban Sahibs: Three Immigrant Families and Their Passage from India to America (Kalita), 49
"Such Were the Joys" (Orwell), 81
Sullivan, Tim, 119–120
Summary narrative, 111–112
Summer of '49 (Halberstam), 10
Suspense, 144

Talese, Gay, 6–9, 13, 30, 237
Talk magazine, 185
Tape recording, 28–30, 43
Tavernier, Bernard, 202
Team storytelling, 243–245, 251–254, 256–259
Teammates, The (Halberstam), 10, 11
Telegraph, invention of, 116–117
Television news, 10, 156
Temple Bombing, The (Greene), 88–89, 274
Tension, 144, 235–236, 250
Texture, 237
Thematic details, 237
Themes, 28, 53, 101, 209
  Moral, 282–282
Things They Carried, The (O'Brien), 4–5
Thoma, Geri, 278–280
Thompson, Hunter, 233
Three Farms (Kramer), 137
Thurber, James, 232
Till, Emmett, 130
Time
  management, 168, 268–271
  photography and, 255
  as writing element, 12, 139–140
Time magazine, 8, 28
Time-Warner, 9
Tizon, Tomas Alex, 5, 71–73, 246–251
Todd, Richard, 53, 138
Tone, 238
Toobin, Jeff, 274
Topics (*see also* Ideas)
  book-length, 274–276
  evaluating, 24–28
  finding, 20–24, 239–243
"Town Is Born, A" (Anthony), 118–119
Trade publishing, 278–279
Transitions, 28, 141
Translation, 29, 47, 105, 108, 125, 188
Travel writing, 66, 74–78

Treasury of Great Reporting, A (Snyder and Morris), 231
True narratives, 217–218
Twain, Mark, 231
Typographic indicators, 239

Ung, Loung, 187–189
Unifying devices, 239
Universal truths, 22
University of Iowa Writers' Workshop, 53
University of Missouri, 7
U.S. News & World Report, 108

Vanity Fair, 11, 71
Vargas Llosa, Mario, 156
Vast Conspiracy, A (Toobin), 274
Verbs, use of, 140, 236
Verrengia, Joseph P., 119
Vignettes, 236, 237
Virginian-Pilot, 243–244
Voice, 53, 58, 238
    development of, 79, 125, 158–159, 202, 230, 283
    effective, 126
    of newspapers, 227–228
    structure and, 126
    variations within, 199–200
Volume, sense of, 137

Walcott, Derek, 199
Wall Street Journal, 13
Ward, Ned, 231
Warren, Jim, 271
Washington Post, 13, 15, 44, 50, 81, 84, 107, 141, 154, 155, 170, 171, 230
Washington Post Magazine, 128, 148
"What Price the News?" (Stewart), 118
White, E. B., 79, 199
Whitman, Walt, 231
"Who Shot Johnny?" (Dickerson), 184–185
"Why I Write" (Orwell), 150
Wilkerson, Isabel, 30–33, 172–176
Winburn, Jan, 22–24, 202–205, 228
Wolfe, Tom, 101, 113–114, 129, 149–154, 166, 233, 275
Woodward, Bob, 274
Word choice, 159, 200, 207–208
Writing, passion for, 284–287
Writing for Story (Franklin), 203
Writing group, 256–259
Writing process, 16, 28, 42, 51, 53–54, 58, 205, 253–254

Yale Review, 166
Yankee magazine, 267, 268, 277

Zeman, Ned, 71